TRANSFORMATIONS

TRANSFORMATIONS

Change Work across Writing Programs, Pedagogies, and Practices

EDITED BY
HOLLY HASSEL AND KIRSTI COLE

UTAH STATE UNIVERSITY PRESS
Logan

Published by Utah State University Press
An imprint of University Press of Colorado
245 Century Circle, Suite 202
Louisville, Colorado 80027

The University Press of Colorado is a proud member of
the Association of University Presses.

The University Press of Colorado is a cooperative publishing enterprise supported,
in part, by Adams State University, Colorado State University, Fort Lewis College,
Metropolitan State University of Denver, Regis University, University of Colorado,
University of Northern Colorado, University of Wyoming, Utah State University, and
Western Colorado University.

∞ This paper meets the requirements of the ANSI/NISO Z39.48–1992 (Permanence of
Paper)

ISBN: 978-1-64642-141-1 (paperback)
ISBN: 978-1-64642-142-8 (ebook)
https://doi.org/10.7330/9781646421428

Library of Congress Cataloging-in-Publication Data

Names: Hassel, Holly, editor. | Cole, Kirsti, editor.
Title: Transformations : change work across writing programs, pedagogies, and practices
/ edited by Holly Hassel and Kirsti Cole.
Description: Logan : Utah State University Press, [2021] | Includes bibliographical refer-
ences and index.
Identifiers: LCCN 2021021089 (print) | LCCN 2021021090 (ebook) | ISBN
9781646421411 (paperback) | ISBN 9781646421428 (ebook)
Subjects: LCSH: English language—Rhetoric—Study and teaching (Higher)—United
States. | English language—Rhetoric—Study and teaching (Higher)—Administration. |
English teachers—Training of—United States. | College teachers—Training of—United
States. | Writing centers—United States—Administration. | Academic writing—Study
and teaching (Higher)—United States.
Classification: LCC PE1405.U6 T735 2021 (print) | LCC PE1405.U6 (ebook) | DDC
428.0071—dc23
LC record available at https://lccn.loc.gov/2021021089
LC ebook record available at https://lccn.loc.gov/2021021090

This volume is dedicated to college writing teachers, particularly those who do the majority of the labor we address in this collection: the dual-enrollment high school teachers, contingent faculty, lecturers, and other teaching-track faculty who support student writers in the first year and beyond, as well as our two-year college colleagues who teach in basic writing and first-year writing courses across the United States. We recognize, as well, the graduate student teachers, faculty, and writing program administrators who work to build programs that have integrity, that are equitable, and that are transformative: you do incredible, often invisible, always undervalued work, and it helps people write better lives into existence for themselves every day.

It is crucial that teachers, administrators, and scholars learn to work across institutional hierarchies while recognizing and responding to the rapidly eroding boundaries between disciplines, institutions, and the corporate world. Their ability to do so depends on their willingness to confront and not displace mounting anxieties about the nature of their work in relationship to the realities of disciplinary, institutional, and socio-economic interrelationships and change.

Carrie Byars Kilfoil, "The Nature and Value of Work in Rhetoric and Composition," *JAC*, Vol. 32, No. 3/4, Economies of Writing (2012): 731–37.

CONTENTS

ACKNOWLEDGMENTS

I would like to acknowledge the inspiring work of my mentors, Maureen Daly Goggin, Sharon Crowley, Valerie Renegar, and Kristin Swenson. I am grateful for my wonderful colleagues in composition, TESOL, and technical communication at Minnesota State University, and for the students in my master's program, whose insights and weekly discussions constantly motivate me. Holly Hassel, my coeditor for the third time—it's a pleasure to work with you, learn from you, and grow in my thinking every time we write together. Finally, a big thank you to my parents, Nancy and Scott, my partner, Joshua Preiss, and my sons, Oliver and Beckett, who always cheer me on.

—KIRSTI

I am grateful to the many partners I have had in institutional change work: Joanne Baird Giordano, Cassie Mach Phillips, Jessica Van Slooten, Iris Ruiz, Nancy Chick, Lisa Arnold, Jill Stukenberg, to name a few. I am also grateful for all that I learned from my colleagues and friends in the University of Wisconsin Colleges (now dissolved) during my work there from 2002 to 2018. The generative and generous collaboration that started when Kirsti Cole and I met at a Conference on College Composition and Communication (CCCC) convention several years back, continuing now through our third edited collection, continues to energize me. Thank you for being an amazing coauthor and coeditor. Last, I thank my family—Ben, Trixie, and Gus—for their inspiration, support, and humor.

—HOLLY

TRANSFORMATIONS

INTRODUCTION
Transformations in a Changing Landscape

Kirsti Cole and Holly Hassel

If writing programs in the United States have anything in common it is this: they change. As our teaching practices adapt to changing technologies, budgetary constraints, new student populations, and changing employment practices, writing programs remain full of people dedicated to helping students improve their writing. However, as we know from the long and diverse histories of composition in the university, writing programs are typically sustained by the most vulnerable individuals in the institution. Although we have made great strides in recognizing the institutional value of writing programs, in making recognizable our professionalization efforts for writing program administrators (WPAs) and faculty hired on the tenure-track to teach writing, a large portion of our courses are offered by non-tenure-track faculty and graduate students in other programs. According to Emily Isaacs, 82 percent of writing programs are in institutions in which writing is embedded in English departments (Isaacs 2018). We know that part of the precarity of composition and rhetoric is simply the fact that we have been, for so long, embedded in such departments (Goggin 1995). Even though this is changing, particularly at research-intensive institutions, the majority of programs are still struggling for disciplinary recognition as a part of a larger interdisciplinary space, training, and expertise are directly impacted. As such, coordinating writing programs outside of a research-intensive context involves a kind of labor that people are not regularly trained to do.

This book speaks to common issues that might arise in the majority of those situations and proposes solutions to problems that faculty may not know that they will face. In using the prism of transformation as the organizing principle for the collection, the chapter contributions present a series of strategies, situated within the ecology of the campuses, writing programs, and classrooms. In doing so, we hope to highlight the multiplicity of ways that teacher-scholar-activists across institutional sites

https://doi.org/10.7330/9781646421428.c000

bring about change to their work environment. To echo Kathleen Blake Yancey, we have a moment (Yancey 2004). At this moment—at the intersection of austerity, neoliberalism, anti-intellectualism, unprecedented labor issues, and apathy—composition instructors are doing good work. And no one is making these instructors do this work. This collection was already well through the publication process in spring of 2020 when the COVID-19 global pandemic upended higher education, including many of the key assumptions that had underpinned teaching in and managing college writing programs. These included assumptions about how we assess what students have learned, how we teach, what we teach, or where we teach. The changes we made to respond to the pandemic amplified the calls that the authors in this collection make—change work can be initiated locally, or it can be thrust upon us, but it cannot be avoided.

In the three decades since the first PhDs were granted in composition and rhetoric, we've transformed our field. But we still have work to do. In the same way that our pedagogies shift to accommodate new and evolving literacy practices, our labor and institutional presence must also shift. We must articulate what that work is and how we can do that work just as well as we articulate our changing pedagogies. This book offers models for faculty who hope to build new programs or revise existing ones while maintaining a critical eye on our labor practices and external concerns, even in contexts that do not include writing program administrators to do that work.

The call for papers (CFP) for this collection had already gone out when one of the coauthors attended the Council of Writing Program Administrators (CWPA) convention in Baltimore in 2019. She couldn't help but observe the number of sessions she attended in which presenters described struggles they faced, in large part because they held WPA positions at institutions typical of writing programs in the United States—four-year comprehensives, baccalaureate-granting liberal arts colleges, two-year colleges, and in which they sought to influence writing instruction. However, they often were one of a handful, if not the only, writing-studies-trained faculty member in the department, perhaps expected to manage an established program or to oversee adjunct instructors but with little influence to change the current practices or implement best practices recommended in our disciplinary principles statements. Some presenters discussed their work in community colleges, where they are responsible for offering writing classes but without a position or structure resembling writing program administration as it is typically framed in the field.

It is within this context that we offer *Transformations* then—research, stories, studies, and scholarship from the discipline that reflects program work that looks very different from the traditional research 1 / research-intensive / doctoral program model in which a dedicated coordinator leads less experienced and part-time (or apprentice) writing instructors for first-year students. Many of the programs and instructors included in this volume are bringing about effective change in their programs through democratic rather than hierarchical methods. In "Writing Programs without Administrators," Carolyn Calhoon-Dillahunt (2011, 121) identifies some of the challenges to writing program support and development in two-year colleges, ranging from complex or insufficient placement methods to administrative accountability measures to precarious employment status for instructors, and inconsistent disciplinary preparation among instructors (also addressed by Klausman 2008, 2010, 2018). As she writes,

> Working conditions, then, are another significant challenge to effective writing program administration. In two-year college English departments, writing courses tend to make up the majority of the course offerings—composition is, after all, required, but very few of those teaching writing courses have any theoretical background in composition and rhetoric or writing pedagogy. In my own department, most full time and part-time faculty have degrees in literature or creative writing. That said, those teaching composition in community colleges are often experienced practitioners, unlike the graduate students who so often do the work of teaching composition at major universities with well-developed writing programs led by a WPA.

In research-intensive and graduate-degree-granting programs, who teaches composition tends to be more diverse. It may include a WPA, a teaching assistant (TA) trainer, tenured or tenure-track faculty in writing studies or composition and rhetoric, as well as instructors, graduate teaching assistants (GTAs), and contingent, non-tenure-track faculty. In other environments, such as smaller colleges and two-year colleges, people with PhD credentials, graduate students building expertise, and people with job security may not be available to teach composition at all, institutionally or locally. The shape and nature of programs at nonselective universities, without designated WPA positions, require a different type of navigating and negotiating (Dew 2009).

In such an environment, navigating change work in writing programs benefits from Eileen Schell's (2016) admonition in *A Rhetoric for Writing Program Administrators* handbook, "What Is a Writing Instructor?" that "writing instructors, no matter what rank, *are your colleagues*" (223). Our goal here is to present work that reflects the conditions in which most writing instructors and writing program administrators find themselves: working, perhaps, off the tenure track and within the context of English departments, sometimes as the sole member of the department with expertise in writing studies, and working with a highly diverse range of writing instructor colleagues. Perhaps writing courses are staffed by tenure-line faculty who have not been trained in writing studies beyond the requisite "Comp Theory" seminar in graduate school, or with non-tenure-track faculty. Writing program change work in this context is quite distinct from that in International Writing Programs (IWP) or WPA positions in which administrators are responsible for supervising almost exclusively a cadre of graduate student teaching assistants and non-tenure-stream faculty.

Such positions require distinct skills that include navigating complex political landscapes, working with a wide range of diversely trained—and largely autonomous—instructors, and designing and assessing writing programs that serve students who may not be like those at the institutions in which they were trained. Eileen Schell rightly describes the responsibilities of those doing writing program work in such contexts as to "find ways to establish a *shared and mutual pedagogical culture and community* that successfully bridges and addresses differences in knowledge, training, and approaches or that at least attempts to do so through conversation and dialogue" (223). Program work within English departments in comprehensive regional universities, in two-year colleges, or in other teaching-intensive and access-focused institutions also required extensive collaborative decision-making with administrators—department chairs, deans and associate deans, general education committees, coordinators for related programs (perhaps developmental education, reading support programs, or ESL program coordinators). Certainly, when writing programs are embedded in English departments, unilateral budget cuts to the department can detrimentally impact how many sections of composition are offered. Many administrators do not consider such issues at all in the face of ever-declining state funding and potentially low enrollment numbers. However, such considerations are necessary and require dedicated work on the part of the writing faculty in order to move a program's work forward or to make changes that will have a positive impact on retention, student success, or instructor support, conversations.

This is the context for this collection. The aim of these chapters is to equip readers with a set of schema to advance change for equity within their own contexts. In the contemporary higher education milieux, issues of increasing urgency and complexity face writing programs and department chairs, English departments and writing teachers, issues we center in this volume—in particular, these rapid changes are disproportionately affecting the kinds of institutions we focus on here, those that value access over selectivity. These challenges will only intensify in the postpandemic landscape. These include

- Remediation, developmental coursework, and the status of basic writing program interventions and reforms, such as the Accelerated Learning Program, studio models, the "Stretch" approach, and other corequisite support models serving marginalized and underprepared student populations

- Developments in technology, including online courses, blended writing courses, and other efforts that require supporting students in using technology for learning, as well as increasing the access to quality educational experiences for diverse students

- Gendered and racialized gaps in emotional labor, care work, and service in higher education, whether in types or level of instruction, or in the "outside the classroom" work required to manage writing programs including mentoring, advising and supporting students and instructors, serving on committees, and advocating administrators

- Labor, equitable, and just working conditions, the intensifying demands of graduate workers and contingent faculty resulting from the casualization of labor, the unstable and shrinking market for tenure-line work in higher education, and levels of "doing without / taking on" faced by instructors: additional debt, unmet material and teaching needs, lack of healthcare as just a few examples

- Calls (or the desire by faculty) to do curricular reform, whether through innovative curriculum approaches, as efforts to integrate high-impact learning, or as the result of assessment data or external mandates, as a need to respond to changes in student populations within the institution (including linguistically diverse, first-generation, low-income, nontraditional, and other growing student populations)

This is not to say that no recent scholarship tackles these issues. James Porter et al. introduced the notion of "institutional critique" in their 2000 *CCC* article, "Institutional Critique: A Rhetorical Methodology for Change," which they describe as

a method that insists that institutions, as unchangeable as they may seem (and, indeed, often are), do contain spaces for reflection, resistance, revision, and productive action. This method insists that sometimes individuals (writing teachers, researchers, writers, students, citizens) can rewrite institutions through rhetorical action. We see institutional critique as a way to supplement the field's current efforts and to extend the field into broader interrogations of discourse in society. (612–13)

Likewise, Michelle LaFrance and Melissa Nicolas's (2012) account of institutional ethnography (IE) provides a map for, as they describe it,

> how things happen—what practices constitute the institution as we think of it, how discourse may be understood to compel and shape those practices, and how norms of practice speak to, for, and over individuals. Institutional ethnography's focus on the day-to-day work life of individuals, as well as its emphasis on describing how individuals choose to interact with/in their institutions, provides a methodology for explicating, and thereby gaining insight into, the actualities of our academic work lives. (131)

What we want to highlight here, then, is the next step to this work of institutional examination. Porter et al. (2000) argue that "institutional critique is, fundamentally, a pragmatic effort to use rhetorical means to improve institutional systems," (625), and though we agree that a substantive understanding of the material and rhetorical components of the space that requires change, we want to show what *comes after the deployment of institutional critique.* Recognizing the value of Porter et al.'s claim that "a simple spatial reordering, a micropolitical and rhetorical use of space, can constitute an effective political action" (625), we want to show how, in a rapidly changing ideological and material landscape, change work is possible—even big and seemingly impossible change work. We nod here to Debra Dew and Susan McLeod, as well, who have documented change work in writing programs.

The central galvanizing theme of this collection moves from institutional knowledge (whether through a critique or ethnography) to acting on that knowledge. Steve Lamos (2012), for example, in "Institutional Critique in Composition Studies: Methodological and Ethical Considerations for Researchers," describes the methodological considerations of institutional critique—a step that often precedes action-oriented efforts—that are relevant here in that teacher-scholar-activists must employ evidence and data-based approach to their change work. A key in this discussion is the work and how we envision ourselves as faculty; we must see ourselves as workers in an institution and embrace our role at that institution to do this work instead of continually buying into the myth of mobility (Cole et al. 2017). Our collection takes this work one step further in creating maps for how to move from analysis, critique, and ethnography to interventions that can happen in and from a multiplicity of positions and places within our programs.

Writing program change work as documented in this collection shows how faculty from diverse institutional positionalities (contingent faculty and graduate workers, as well as faculty working on the tenure track), and within, or in response to, institutional constraints can navigate these challenges to bring about change for the benefit of students the mission of educational access.

LABOR, INSTITUTIONAL CHANGE, CURRICULUM: A GUIDE TO THE BOOK

Part 1: Transforming Labor focuses on work done by graduate students, non-tenure-track faculty, and tenured allies to improve working conditions in writing programs. In the first chapter, "Braiding Stories, Taking Action: A Narrative of Graduate Worker–Led Change Work," Ruth Osorio, Jaclyn Fiscus-Cannaday, and Allison Hutchison launch our collection with a powerful narrative based on their work with the Labor Census Task Force within the Writing Program Administration Graduate Organization. Their chapter highlights the labor issues rife within composition, rhetoric, and writing studies: the shockingly familiar stories of graduate labor exploitation. Their chapter, however, is one that claims power, agency, and hope in untenable and unsustainable circumstances. Their study illustrates the power that graduate students can hold as leaders of institutional change, especially regarding issues of equity, labor, and diversity. This chapter begins our collections for an important reason. Osorio, Fiscus-Cannaday, and Hutchinson set the tone for the spaces in which our labor practices must and can change, and they emphasize the nature of what grassroots change can look like at our institutions, in our programs, and as a part of our organizing professional bodies. Paulette Stevenson's chapter, "Circulating NTTF Stories to Effect Change: The Case of ASU against 5/5," follows to illustrate the role that non-tenure-track (NTT) instructors can inhabit to improve labor conditions. She sums up the labor of NTT faculty perfectly: "Budgets are balanced, bottoms lines are cut, and tenured faculty lines are paid for by exploiting NTTF" (chapter 1). In her chapter, Stevenson illustrates the ways in which a large, research-intensive state school attempted to force NTT faculty to teach more courses for less pay. She outlines the work that the non-tenured faculty did to fight even more exploitative working conditions by harnessing the knowledge of the discipline, conveying the pitfalls of the higher course load to a wider public, and getting coverage from popular and academic news outlets. Building off of chapter 1, this chapter highlights the kairotic and rhetorically cunning work that can happen in the face of institutional misuse of vulnerable workers.

In chapter 3, "'From 'Expendable' to Credentialed: Transforming Working Conditions through the HLC's New Guidelines for Faculty Qualifications," Megan Schoen and Lori Ostergaard contextualize how our field remains torn between two contradictory instincts: to improve labor conditions for part-time and contingent faculty, many of whom possess few credentials in the field of composition, or to assert our (exclusive) disciplinary expertise. Locating their chapter in the history of the Wyoming Conference Resolution, they argue that though our scholarship has spent a great deal of time talking about labor, there has been no move to enact the recommendations from the 1987 conference. Schoen and Ostergaard argue that instead of developing a single, national credential for writing instructors, writing programs may be able to leverage the "faculty qualification guidelines handed down from higher education accreditation agencies to develop local, departmental standards for disciplinary expertise in the field" (chapter 3) to improve job security and professional status. Rachel Hall Buck and Susan Miller-Cochran in chapter 4, "Advocating Together: Pros and Cons of Cross-Rank Collaboration as a Strategy for Advocacy," round out the first part of the collection by focusing on cross-rank collaboration: the often messy but rewarding work that happens when faculty across ranks and graduate students work together to navigate the administration of a writing program. This chapter illustrates, in part, what was missing in the change work of the first two chapters—the support of tenured faculty for those who are in precarious labor situations in their programs. Hall Buck and Miller-Cochran use their work collecting data to keep a lower course cap in composition courses to illustrate ways in which cross-rank collaboration can impact and improve labor conditions at colleges and universities.

Authors in Part 2, "Transforming Institutions," direct our attention to the sometimes ignored and often confusing institutional practices that writing studies professionals must navigate to do the work of writing programs. In chapter 5, "Time, Care, and Faculty Working Conditions," Heather M. Robinson provides a useful transition from labor practices to institutions by centering care work as what academics do. Her chapter gives readers a context for the larger foci of this section. By emphasizing care work, she opens space for the various programs that proliferate in or on the edges of writing programs: Writing Across the Curriculum, Accelerated Learning Programs and developmental writing courses, and digital mediated courses. She advocates that we change the discourses that we build around care and, by extension, feminized work. Robinson defines care work as the activities that academic staff undertake to support students' learning and to support students' and other colleagues' emotional health and academic advancement. In this chapter, Robinson focuses on care work as the affective parts of teaching, service, and research, rather than as the content of what we teach and do in our academic work. By countering often all-consuming discourses of productivity, this chapter uses the slow scholarship movement to resist and demonstrate the ways in which what counts as academic labor might be revised through the governance process at colleges and universities.

Tiffany Rousculp, in chapter 6 "Everyone Writes: Expanding Writing across the Curriculum to Change a Culture of Writing," focuses on another cross-institutional writing program, Writing Across the Curriculum (WAC). Rousculp argues that "WAC programs and their 'agents' increase, foster, create, promote, transform, and make change; they do not stand still nor do they accept the status quo of writing at a given institution." However, she highlights the ways in which, though powerful spaces for institutional change work, very few WAC programs are sustained or sustainable. They tend to come and go with funding models, accreditation initiatives, and faculty willingness to do the work. This chapter points to how much more complicated the work of WAC becomes at community colleges. Rousculp illustrates the history of three different versions of WAC at her institution in order to discuss strategies for establishing a culture of writing in a transitional educational space. Her chapter illustrates the labor, and in connection to the first chapter in this section, the care that it takes to establish a sustainable program that supports faculty and students. Transitioning to another common model of writing program instruction, Leah Anderst, Jennifer Maloy, and Neil Meyer discuss Accelerated Learning Program (ALP) models in chapter 7: "Mapping Trajectories of ALP within Developmental Writing Education." The authors contextualize ALP within the histories of basic writing and argue that ALP can serve those who are invested in providing additional support to underprepared students because it is one of the few acceptable alternatives to traditional remediation. They argue that discourses of austerity and a new literacy crisis can circumvent key stakeholders in developmental educational curriculum, and they highlight the importance of our disciplinary position statements and white papers in doing institutional change work that keeps attention on the voices of educators and their students.

In the final chapter of this section, chapter 8, Rochelle (Shelley) Rodrigo and Julia Romberger focus on another writing program initiative that is sweeping our institutions: digital mediated courses. In "Actors and Allies: Faculty, IT Work, and Writing Program Support," they contextualize the impact of information technology (IT) in the academy and in writing programs, and they share their study results that introduce and define writing program technologists to discuss how and why they might be helpful to both WPAs and their institutions at large. Writing studies experienced the impact of rapidly changing computer technologies very early in higher education, and it is an ongoing issue as our programs move to online instruction; multimodal pedagogies; and research in digital rhetoric, media, and composing. Rodrigo and Romberger provide a map in for how writing program administrators, faculty, and instructors can effectively work with "techies" in various roles and at different ranks within writing programs and across individual institutions.

In the final section of the collection, part 3, "Transforming Curriculum," authors highlight curricular initiatives and innovations that have been increasingly important in composition and rhetoric in the last few decades. Debates about basic writing and developmental education, multilingual writing and writers, and online writing programs discussed in part 2 are explored here in detail. The authors in this section focus on transformative course design by highlighting our methods in practice: archival work, multimodal, multilingual, and developmental writing. In the first chapter, chapter 9, "Personal Choice: Connecting Lived Experience to Academic Experience as Essential Empowerment in Basic Writing," Ruth Benander, Brenda Refaei, and Mwangi Alex Chege discuss curriculum reform at an open-access institution for developmental writing. Like Anderst, Maloy, and Meyer in chapter 7, these authors were guided by the "Two-Year College English Association (TYCA) White Paper on Developmental Education Reforms" to redesign a course that serves the majority of English language learners and generation 1.5 students. What sets their chapter apart in terms of curriculum design is their focus on student choice and flexibility to accommodate a diverse student population through a culturally responsive pedagogy.

In "Leveraging the Translanguaging Labor of a Multilingual University: SJSU's Transformation to a Postremedial Writing Community," chapter 10, Cynthia Baer asks "if [her institution] can leverage our internal dissensus to transform diversity into learning, what work might we do to develop public consensus for a working, thriving democracy?" Moving beyond developmental writing curriculum, Baer's chapter focuses on a response to rapidly changing student demographics that include multilingual writers. She narrates her program's move to a Stretch model that emphasizes the labor of translanguaging to support an inclusive, equitable, and sustainable multilingual learning community. This chapter works to contextualize curriculum transformation not only within the institution but within the transformative scholarship that supports multilingual writers and their teachers. She argues that remediation in higher education has been an academic intervention to contain the difference (at its perceived source) and thereby increase communication efficiency (readability) for listeners and readers already expert in the target language of the community. It is a labor policy—and one that has been anything but efficient. In connection to Baer's work, Sarah Henderson Lee and Shyam B. Pandey also focus on multilingual populations in their chapter, chapter 11, "World Englishes in the First-Year Composition Classroom: Perceptions of Multilingual Writers." Henderson Lee and Pandey locate their chapter in the shift in the international student population that they argue stems from a number of factors, including increased globalization and the strong reputation and prestige associated with US higher education and related degrees. They gather and analyze multilingual writers' perceptions of the incorporation of World Englishes texts in an academic writing course at a large state institution. They report on their participants' movement toward language variation that supports a revised first-year writing curriculum that prioritizes the development of global literacy among all undergraduate writers. They found that their students moved from resistance to curiosity to acceptance as they powerfully navigated the relationship between language, culture, and academics. As our populations in writing programs become increasingly diverse, this focus on World Englishes demonstrates the ways in which writing studies programs can support all of their learners.

Lynée Lewis Gaillet in chapter 12, "Teaching with Archives: Transformative Pedagogy" also highlights how the major in composition has changed. Instead of focusing on demographics, however, Gaillet offers an example of transformative pedagogy in response to the needs of twenty-first-century humanities students in an era of decline. Locating her work in the "archival turn" in writing instruction, this chapter outlines a split-level graduate/undergraduate course in archival research methods, providing a rationale for the course along with reading suggestions and dovetailed assignments that introduce students to digital and material primary investigations. She highlights student voices as primary researchers as a way for instructors to enact larger concepts integral to writing studies: multidimensional collaboration, opening access, rhetorical activism, and dissemination of student writing. The level of detail that Gaillet provides in her chapter gives instructors interested in exploring such a course a blueprint and a series of tools to enact primary research in their classrooms. By pairing her course design with her students' voices, Gaillet powerfully demonstrates the role of primary research in twenty-first-century writing education.

The final chapter of the collection also moves us powerfully forward in terms of twenty-first-century writing instruction. In chapter

13, "Designing an Open-Access Online Writing Program: Negotiating Tensions between Disciplinary Ideals and Institutional Realities," Joanne Baird Giordano and Cassandra Phillips discuss the ways in which online writing instruction (OWI) principles as outlined by the OWI Committee lay a foundation for developing an online writing program based on writing studies theory and practice while also arguing for disciplinary values and ethical standards, including manageable class sizes, instructor control over course content and teaching, fair compensation, and faculty training. For Giordano and Phillips, however, many of the OWI principles can be difficult to implement fully at two-year open-access institutions and some public four-year institutions because of institutional mandates, limited financial and professional resources, contingent staffing, and limited instructor agency. This chapter describes the complicated process of designing and implementing change within an online writing program at a two-year, open-admissions college. The authors outline the process of negotiating disciplinary tensions, conditions of austerity that impacted their work, and the ways in which they met the needs of diverse learners. Like the previous chapters on multilingual writing, primary research, and the needs of diverse learners in the composition classroom, these authors highlight the affordances and constraints of best practices in new pedagogical trends at different institutional types.

We organized this collection out of a sense of ambition for what it could be and what the implications are: change can happen in positive ways for our teachers and our students. While the material experiences of being underpaid, overworked, and overwhelmed in higher education is a reality of the job, writing teachers navigate change and work to better the educational experiences of their students all the time. Some of this pedagogical work can happen individually and does because composition instructors put their heads down, teach their classes, grade mountains of papers, and make it better the next time they do it. But, the work that is outlined in this collection cannot happen independently or individually in our classrooms only. The chapters in this collection that focus on curriculum contextualize curricular work in collaboration for a reason. And that is what these authors speak to collectively: collaboration. In reaching out to others, building coalitions beyond our immediate spaces and environments, we resist the isolation that unfolds at many institutions. This collection asks us to move beyond our cloisters, dynamically, by forging alliances even if they seem unlikely or challenging.

If there is one thing that all of these chapters demonstrate, it is that even seemingly impossible tasks are doable. But they require us to think strategically about the role of composition in the university. The field is past the point where we can bemoan the reality of our curriculum, and our students, and our precarity. Compositionists know the business of the university, perhaps better than people in any other discipline. By leveraging that longitudinal knowledge, understanding the systems in which we labor, and forging alliances with people who are as invested as we are, we can create educational spaces that are true to our values. And as we all begin to process the political, social, economic, and institutional changes that have been foisted upon us by the COVID-19 pandemic, it will be more important than ever that we articulate these values to ourselves, our colleagues, and our discipline as we face unprecedented and swift calls for change.

What are these values? Those haven't really changed. We strive to support literacy development for our students, in ways that meet their needs, that are sustainable and responsive, and that help students name and achieve their educational goals. For those of us who are in positions with some stability and agency, we make it (and must work harder to make it) a priority to support and respect the people who are working with our students, all of the people across rank and institution type. Advocating for all the best practice models and conditions brings us part of the way to that goal, but the work discussed in these chapters makes it a reality. Knowledge about how students become better writers has been established and fine-tuned for decades, and so, in this collection, we ask readers to commit to making strategic and intentional decisions that move us closer rather than farther away from the ideals they espouse. We have to care about all students. We have to care about all instructors. The individuals in our ecosystems have the capacity to do the work and must be afforded every opportunity to fulfill their potential. The individuals writing in the collection focus, in a way, on one big question: Am I making the learning environment for writers, students, and teachers better? And they demand of our readers: are you?

REFERENCES

Calhoon-Dillahunt, Carolyn. 2011. "Writing Programs without Administrators: Frameworks for Successful Writing Programs in the Two-Year College," *WPA: Writing Program Administration* 35.1: 118–34.

Cole, Kirsti, Holly Hassel, and Eileen Schell. 2017. "Remodeling Shared Governance: Feminist Decision Making and Resistance in Academic Neoliberalism" In *Surviving Sexism in Academia: Strategies for Feminist Leadership,* edited by Kirsti Cole and Holly Hassel, 13–28. London: Routledge.

Dew, Debra Frank. 2009. "WPA as Rhetor: Scholarly Production and the Difference a Discipline Makes." *College Composition and Communication* 60.2: W40–W62.

Goggin, Maureen Daly. 1995. "The Disciplinary Instability of Composition." In *Reconceiving Writing, Rethinking Writing Instruction*, edited by Joseph Petraglia, 27–48. Mahway, NJ: Laurence Erlbaum Associates.

Isaacs, Emily. 2018. *Writing at the State U: Instruction and Administration at 106 Comprehensive Universities*. Logan: Utah State University Press.

Klausman, Jeffrey. 2008. "Mapping the Terrain: The Two-Year College Writing Program Administrator." *Teaching English in the Two-Year College* 35.3: 238–51.

Klausman, Jeffrey. 2010. "Not Just a Matter of Fairness: Adjunct Faculty and Writing Programs in Two-Year Colleges." *Teaching English in the Two-Year College* 37.4: 363–71.

Klausman, Jeffrey. 2018. "The Two-Year College Writing Program and Academic Freedom: Labor, Scholarship, and Compassion." *Teaching English in the Two-Year College* 45.4: 385–405.

LaFrance, Michelle, and Melissa Nicolas. 2012. "Institutional Ethnography as Materialist Framework for Writing Program Research and the Faculty-Staff Work Standpoints Project." *College Composition and Communication* 64.1: 130–50.

Lamos, Steve. 2012. "Institutional Critique in Composition Studies: Methodological and Ethical Considerations for Researchers." In *Writing Studies Research in Practice Methods and Methodologies*, edited by Lee Nickoson and Mary P. Sheridan, 158–70. Carbondale: Southern Illinois University Press.

Porter, James, Patricia Sullivan, Stuart Blythe, Jeffrey T. Grabill, and Libby Miles. 2000. "Institutional Critique: A Rhetorical Methodology for Change." *College Composition and Communication* 51.1: 610–42.

Schell, Eileen. 2016. "What Is a Writing Instructor?" In *A Rhetoric for Writing Program Administrators*, 2nd ed., edited by Rita Malenczyk, 219–32. Anderson, SC: Parlor Press.

Yancey, Kathleen Blake. 2004. "Made Not Only in Words: Composition Is the New Key." *College Composition and Communication* 56.2: 297–328.

PART 1

Transforming Labor

The worst-kept secret in academia is exploitative labor practices. In fact, it is not a secret at all. Precarious labor is simply our reality. We talk about the labor problems haunting our field at length but in reality, we do little to combat them. There are a number of reasons for exploitative labor, and in writing studies we are familiar with them all: cheap labor in high demand to meet curriculum requirements, administrative bloat, increasingly little monetary support from state and federal legislative bodies, neoliberalism, and American anti-intellectualism that posits all teachers as simultaneously out of touch with the needs of the public and disconnected from mainstream values.

In writing studies, in particular, labor inequities are amplified by an increasing class of faculty with training in writing studies who take on primary material and intellectual responsibility for writing programs—and an apprentice model that staffs courses taught to first-year students with minimally prepared graduate students and poorly supported contingent faculty, in part because assertions about the "disciplinarity" of writing studies and its establishment as a field have not been aligned with the reality of what and whom we teach.

For us, it was imperative that any collection focused on change work in writing studies start by acknowledging the problems and by demonstrating that there are ways to work within the system to positively improve the labor conditions of everyone. In Part 1, "Transforming Labor," contributing authors highlight work done by graduate students, non-tenure-track faculty, and tenured allies to improve working conditions in writing programs. These are powerful chapters and powerful voices that do not simply succumb to the tales of neoliberalism haunting our institutions. These chapters give us disciplinary, institutional, departmental, and programmatic strategies to make a difference. The authors demand that we face the stories of the people who do the support work, often unacknowledged and always underpaid, in our departments. They

https://doi.org/10.7330/9781646421428.p001

also reflect the voices of *those who do the vast majority of the teaching of first-year writing*—graduate students and contingent faculty.

By shining a light on our systemic labor problems, each chapter poses a set of strategies that, with some organizing and collaboration, could work in most contexts. Stories matter. But perhaps these chapters reveal the shortfalls of relying only on stories without action. These chapters show us how to take action, powerfully, to create more equitable labor practices.

1

BRAIDING STORIES, TAKING ACTION
A Narrative of Graduate Worker–Led Change Work

Ruth Osorio, Jaclyn Fiscus-Cannaday, and Allison Hutchison

"I know I'm at one of the better universities in the country, so I find it depressing that I have to continue to take out loans because I don't make enough. I can't even fathom how I would survive with less of a stipend or without health insurance. My department fights for my rights, but it's a constant battle against the university."

"Women's or trans procedures barely or not covered [by healthcare offered to grad workers]; insurance over the summer is an extra $600 on top of the academic yearly $1,400 for two people."

"Having children is also a blessing, but personally it puts me at a disadvantage when it comes to my teaching preparation and research. There is little to no support to mitigate this, and our university yanked dependent coverage from us last year which put more of a strain on our finances and time."

"As far as I know, the only mental healthcare we have access to is the resources available to us as students—and that usually means talking to someone who's getting a master's in clinical psychology instead of speaking to a licensed medical practitioner."

"I understand why the suicide rate is so high. These are inhumane conditions."

We collected these stories as part of a 2017 nationwide survey about the labor conditions of graduate student workers in writing programs (LCTF 2019).[1] These stories both shocked us and felt familiar. As grad workers at the time, we had so many of our own stories that we experienced, observed, or overhead. If you work in a writing program, you probably do, too. The goal of our survey was to gather data that would shine light into the systemic exploitation of grad labor. We did so as graduate students,

https://doi.org/10.7330/9781646421428.c001

Figure 1.1. Timeline of Labor Census Task Force activities.

workers, and researchers on the Labor Census Task Force (LCTF) within the Writing Program Administration Graduate Organization (WPA-GO). In response to the University of Missouri healthcare crisis in summer 2015, Ruth worked with the WPA-GO to begin our group, and Allison and Jaclyn joined when the LCTF officially began its work in summer 2016. Inspired by the depth of adjunct organizing in the field of writing studies, we designed, circulated, and analyzed a nationwide survey about the labor and labor conditions of graduate workers in writing programs together with ten other people (see figure 1.1).

Our LCTF quantitative findings tell a compelling story: 71.6 percent of the 344 grad workers surveyed declared that their stipends did not adequately cover their basic needs, 36 percent expressed that their university's health plans did not adequately cover their health needs, and 62.8 percent reported working more than their contracted hours. The LCTF circulated these data to the WPA-L (the central listserv for folks interested in writing program administration) and social media on March 20, 2019, as a six-page PDF report titled "Report on Graduate Student Instructor Labor Conditions in Writing Program." We hoped that the data would change the status quo of grad workers in writing programs. The response was electric: leading scholars in the field of writing studies replied with dismay and outrage, expressing solidarity with grad workers at their institutions. Grad workers responded as well, telling us that they were using the document to initiate negotiations for higher pay and better benefits at their home institution.

The stories, data, and responses to the survey highlight the liminal space graduate workers occupy in writing programs. As Tressie McMillan Cottom so bluntly states when she criticizes the inequity of the graduate student experience, "In the academic hierarchy, [graduate students] are units of labor. They can be students but not just students. They are academics in the making" (2019, 2). As both students and workers, graduate students perform essential work for the campus by teaching introduction classes, running labs, supporting administrative work, and more. And the struggles described in the stories above emphasize that often the biggest barriers faced by graduate students are tied to their status as workers: low pay, limited benefits, little to no support for parents and caregivers—the same issues that unite the larger labor movement in the United States. Even though the National Labor Relations Board ruled that grad workers at private universities are indeed employees in 2016, university administrators and some faculty insist that grad workers are students first and apprentices second. Such framing allows universities to benefit from the cheap labor of graduate workers, especially in a time of underfunding for the humanities (Chaput 2000, 184). In particular, writing programs depend on grad workers, with grad workers teaching nearly 40 percent of first-year writing sections at PhD-granting institutions and 15 percent at MA-granting institutions ("MLA Survey of Departmental Staffing" 2014). Therefore, we ask ourselves and our readers: What are writing programs, pedagogies, and practices doing to change the status quo of graduate worker exploitation?

We—Ruth, Jaclyn, and Allison—believe that the story of the LCTF's behind-the-scenes work of developing, distributing, and analyzing the study illustrates the power that graduate students can hold as leaders of institutional change, especially regarding issues of diversity, equity, and labor. We all served as chair or co-chair of the LCTF at some point in the task force's tenure, shepherding the project from brainstorming sessions to IRB approval to survey circulation to analysis to reporting. As graduate students at the task force's formation, we joined for a variety of reasons, but one motivation united us: a belief in the potential for grad workers to enact structural change in their departments, universities, and disciplines. If institutions truly value diversity, equity, and labor, they should support grad-worker-led initiatives. And, because Writing Programs are often fueled by grad worker labor, we argue the field of writing studies is a ripe site for supporting graduate-student-led initiatives that will reshape labor practices.

Just as we began the chapter with stories, we move onto our own stories of leading this study. Following cultural and feminist rhetorics methodologies, we evoke storytelling as our method of theory making (Ahmed 2017; Cottom 2018; Powell et al. 2014; Royster and Kirsch 2012). In the following two sections, we focus on two feminist rhetorical practices that fueled our work: (1) honoring lived experiences as sources of knowledge and (2) creating equitable models of collaborative leadership. In each section, we speak in a collective voice to situate the following stories in larger conversations within writing studies, and include our own reflections on the work. We hope that sharing our stories will function as a theoretical tool for inspiring other transformational change work led by graduate workers. Not only did the graduate students of LCTF function as academics reporting their own research, but we also validated graduate workers as knowledge makers by centering them as research subjects. We hope that in sharing our stories about our LCTF experience, we reveal the power of grad workers to research, organize, and lead the way in transforming the labor practices of writing studies.

CREATING CHANGE BY CENTERING GRADUATE WORKER EPISTEMOLOGY

Feminists have long argued that the "personal is political," using it not only as a rallying cry but also a method for incorporating lived experiences as evidence: "for black and Chicana feminists, as for white feminists in women's liberation, personal experience was the beginning point for their critical resistance to masculine ideologies" (Hesford 2013, 13). Because we too are intersectional feminists who value personal experience as evidence for systemic oppression, the lived experiences of graduate students served as the catalyst for our research study. Each of us seemed to know innately that our labor conditions as graduate student workers—and for Allison, as a former adjunct college writing and reading instructor—were less than ideal, but we didn't necessarily have any empirical evidence. We knew, though, that our own personal experiences could do the important work of guiding us in designing our LCTF survey, gathering the evidence we needed for change work done for graduate labor practices.

We see our work at LCTF and our reliance on graduate student epistemology as influenced by the work of feminist scholars such as Jacqueline Jones Royster, who argued in her influential article on rhetorical history that "in recognizing knowledge as an interpretive enterprise, a social construction, the imperative becomes the task of connecting theory with scholarly action in order to both theorize and engage in other scholarly activities more systematically" (2003, 149). While Royster was addressing what constitutes knowledge in rhetorical studies, we would like to extend her point that "other views participate kaleidoscopically in the knowledge-making process" (149) to our own work leading the LCTF. We support the view that narrative and perspective are both an epistemological orientation and a research method. Like Deborah Journet (2012), we believe that "it is important to articulate what qualities of observation, analysis, or representation we require if we are to accept any particular narrative account as a persuasive instance of research" (17). However, our project in this chapter is not necessarily to distribute knowledge generated from our survey, but rather to offer knowledge we have generated on instituting programmatic change as graduate student leaders and researchers in writing studies.

Ruth:

I first saw the story on Facebook in 2015: the University of Missouri had abruptly canceled its health insurance plans for graduate workers. I was states away, attending the University of Maryland, College Park, as a PhD student. I had no connection to Mizzou. But still, I shared the outrage, shock, and sense of betrayal the grad workers were expressing on social media. In a news article about Mizzou grad worker organizing, I saw a picture of a pregnant grad worker; *how could she afford prenatal, labor and delivery, postpartum, and newborn care without insurance?*

These questions were fresh on my mind because I had just had my first child, and the medical care had been almost entirely covered by my insurance from the University of Maryland. I chose my PhD program based on the same things other prospective students think about: my potential advisor, job placement statistics, and opportunities for professional development. But I also prioritized programs that offered quality, affordable healthcare and paid parental leave. I wasn't a mom yet, but I knew I wanted to be one and soon.

I joined the Facebook group for Mizzou grad workers organizing in the hopes to help in any way I could. They wanted to know how other grad programs do grad student healthcare, so they could sharpen their demands to the university. What they needed was information, but that information was largely unavailable. There was no easy-to-find census of grad student labor conditions.

At the same time, I emailed all the professional organizations I belonged to at the time, asking them to make a statement about the crisis at Mizzou. They all declined, saying that they don't take positions in political matters. I was frustrated because so many of these organizations had been writing about the relationship between labor conditions and writing instruction, but they didn't seem interested or concerned about grad workers en masse losing healthcare. That's when I realized that any response to Mizzou had to come from grad students. I was lucky enough to be on the WPA-GO Committee, and my grad student colleagues agreed with me:

we also saw how quickly a university could threaten the health of its grad workers, and we were afraid and pissed off.

Eventually, because of fierce and dedicated grad worker organizing, Mizzou restored its health insurance plan for grad students. But the fact remained: grad workers don't know what we don't know. What is the status of grad worker pay, insurance, and leave? How do grad workers feel about their labor conditions? How do they think programs can do better? With the support of the WPA-GO committee, I put together a pilot survey and circulated it among the committee members. When I talked about the study, which highlighted the concerns our committee members had about their pay and benefits, we decided to create a task force dedicated to a national survey of grad worker labor conditions.

Ruth's narrative highlights how valuable grad worker emotions can be in evaluating fairness, equity, and diversity in the profession—and, thus, how those emotions can be key in changing the profession. Feminist scholars have long argued for the epistemological richness of lived experiences, particularly emotions; thanks to the work of Sara Ahmed, Laura Micciche, Shari Stenberg, Allison Jaggar, and many other feminist writers, emotions are no longer dismissed as a contrast to or distraction from knowing. Therefore, emotions guided our study: our feelings as grad workers brought us to this work, shaped our work, and pushed us to complete a study completely unrelated to our dissertation research. We knew—as Jaggar, Micciche, and Ahmed argue—that emotions are social and political. And we knew, as workers low in the hierarchy of academia, and as women, our emotions granted us "epistemological privilege," enabling us to "incorporate reliable appraisals of situations" and imagine "possible beginnings of [academia] in which all could thrive" (Jaggar 1989, 168).

But Ruth's emotions could not be the sole driver of the study: in order to conduct a nationwide survey of grad worker labor conditions in writing programs, she needed to form a team of other grad worker-researchers. By fall 2016, WPA-GO put out a call to all its members for committee assignments, listing the LCTF as an option. Jaclyn and Allison became members, along with ten others, and together we talked about what kinds of questions we wanted to see on the survey. As more people joined the task force, our conception of what constituted "labor conditions" expanded. Each member brought their life experience to the team, which shaped our survey design in generative ways.

Jaclyn:
About six months prior to our LCTF brainstorming meeting, I had sat outside the building of my graduate seminar crying. Well, more like hyperventilating. I was having another panic attack. Unable to breathe. Feeling

like someone was sitting on my chest as I spiraled: *Why does it feel like even the simplest tasks are impossible? How is it that the only way I will get dressed is I have to teach? I haven't read for my grad classes yet this semester and we're three weeks in. Why am I avoiding any professionalization opportunity? I can't even get myself to grocery shop. How am I going to finish this PhD? I can't even imagine getting through tomorrow. I can't live like this anymore.*

I was frozen in a cycle of depression and anxiety, and I finally had the courage to call our on-campus health center for mental health screening, thanks to my fellow graduate students' encouragement, only to find out the center did not have availability for months. I knew I could not make it months. The on-campus health center was the only affordable option on our graduate student healthcare plan. I made the only choice I had: I went into debt to pursue other mental health care. And, so, in this brainstorming moment I pitched the idea that we should not just focus on healthcare, generally, but also ask questions about mental health care more specifically. The group heard me. We added a section about mental health care in the hopes that the data would help other graduate students negotiate for better mental health care coverage.

Ruth:

Like Jaclyn, my health experiences shaped what questions I wanted to see on the survey. Because I was a grad worker and a mom, I was particularly curious about how different campuses approached support for graduate workers with children, including parental leave and childcare. As we were drafting the survey questions, I was surprised to receive pushback from another LCTF member, who questioned why we had included such a focus on parents in the survey. This focus didn't make sense to the member because in their program, they explained, no one had kids. It was an interesting, and honestly frustrating, moment for me: less than 10 percent of the questions focused on the question of support for families. After I pointed that out, the other member agreed that it was important to keep the questions in.

The interaction also made me ponder how many programs unwittingly (or maybe somewhat consciously) preclude diversity by not offering support for varied life experiences. In other words, could the reason the other member's program had no parents be because the program does not offer parental leave? How do the labor conditions offered or not offered shape the embodied realities of the people who attend a particular program? As a former adjunct, I know this question applies to all laborers, but since grad students are rarely framed as laborers, this question stayed with me throughout the survey design, circulation, and analysis.

As a result of Ruth's insight, we did try to safeguard against our lived experiences being the only ones that shaped the kinds of questions we asked and therefore the kinds of knowledge we could draw upon. At multiple points in our survey drafting process, we incorporated usability testing. First, we did this testing in-house with members taking the survey, and, later, we shared survey drafts with others for feedback: graduate worker colleagues, Council of Writing Program Administrators (CWPA) and Conference on College Composition and Communication (CCCC) conference participants, WPA-GO leadership, and the faculty primary investigator (PI) for our IRB process. But, while gathering others' perspectives in the hopes that their lived experiences would become exigencies within our transformational change work, we were also wary of changing the focus of our research. It was important that the voices of graduate students were the most instrumental in shaping the kinds of data that were collected and how the data were distributed.

Allison:
My experiences framed the survey in certain ways that were both beneficial and insulated. As someone who entered a PhD program seven years after earning my master's degree, I had been working and teaching in higher education settings before joining the LCTF. In some ways, I had more of an administrative than a graduate student perspective because of my professional experience. Nevertheless, I was familiar with my expertise being undervalued because I had been employed as a staff member and adjunct instructor, not a faculty member. Straddling this divide was quite similar to the status of a graduate student: I felt like my teaching and administrative experience wasn't always acknowledged by faculty who I had become used to interacting with as colleagues. Being the student again, I had difficulty adjusting to the idea that I was a novice in many regards and yet still had familiarity with academic hierarchies, curricula, and institutional structures.

The survey creation for this project was a new and empowering experience for us because we shifted from our novice roles to that of researchers. Although we worked with a PI as part of IRB protocol, to whom we are grateful for their service, we the grad workers took ownership of the study design. During initial survey drafting, the PI noted that the survey questions seemed institutional and programmatic, so the PI suggested that we survey writing program administrators and directors of graduate studies. After deliberation, we decided not to take that suggestion because we were not just interested in the facts that administrators could report; we wanted to learn what graduate students were experiencing. We wanted our project to offer graduate students' stories, honoring their personal experiences as evidence of the systemic oppression that graduate students face. As a result, we added questions that would elicit knowledge that only graduate students could share, like: *Is your stipend adequate for covering your living needs?* And, *is your university or program's healthcare plan adequate for covering your health needs?* We thought these questions were important because (1) only graduate students themselves could answer, and (2) the answers provide significant data about the status of graduate student laborers and how material circumstances affect their lives. Because this survey emerged out of our own lived experiences, we felt empowered to design a survey that centered on the lived experiences of our respondents. This was the moment when we realized that, even though we needed faculty to legitimize the study, we as grad workers were the leaders of this project.

As leaders of the project, we honored our belief that transformational change work should come from fellow graduate students. For example, if an administrator was taking that same survey, they may list that there is a six-week course release policy. But graduate workers taking the survey can explain that though such a policy exists on the books, grad workers in their writing program are discouraged from taking time off of teaching for birth or adoption. Indeed, many respondents shared that exact observation with us, describing the pressures grad workers faced to either teach through birth and recovery or take the semester off without pay or benefits. In allowing graduate workers' lived experience to be evidence, we learned not just the official labor policies but what was practiced. This was what made our work unique: we trusted graduate workers to tell us the status of their labor conditions, and with that data, better understood how policies were implemented and experienced in their daily lives. By privileging the voices of grad workers over administrator reporting, we were able to paint a picture of the grad worker experience and identify specific labor practices that grad workers can organize around.

And yet, there are dangers to relying solely on the life experiences of those present. For example, we were all white on the task force, so we did not have lived experiences of racism to draw upon when brainstorming questions for the survey. Looking back, especially at the overwhelming whiteness of the survey respondents (79 percent), we realize that we overlooked how race impacts working conditions when creating and distributing the survey. How would our survey, its circulation, and our analysis have looked if grad workers of color led the initiative? We share this absence as a cautionary tale: experiences can help illuminate what change work is necessary, but change work must incorporate diverse experiential knowledge in order to transform power structures in academia. We hope that future studies of graduate student instructor (GSI) labor will articulate the relationships among identity, power, and labor and elevate the voices of Black, Indigenous, and other people of color from start to finish.

COLLABORATORS OF CHANGE: A FEMINIST
APPROACH TO LEADERSHIP

Another key component that helped the LCTF's success was our unique leadership strategy: a feminist approach to activity theory informed by the feminist rhetorical scholarship of Lindal Buchanan, Jacqueline Jones Royster, Gesa Kirsch, and more. Activity theory relies upon relationships and connections between six main elements: instruments, collaborators, domain knowledge, community, division of labor, and object/outcome. As Clay Spinuzzi puts it, "Activity theory posits that in every sphere of activity, *collaborators* use *instruments* to transform a particular *object* with a particular outcome in mind" (2003, 37). By bringing together feminist methodology and activity theory, we developed models of leadership and created a network of collaborators that valued equity, self-care, and institutional change.

Our view of collaboration draws productively from both feminist and activity theory. Collaboration, in our minds, is similar to the view of Buchanan, who considers collaboration "a cooperative endeavour involving two or more people that results in rhetorical product, performance, or event" (2003, 43). Like Buchanan, we honor both "productive collaborators," who directly collaborate on the material product, and "supportive collaborators," who indirectly collaborate by supporting personal life, as integral in making the LCTF collaboration possible. But, we also see our collaboration as being not just between human agents, but also nonhuman agents. As the previous section demonstrates, emotion and past experiences were integral into our collaboration's success. Further, things like affect—the nebulous and fleeting feelings we experienced of joy, motivation, despair, or anything between—and material support, like our access to and experiences with social media tools, functioned as co-collaborators in this project.

Ruth began the group and chaired it from initiation to survey creation, Allison and Jaclyn co-chaired from survey creation to survey distribution, Allison chaired during the coding, and Ruth and Allison co-chaired during the report distribution. As the leadership shifted, members also "tacked in" and "tacked out" (Kirsch and Royster 2010) of the LCTF. Identity changes from member to chair to nonparticipating ally were made because of labor issues we experienced: we were graduate students electing to do unpaid labor about graduate working conditions while experiencing the same labor issues we were documenting. We experienced pressures from graduate school to juggle coursework, study for exams, and go out on the job market all while being teachers and parents and/or partners, experiencing health crises, and wanting to work for social change. As co-chairs of the task force, each of us took on responsibility at different points in time according to our individual situations.

Ruth:

I had enjoyed serving as the chair of the LCTF, which mostly involved setting up meetings and then asking the group to discuss and decide on our priorities, goals, and strategies. It was so rewarding for me to be moving toward concrete action toward change after my outrage at Mizzou one year earlier.

As rewarding as chairing the LCTF was, at the end of 2017, I realized I couldn't continue leading the project. I was preparing for the academic job market, my dissertation defense, and most importantly, the birth of my second child. For my and my family's well-being, I had to cut out all nonessential projects from my agenda. When Jaclyn and Allison agreed to act as co-chairs, I felt such relief. I was confident they would keep things moving. In an email to Allison and Jaclyn dated June 7, 2017, I wrote,

Thank you both so very very very much for agreeing to step into leadership roles for this task force! You are lifesavers. I'm thinking we could all work together as Co-Chairs, since everyone has a big Fall ahead of us. Then, once I step down in November, you two will remain and no transition will be needed.

Allison:

When I initially joined the task force, I took on a sort of secretary role by setting up a shared Google Drive folder and a Google Group email address, recording notes, and emailing summaries of our meetings to the LCTF. Perhaps due to my previous experience in administrative roles in higher education, I was comfortable with this work. In addition, in February 2017, I encouraged the LCTF to seek IRB approval for our survey. I sought the help of Dr. Jennifer Sano-Franchini, now an associate professor at Virginia Tech, to become our primary investigator. Later that year, after we received feedback on our survey questions, I submitted the IRB protocol, which was approved in September 2017.

Around the same time, I spearheaded a conference proposal to CWPA. Our proposal was subsequently accepted, but unfortunately, due to a lack of summer funding for everyone involved, no one could attend the conference. This was a crystallizing moment for me on the LCTF because the funding structures in our individual programs caused a collective setback in our research. The process of researching graduate student labor conditions while simultaneously experiencing difficulties in sharing our research activities with the writing studies field got me even more fired up.

A short while later when Ruth approached me about becoming a co-chair, the transition felt natural because I had already been highly involved in the LCTF. I felt honored that Ruth was acknowledging my labor by asking me to step into a leadership position.

Jaclyn:

Seeing Ruth's note, there was no hesitation. I was in. Taking on more responsibility worked with my life at the moment. And, when I found out that Allison had also stepped up, I thought, *Yes! Two heads are always better than one. Let's do this.*

About a year later, my life circumstances shifted, making it impossible for me to commit the time and energy I needed to be the kind of co-chair I wanted to be to Allison. I tacked out of my leadership role to a member role, and Ruth was in a place to tack in as co-chair once more. The two finished out leading the LCTF, and I felt so grateful they could do that important work.

I'm so glad that I had the opportunity to learn about leadership throughout these experiences watching and participating in the LCTF leadership structure of Ruth as chair, all three of us as co-chairs, Allison and me as co-chairs, and Ruth and Allison as co-chairs. We did things I had never done before—designing and executing a large-scale research project, soliciting responses from nationwide research participants, being a liaison to a national organization about our progress—and this gave me tangible skills that I use in my career today. But, what I really learned most, I think, is about the importance of treating ourselves as whole humans while we do this kind of change work. I learned that change work is about working together, taking on more when possible, and stepping back as necessary. My experiences taught me that change work is at its most successful when it relies on compassionate collaborations.

Our leadership model, we realize now in retrospect, developed because Ruth, Allison, and Jaclyn all identify as feminists and that identity influences how we live our daily lives. As Tanice Foltz (2000) explains, doing feminism "permeates [her] relationships and interactions, and shapes [her] professional goals as well as [her] dreams." And, much like Lauren Rosenberg and Emma Howes (2018), whose feminist identities shaped their research methods, our feminist identities shaped our leadership methodology for LCTF. Our model of moving between organizing and member and nonparticipating ally roles as labor issues unfolded is the kind of feminist leadership model that helped this group thrive. The collaborative, empathetic spirit of our group and the leadership allowed each of us to participate as we could and protected us from territorializing behavior that may have resulted in the LCTF postponing its work or folding all together. Therefore, we see this practice as being integral in future change work.

While serving as chairs and/or co-chairs at different stages of the LCTF's progress, we kept the feminist rhetorical practice of collaboration as integral to our success (Kirsch and Royster 2010; Peck and Mink 1998). We collaborated with members, serving as organizers of meetings where goals were collectively shaped and set, shepherds of action toward the goal progress of the collective, and liaisons between LCTF and WPA-GO. We had a "benevolent hierarchy," a leadership structure that used emancipatory, democratic, and relationship-building principles to create a lateral organizing structure (Spatig et al. 2005); chairs served as leaders, but both chairs and members shaped the group's work and trajectory. Our work was so successful because it incorporated feminist collaboration principles—and because we therefore drew from our collective network of experiences.

Perhaps the most important co-collaborator in our work with LCTF was the shared community of WPA-GO, which enabled success in our research activity because WPA-GO not only legitimized our work with the stamp of approval from a national organization, but also supplied a network of like-minded volunteers. The Writing Program Administration Graduate Organization enabled the LCTF to embody a decentered form in relationship to the larger field of writing studies; furthermore, this structure allowed LCTF members from different institutions to collaborate in an environment in which we, the leaders of the LCTF, could divide labor effectively. In other words, we were acting almost entirely independently of our programs—with the exception of our PI and the Virginia Tech IRB—in order to invoke our own domain knowledge as graduate students. Because of the relationships among our human and nonhuman co-collaborators, we were able to do transformational change work, creating a survey with room for open-ended responses for participants to tell their own stories of graduate student labor conditions—and then distributing those stories to others. We hope our stories will help others as they embark on their own change work.

CONCLUSION: USING OUR STORY TO WRITE YOUR OWN

Let us conclude in the same way we began: with stories. But this time, we will share the stories people shared with Ruth over email after she circulated the report.

> I wanted to relay my gratitude to you and the committee for this work. I have shared it with the chair of the English grad student organization at my previous institutional workplace and with the Council on Basic Writing Facebook page.
> Thanks to you and your collaborators on that grad student labor report. It's been getting ppl talking (in good ways) at [my institution].
> I immediately shared [the report] with my union siblings as we're in contract negotiations currently, pushing back with the university about these very things—workload, living wages et al.

After years of collecting the stories of grad student labor conditions in writing programs, we were finally ready to circulate our findings. Ruth sent the report to the WPA-L, and the LCTF as a whole shared it widely on social media. The report sparked the kinds of conversations we were hoping it would. Tenured and tenure-track professors expressed shock and dismay on WPA-L, many vowing to advocate for better labor conditions within their programs. Lecturers expressed solidarity with grad workers on Twitter. And, most important, grad students privately expressed gratitude for a resource that told their stories as workers in higher education, a resource several planned to use when negotiating for improved pay, benefits, and support. The response validated a hunch we long had: that our stories as grad workers could make community, knowledge, and change within the field of writing studies.

We imagine at least two generative ways to use the survey data to initiate local organizing and to advocate for graduate worker equity in writing programs:

1. *WPAs and Directors of Graduate Studies*: Bring the LCTF report to meetings with university administrators and advocate to increase stipends for graduate students. Given the competition among graduate programs, fair labor conditions and compensation make your program's recruitment package more attractive to prospective students. Most important, WPAs and directors of graduate studies (DGSs) can use this report to create meeting agendas with their own graduate workers: listen to their local concerns, offer solidarity, and then bring grad worker concerns to administrators. Clarifying leave procedures and healthcare coverage were two big areas of confusion, according to our survey results.

2. *Graduate Students*: Use the report data when discussing labor conditions with WPAs, DGSs, and administrators, especially ones that serve in the faculty senate and/or as representatives for union meetings. Attend your program's and/or graduate school's advisory board meetings and participate as a graduate student member if possible. The survey can also help when rallying other grad workers to start a union and organize.

As the 2020 graduate worker strike in the University of California system demonstrates, graduate workers hold incredible power on their campuses (Busch 2020). Universities depend on grad labor in order to function, and we hope that the report empowers grad organizers to craft persuasive lines of argument for fair and just labor conditions.

Our suggestions are firmly rooted in the purpose and goal of our research: to center the lived experiences of graduate students' labor. We described how this research took shape earlier in the chapter, which included many email exchanges between our LCTF members as we worked remotely in multiple areas of the country. During one of those exchanges, we believe the following email excerpt from LCTF member Katie McWain, dated March 2017, illustrates why graduate students themselves must be the driver for change in labor conditions:

While I love and respect the WPAs in my department, they haven't lived the GSI [graduate student instructor] experience here and they can't keep track of the arc of every GSI's workload or responsibilities over time. As a result, I worry they sometimes have a more rosy view of the labor conditions than the reality I experience from semester to semester. . . .

What might be more important, then, is to frame the survey results—whenever we distribute them—as GSIs' labor *experiences* or as one piece of the much larger puzzle of labor conditions in our field.

Katie's words here perfectly encapsulate why the LCTF report has the potential to be so powerful in negotiations: the data offer graduate students' insights about how their labor *experiences* shape their reality. As Katie pointed out, those who haven't lived this reality may not quite understand how to advocate or even what to advocate for. The LCTF report is indeed a puzzle piece that begins to fill in the bigger picture of new and improved labor conditions.

Through our research, collaboration, and leadership, we forward the LCTF as proof that graduate students are more than apprentices. The graduate students who teach in, and largely sustain, our writing programs are *workers*, and we used our personal experiences with graduate labor as a catalyst for institutional change. We know as a result of our survey research that graduate students in writing programs across the United States feel underpaid and overworked, are often unaware of leave policies, and have difficulty accessing mental and healthcare services. Amid these alarming facts, graduate students are teaching the overwhelming majority of first-year writing classes. And despite this confluence of facts, graduate workers are generally not regarded as leaders of change in the field of writing studies (though, thanks to grad collectives like WPA-GO and nextGEN, grad workers are indeed challenging that perception).

Without framing graduate student teaching and research activities as *labor*, and *labor* that is enacted by a collective epistemology born out of our experiences, we are doubtful that institutional change will ever surface. Like Marc Bousquet, we support the notion of "a *labor* theory of agency and a rhetoric of solidarity, aimed at constituting, nurturing, and empowering collective action by persons in groups" (2002, 494). Graduate students are important members of a group that constitutes teachers and researchers in writing studies. Imagining grad workers alongside their contingent colleagues as the core of the instructional force of a writing program rather than the periphery could radically improve labor conditions, departmental politics, and writing instruction. Furthermore, such revising can lead to continued organizing within and among institutions. Groups such as WPA-GO have formalized sustainable models of organizing, allowing grad students to cycle in and cycle out of leadership, so their organizing continues despite the temporary nature of grad student-ness. We hope more professional organizations will readily support grad-worker-led initiatives that will galvanize structural change in writing programs.

Our stories of grad labor catapulted an effort to collect and amplify the stories of our peers across the nation, which led to more stories of grad-worker-led institutional change. Throughout the project, we embodied what Linda Adler-Kassner describes as "a commitment to changing things for the better here and now through consensus-based, systematic, thoughtful processes that takes into consideration the material contexts and concerns of all involved" (2008, 32–33). As graduate students in precarious situations and negotiating competing priorities, it was impossible for our story to have one author. None of us knows the entire story of LCTF because we all took turns leading it, but we also stepped away as needed. Furthermore, we undertook this project not as a part of our dissertation research nor as a part of our paid assistantships: the LCTF was and still is a passion project, one born out of our collective frustrations with grad labor exploitation and a commitment to feminist praxis. We had to create our own activity system and models of leadership with very little institutional support, under the same exploitative labor conditions that we were reporting on. Since the start of the study, we have all moved onto faculty positions, shifting our roles from grad worker–researcher–activists to faculty advisors, advocates, and accomplices to grad workers. So, to our grad worker readers, we say: your stories are valuable, and you can create meaningful change by making knowledge from your lived experiences as grad workers. And to our fellow faculty and WPAs readers, we ask: what are we doing to foster, value, and tangibly support the transformational work of grad workers?

ACKNOWLEDGMENTS

We would like to thank all of the task force members who made this work possible: Alexander Champoux, Sarah Primeau, Molly Ubbesen, Julianna Edmonds, Leah Heilig, Laura Matravers, Katie McWain, Stacy Rice, and Hillary Yeager. We are grateful for your time, energy, and emotional investment in our work together, and we look forward to seeing the change for graduate student labor conditions that will come as a result of our work. We also want to make a special acknowledgement to Katie McWain, PhD, who died in 2019. Katie emailed WPAs and directors of graduate studies to encourage their students to complete our survey while she was on the job market in 2017. She was an adamant supporter and doer of this research, which wouldn't have been possible without her contribution.

NOTE

1. These data were collected in accordance with Institutional Review Board (IRB) Protocol #17-275 at Virginia Tech.

REFERENCES

Adler-Kassner, Linda. 2008. *The Activist WPA: Changing Stories about Writing and Writers.* Logan: Utah State University Press.

Ahmed, Sara. 2017. *Living a Feminist Life.* Durham, NC: Duke University Press.

Bousquet, Marc. 2002. "Composition as Management Science: Toward a University without a WPA." *Journal of Advanced Composition* 22.3: 493–526.

Buchanan, Lindal. 2005. *Regendering Delivery: The Fifth Canon and Antebellum Women Rhetors.* Carbondale: Southern Illinois University Press.

Busch, Clare. 2020. "Tenured Faculty Should Be Showing up for Striking Grad Students." *Outline,* March 25. https://theoutline.com/post/8874/uc-grad-students-cola-strike-tenured-faculty.

Chaput, Catherine. 2000. "The Rhetoric of Globalization, Graduate Student Labor, and Practices of Resistance." In *Professing Rhetoric: Selected Papers from the 2000 Rhetoric Society of America Conference,* edited by Frederick J. Antczak, Cinda Coggins, and Geoffrey D. Klinger, 179–86. Washington, DC: Routledge.

Cottom, Tressie McMillan. 2019. *Thick: And Other Essays.* New York: New Press.

Foltz, Tanice G. 2000. "Women's Spirituality Research: Doing Feminism." *Sociology of Religion* 61.4: 409–18.

Hesford, Victoria. 2013. *Feeling Women's Liberation.* Next Wave: New Directions in Women's Studies. Durham, NC: Duke University Press.

Jaggar, Alison M. 1989. "Love and Knowledge: Emotion in Feminist Epistemology." *Inquiry* 32.2: 151–76.

Journet, Deborah. 2012. "Narrative Turns in Writing Studies Research." In *Writing Studies Research in Practice: Methods and Methodologies,* edited by Lee Nickoson and Mary P. Sheridan. Carbondale: Southern Illinois University Press.

Kirsch, Gesa E., and Jacqueline J. Royster. 2010. "Feminist Rhetorical Practices: In Search of Excellence." *College Composition and Communication* 61.4: 640–72.

Labor Census Task Force (LCTF). 2019. "Graduate Student Instructor Labor Conditions in Writing Programs." WPA-GO. https://csal.colostate.edu/docs/cwpa/reports/wpago-gsi-2019.pdf.

"MLA Survey of Departmental Funding." 2014. https://www.mla.org/content/download/103529/2303971/2014-Staffing-Survey.pdf.

Peck, Elizabeth G., and JoAnna Stephens Mink. 1998. *Common Ground: Feminist Collaboration in the Academy.* New York: State University of New York Press.

Powell, Malea, Daisy Levy, Andrea Riley-Mukavetz, Marilee Brooks-Gilles, Maria Novotny, and Jennifer Fisch-Ferguson. 2014. "Our Story Begins Here: Constellating Cultural Rhetorics." *Enculturation* 18. http://enculturation.net/our-story-begins-here.

Rosenberg, Lauren, and Emma Howes. 2018. "Listening to Research as a Feminist Ethos of Representation." In *Composing Feminist Interventions: Activism, Engagement, Praxis,* edited by Kristine Blair and Lee Nickoson. Fort Collins: The WAC Clearinghouse and University Press of Colorado. https://wac.colostate.edu/books/perspectives/feminist/.

Royster, Jacqueline J. 2003. "Disciplinary Landscaping, or Contemporary Challenges in the History of Rhetoric." *Philosophy and Rhetoric* 36.2: 148–67.

Royster, Jacqueline Jones, and Gesa Kirsch. 2012. *Feminist Rhetorical Practices: New Horizons for Rhetoric, Composition, and Literacy Studies.* Studies in Rhetorics and Feminisms. Carbondale: Southern Illinois University Press.

Spatig, Linda, Kathy Seelinger, Amy Dillon, Laurel Parrott, and Kate Conrad. 2005. "From an Ethnographic Team to a Feminist Learning Community: A Reflective Tale." *Human Organization* 64.1: 103–13.

Spinuzzi, Clay. 2003. *Tracing Genres through Organizations: A Sociocultural Approach to Information Design.* Cambridge, MA: MIT Press.

2

CIRCULATING NTTF STORIES TO EFFECT CHANGE
The Case of ASU against 5/5

Paulette Stevenson

In 2014 the English Department chair at Arizona State University Tempe approached writing program instructors, full-time non-tenure track faculty (NTTF) with a proposal to teach more classes for no additional pay. Budgets are balanced, bottoms lines are cut, and tenured faculty lines are paid for by exploiting NTTF. Because NTTF often lack the power to combat exploitation, the injustices of these policies and the process by which they become normalized are often regulated to the NTTF table at the department's annual meeting or the copy room near the NTTF office space. A group of ASU Instructors decided that our department's unethical proposal would not stay in the shadows; we would use our training as rhetoricians and writers to circulate our story and fight for better working conditions.

What follows is the story of how ASU instructors, without much support from tenured faculty in the department, harnessed the knowledge of the discipline and conveyed the pitfalls of the higher course load to a wider public, getting coverage from popular and academic news outlets. It was ultimately the high-profile nature of this story that led to the vice provost's willingness to renegotiate the terms of the instructors' contracts. While gains and losses did come from this renegotiation, this narrative provides writing instructors, writing program administrators (WPAs), and higher education leaders a blueprint for cultivating a kairotic and rhetorically cunning labor campaign that uses the contexts of the public, the university, and the local and national situations to its advantage. In this chapter I use the method of narrative, and I also out myself as one of the architects of this campaign. Thus, my own positionality and memory are part of the data here. Also, I draw from the publicly available materials we collectively produced to run the campaign. Although this is not a transnational feminist rhetorical analysis, I

https://doi.org/10.7330/9781646421428.c002

use Rebecca Dingo's idea of networking arguments to think about how ASU instructors produced networked arguments that linked to existing communities and arguments to more effectively circulate their message. Finally, I make assessments of the gains and losses, describing in detail the losses in professional development and service as ceding epistemological terrain. As such I offer that the next terrain of action and activism must be NTT faculty finding ways to engage in the discipline, their college, and their departments as knowledge makers. I offer ways that this might be realized.

NARRATIVE METHOD

While narrative can sometimes be seen as a biased and an unscientific method to create and produce knowledge, feminist standpoint theory counters this claim, maintaining that objectivity is only realized through listening to multiple voices. Sandra Harding (1993) argues, "social situated grounds and subjects of standpoint epistemology require and generate stronger standards for objectivity than those that turn away from providing systemic methods for locating knowledge in history" (50). Feminist Standpoint theory understands that traditional, empirical methods are too weak to *systemically* identify and eliminate from results of research social values, interests, and agendas of an entire community (i.e., bias). In this view, narratives, especially those voiced by marginalized communities, become a systemic provider of scientific and epistemological resources rather than a barrier (53). In Harding's view, objectivity is analyzing and acknowledging knowledge as it is extremely socially situated (in deep contrast to how empiricists see objectivity as removing all bias). Therefore, as a knowledge project in the university, hearing stories of NTTF from their positionality helps correct and complete the historical record, even as those in power have tried to silence and erase these stories, or in our case, tried to cover up these stories by providing incremental changes in pay and working conditions. The story of speaking back to a university and a department adds a counter to the historical record often told as progress, but it also provides a productive starting point to think about knowledge creation by nontenured and adjunct academic labor.

Narrative also allows for a richer understanding of rhetorical context. In her foreword to *Contingency, Exploitation, and Solidarity: Labor and Action in English,* Eileen E. Schell (2017) asserts that "the institutional case, informed by the larger discourses of organizing and scholarly work on labor and higher education, thus can become a space from which to analyze, assess, and dissect local reform and organizing strategies" (xi). Telling the specific ASU narrative of NTTF exploitation and organizing allows others to fully see the local and rhetorical context of our situation. Without the fullness of these stories and their local situations, told from the position of those with the least power, the academy will continue to scapegoat others—state legislators, a weak economy, declining enrollment—instead of holding itself accountable for exploiting cheap and contingent labor. Thus, I add the story of our struggle at ASU to the historical record of contingent labor exploitation, in hopes that more narratives will help speak truth to power.

I tell this story on behalf of myself and my colleagues and for contingent faculty facing exploitation. I write this narrative as a single individual who had a significant role in organizing ASU instructors. When I feel it is ethically appropriate, I use the "we," but when I don't, I use "I." As a group of sixty people, not everyone was engaged in the planning and organizing, and not all those involved in the organizing and planning were in agreement about the actions we took. Finally, narratives are subject to misrememberings and overexaggerations. While I have consulted notes and peers to help keep these lapses down to a minimum, my subjective bias simply cannot be wiped from this project—it consumed and continues to consume my life.

BACKGROUND

Arizona State University's instructor position was created in the early 2000s out of need and convenience. The department needed a stable workforce to teach first-year writing to the university's growing freshman population. Also, a full-time, benefits-eligible job at ASU was attractive for location-bound graduates and PhD students who had exceeded their funding allowance (ASU allows for five years). The job was originally defined as a 4/4 load with 80 percent of the load being teaching and 20 percent of the load split between teaching and professional development. In 2014, the starting salary for instructors was $30,000/year for MAs and MFAs and $32,000/year for PhDs. Instructors had tried for years to obtain raises and better working conditions, but the department and college never followed through until 2015.

At a meeting between instructors and the department chair in fall 2014, our department chair proposed a significant change to instructor job definition. He said that the university was moving to defining all Instructor positions as 5/5, 100 percent teaching, and as such, we would be teaching a 5/5 load starting in fall 2015 for no additional pay. Without exaggeration, I can confidently say that everyone hated this idea. Our rank was split between people who would happily take more money for the extra classes and the people who just wanted to do the same job for better pay. Some people liked the service assignments they were performing, while others saw service as nonessential and time consuming (a split that also pervades nearly all of academic jobs, tenure and nontenure). Also, based on department need, many of us had taken overloads in courses for additional pay; thus, some of us were teaching 5/5 for + $6,000/year on top of our base salary with an official release of service and professional development duties for the semester service and professional development. So, for some, this would be a pay reduction.

After this meeting, most people felt defeated. Those that had been lobbying administration for years to raise our salaries saw this as the ultimate slap in the face—pay raises were no longer on the table, administration had changed the narrative and forced us to go on the defensive to just protect our current jobs. Administration moved the Overton window. Newer instructors, happy to have the benefits of the job, were just wondering how they could add more students, more papers, and more grades to a job that they were already underpaid to do.

Our situation aligned with increased media attention on NTTF and contingent labor. In 2013 Margaret Mary Vojtko, a long-term adjunct professor at Duquesne University, died of health problems that might have been avoided had she had access to healthcare, and national media outlets like *NPR*, the *Huffington Post*, and the *New York Times* were forced to confront the adjunct problem. The NTTF conversation had reached a pitch in late 2014, when on social media the question was posed, "What would happen if adjuncts across the country turned that invisibility on its head by all walking out on the same day?" The first ever National Adjunct Walkout day was scheduled for February 25, 2015, right in the middle of contentious talks with our department. The conversation was changing around us, and national attention on NTTF and contingent labor would only help our cause.

This was precisely the available means that we needed to persuade the public. We had a local situation that literally could not get worse and a national conversation that was ramping up. On top of this, ASU needed us. We taught over 50 percent of courses in the Writing Programs, and the freshman population was only growing. Finally, ASU was at the tail end of rebuilding its public image. President Michael Crow helped rebuild the ethos of ASU from being named a top party school in *Playboy* magazine to one of the top public universities in the country. Negative media attention from underpaid and overworked writing instructors would surely reach President Crow's desk. In this rhetorical environment, we were well positioned to be heard, if we decided to speak out.

ORGANIZING

Our organizing started with some talks, mostly on private social media channels, about what to do next. Which administrators could we meet with? How could we leverage tenured professors in the fight? Should we call the local media? These, I would argue, were traditional methods: go up the chain of command, find allies in powerful spaces, but the people in power that drafted this bad deal *were* our allies (or should be). To some of us they taught our graduate classes, to others they were our MA advisors, and, even, to some, they were our dissertations committee members and chairs. It was in their best interest to the future of the program, to their reputation, to see to it that we had "good jobs"—that we were placed well. However, they had succumbed to administrative pressures. The department chair's response to the original reporting from *Inside Higher Ed* made his allegiance clear: "This does not make me happy but given the budgetary constraints under which we operate this change (which has already arrived in most locations across the university) will quite likely become necessary" (Warner 2014). Our tenured allies would be few and quiet, and our chair's first response only confirmed that our fight could not go through official channels.

At the time of the proposition, I was a full-time instructor and a full-time PhD student in what is now called the Writing, Rhetoric, and Literacies program. I had begun coursework in digital media and was starting to look at the power of tapping communities on the web. Taking my coursework from theory to practice, I spent one December day setting up Facebook, Twitter, and WordPress accounts with the name ASUAgainst55. I put this all together with little communication between myself and sixty instructor colleagues for fear that too many cooks in the kitchen would mean that nothing got accomplished. Besides, I also envisioned this being a collaborative project; I'd build the shell, and then others would sign on to help do some writing.

Within two days we received our first request for an interview from Colleen Flaherty of *Inside Higher Ed* wanting to know more about the 5/5 policy. We had to develop a message and a focus, much like political campaigns do. What was our message? There were internal conversations about this, and, ultimately, we decided we wouldn't make this about our lives and our own struggles, even though most everyone in our rank had a compelling tale of exploitation and personal hardship; we needed to be strategic about the arguments composed, with special consideration into how these arguments could/would travel and circulate.

NETWORKING ARGUMENTS

In her book *Networking Arguments* Rebecca Dingo argues that rhetoricians must "examine how rhetorics travel—how rhetorics might be picked up, how rhetorics might become networked with new and different arguments, and how rhetorical meaning might shift and change as a result of these movements" (Dingo 2012, 2). Rhetorics travel. They take up space in places that we expect and those that we don't. Arguments get taken out of context and get picked up by unexpected groups. We had to be aware of likely possibilities of where and how our arguments would travel, and which ones would travel the farthest, linking to the most consequential publics, and which ones would stop our movement from gaining traction. To fully analyze our campaign and its successes (and failures), it is imperative to evaluate the network of arguments that we built, those we ignored, and those we failed to identify.

Thinking rhetorically about our campaign, we imagined the following as potential audiences for our work: ASU administration, ASU students, ASU parents, local AZ public (taxpayers, lawmakers), the Modern Language Association (MLA), Conferences on College Composition and Communication CCCCs, Rhetoric Society of America (RSA), professors working in English departments, and other NTTF. There was a sense that our story could be bigger than just us. Arizona State University's own growing reputation as an innovator in higher education would mean increased media attention, and, perhaps, our story (especially if the outcome was positive) could help others. The arguments we networked were about impact to students, disciplinary workload, service loss, and graduate student retention (because many of us had received our graduate degrees in the department). These arguments could easily be picked up, and circulated, and recirculated by groups, individuals, and influential professionals.

Impact to Students

Our strongest message was about how moving to a 5/5 load would impact students. At the time, most of us taught between 100 and 150 ASU students a semester, so we could easily imagine ways our increased teaching would affect students, and having clear numbers helped us communicate clearly what an increased workload looked like in time and essays. We ran data that showed instructors would be grading, in proposal, draft, and final format, 150 more essays a year. Based on the National Society for Experiential Education's suggested fifteen minutes/essay, an extra course per semester would add 18.75 more hours of grading final essays to our workload. Most of us also read student drafts so that would add 37.5 hours (approximately an extra week of work) of reading and grading essays to our workload every semester.

Another impact to students that we stressed was the strain to hold individual conferences. Most instructors hold individual conferences to discuss drafts and/or grades, and these had been encouraged by ASU's teaching training (something that most of us went through as graduate students) as a tool to connect with and retain students. Although holding conferences is a huge time inconvenience (cancelling class, meeting outside of class), the benefit outweighs the cost. When looking at the data, it would take 6.5 additional hours to hold a conference for one additional class each semester.

We anticipated that the story about student impact would quickly reach the local public, but it wasn't until nearly the end of our fight (June 2015) that local media took interest in our story. I spent time on the phone discussing the situation with Anne Ryman, *Arizona Republic*'s higher education reporter; she ultimately never published the story. However, *Phoenix New Times* interviewed three instructors and reported quotes like "Writing composition classes are capped at 25, so the teachers are among the only faculty to build a relationship with students, whose other classes often have between 100 and 300 students" (Stuart). Also, one of our brave instructors sat for an on-camera interview with one of the local news stations. We found that in talking to reporters, we had to act much like politicians to get the message across that we wanted. The reporters wanted to ask us how the increased workload would affect us, but we really needed to talk about how it would affect students, especially to get the tax-paying public and tuition-paying students and parents to care. The on-camera interview was a mix of how it affected the instructor personally (student loan debt, raising a family), but it also included her saying, "It really breaks me up to think that students will have to pay an increased tuition and get less than ever before." In the end, we never got wind of how many people in the Arizona public reached out to the university, but the impact of local news stories (one on camera, and one in a popular, online publication) was certainly felt at the highest level of ASU administration.

While we tried to focus on things more than salary, the funding discussion produced a lively debate among chairs and deans on the

WPA-L, suggesting that our labor made the university much more than we were offered. John Warner, a blogger for *Inside Higher Ed* and a contingent faculty member himself, did some of the public work for us by writing about these figures in an article titled "Yes, Small Class General Education Courses Do Make Money" (2014c). In the article he offers figures for his current university and how much money general education courses make for the university, and it circulated back to us, where we ran the numbers for ASU, showing that the university could afford to pay us much more money for the work we do.

Disciplinary Workload

While unfair and untenable workloads have been placed upon adjunct and NTTF for quite some time, our story gained traction in the rhetoric and composition discipline because of the scale. ASU had become one of the largest and fastest-growing universities in the nation. Our writing program is one of the largest in the nation. Thus, at a scale unlike anywhere in the United States, ASU leadership tried to implement one of the largest pay inequities on their writing instructors. To counter the narrative that it is natural or normal for instructors to take on this workload in the university, we did our homework and referenced the disciplinary standards for class size and teaching writing. At the time, CCCCs and MLA were not releasing exact numbers (this would be later rectified), but the Association of Departments of English (ADE) suggested no "more than three sections of composition per term . . . No English faculty member should teach more than sixty writing students a term" ("ADE Guidelines" 1992). The argument about disciplinary workload spilled over into academic conferences that year.

At the MLA Delegate assembly in 2015, a couple of weeks after news broke in *Inside Higher Ed* about our situation, Margert Ferguson, the most recent past president of MLA, was quoted as saying she's "concerned about faculty members having a composition course load of that size" (Flaherty 2019). I personally attended CCCC's for the first time in 2015, slotted to talk about anything but contingent labor, but there was a buzz about the ASU situation. During a break at the Feminist Workshop I outed myself as the person behind ASUAgainst55's social media, and I drew praise. Little did I know that behind the scenes things were happening. As Seth Kahn et al. (2017) recount in the introduction to *Contingency, Exploitation, and Solidarity: Labor and Action in English Composition*, the "Labor Caucus shared and opened for public comment and revision a draft of the Indianapolis Resolution, a reworking of the Wyoming Resolution, calling for our professional organizations to revise and redouble their efforts in working for adjunct equity" (5). Also, that same year, the CCCC's position statement *Principles for the Postsecondary Teaching of Writing* added class size maximums to their recommendations that mimic the ADE's suggestions. Previously, these were absent, but our campaign was posted on the WPA-L asking for any help that community could provide. Susan Miller-Cochran stated, "I hate to be a squeaky wheel about this, but I am really disturbed that there is no mention of specifics of working conditions in *any* CCCC documents now" (WPA-L, December 16, 2014). While I was not in the room to help discuss these decisions, I am assuming that the statements were altered to help instructors, WPAs, and administration to advocate for class sizes and course loads.

Service Loss

In selling the 5/5 100 percent teaching positions, English Department chair at the time, Mark Lussier, referenced the service requirements of instructors as outside the scope of our work, suggesting that "just teaching" a 5/5 load would be easier. His own idea of the impact of NTTF service was out of sync with the work ASU Instructors did to professionalize the Writing Programs and run Writing Programs–specific programs. Thus, another argument we made on social media and our website was that our service was crucial to the healthy functioning of our writing programs, and our service was a space to give voice to our students on department committees that often focus on English undergrad majors and graduate students.

Our WPA chair, Shirley Rose, had been working to make the Writing Programs more visible and underscore the program's importance to the department and university. We began doing a number of things to showcase the work of teaching, learning, and writing. A project called Visualizing Teaching in Action (ViTA) tasked someone to capture in video, images, and/or text actual classroom teaching. Writing Programs also began participating in the National Day on Writing. We linked the activities to ASU's homecoming celebration and set up a booth in the middle of campus with writing activities. We broadcasted the events to the university and department via social media. Finally, the Writing Programs piloted and adopted Digication, a digital portfolio platform the university enlisted for use in all classrooms. In all of these instances our instructors did much of the work of occupying these spaces.

The AAUP's blog *Academe* picked up the message about our service and professional development and wrote about it. The WPA-L administrators discussed the need of service and professional development as a given; however, I would argue that as a profession the idea of service and professional development loss is inside baseball in the way the class size is not. Parents understand class size, but they are kept in the dark about how teachers also provide service to their institution and need professional development to stay relevant. As a first-generation college student, I was not aware of departmental service until I took the ASU instructor job. To make this travel beyond the disciplines, we need to develop a better way of talking about service and professional development.

Graduate Student Retention

The argument that most angered department administration was about graduate student retention to the instructor position. In 2014–2015, ASU English began a deeper dive into graduate education. Our graduate students, on the whole, were not finishing degrees in a timely manner and were not being placed in tenure-track jobs (or even non-tenure-track jobs) at a rate aligned with the number of PhD students we were admitting. Arizona State University was in talks with the MLA for a grant to help rethink graduate education and retool placement opportunities (i.e., alt-ac). Yet one fact was not being discussed—retention of graduate students. By that, I mean retaining graduate students into the instructor position. Students, either needing an income after they run out of TA funding or struggling to find a job on the academic job market, turned to the ASU instructor position. In 2015, thirty-three of our sixty-one instructors received an MA, an MFA, or a PhD from ASU. By drawing attention to this, we exposed a fault line between tenure-track (TT) faculty and NTT faculty that would erupt.

John Warner wrote about the fact that ASU English retains its graduate students as instructors (a fact that wasn't the most prevalent thing on our report) in his first article on us called "ASU and the Non-tenured Human Shields" (2014a). It was sardonic but shockingly true to what was happening on our end—no TT faculty would stick their necks out for us, except our writing program administrator (WPA), Shirley Rose. Warner's next article, "ASU English by the Numbers: It Ain't Pretty" (2014b), discussed the poor placement of ASU PhD holders. Of the 60 PhDs awarded by ASU English in 2012–14, Warner found that only 6 were placed in TT jobs at 4-year institutions, while 20 were placed in NTT roles at ASU. While Warner doesn't parse the number of placement into NTT jobs at other institutions, TT jobs at two-year colleges, NTT jobs at two-year colleges, jobs at high schools, jobs outside of academia, or those unemployed, the point he makes about ASU retaining its own PhD graduates into NTT jobs is strong. From these numbers he wonders why "the Arizona State PhD program in English exist[s], other than to create a continuous supply of low-paid non-tenure-track faculty and graduate assistants" (Warner 2014b). Beyond being correct, his information was damning to ASU TT faculty and the project of graduate education in ASU English, which before Warner's prodding articles was on life support and hoping to be revived by an MLA grant. Anecdotally, I heard that this grant was in jeopardy because of the treatment of NTTF. In the end we received the grant to hold workshops to help professionalize English PhDs in alternative careers. However, Warner's indictment of TT faculty as complicit in our exploitation reverberated in the halls of our department.

Arguments That Didn't Travel

Sticking to these core issues about impact to our students, disciplinary standards, service loss, and retaining graduate students to the rank meant that other very valid arguments had to get pushed to the side. The overwhelming and largest issue here was not being talked about: the mental and physical ramifications of being a contingent faculty member being asked to take on an increased workload for no more pay. I will return to this issue in the conclusion, but, sadly, this argument would not travel. This argument was used by previous groups of ASU instructors fighting for higher wages, but the administration would not budge and the media was uninterested. Meanwhile, many of us were living beyond our means with student loan debt acquired while attending ASU—the school we now worked at full time. Physical and mental health issues persist in academia, and contingency only exacerbates them. However, to truly get our message across, we need to "stick to the students" as one tenured ally (from afar) would explain to us. We also tried early on to link to political organizers attempting to form unions in Arizona. They helped us plan a march down the main street of ASU campus, right past the college president's window; however, the politics of unions and the minimum wage fight did not sit well with some instructors, and they especially didn't sit well with the Arizona public.

RESOLUTION

On June 19, after much back and forth with department administration, a number of us were invited to sit with the vice provost. He was firm, he couldn't have this story continue in the media, and he had looked at the issue and agreed that we were severely underpaid. He offered current instructors one of the following one-year contracts: 4/4 load for $36,000 or 5/5 load for $40,000 all at 100 percent teaching, no professional development or service required. In fact, he was rather strict about these positions not requiring any service or giving any course releases for service. While this fixed most people's situation, a small number of instructors would not receive better pay under this system.

At the department level, we also received two small wins: voting rights and a Non-Tenure Track Committee. We always sent representatives to the department meetings, but without voting rights, we were invisible (literally sign-in sheets and vote counts ignored us). Now, we would get one representative for every ten instructors, and in 2015–16 we sent six instructor representatives to the department meeting to be our voice. Also, based on our fight, the department established a standing non-tenure track committee, which would deal with issues unique to faculty not on the tenure track.

POSTRESOLUTION

We are nearly four years from our fight, and much has changed in the department, some things have stayed the same, while others have worsened. Since the pay increase for the workload, instructors receive two separate cost-of-living raises that none of us had to fight for. At the point that I am writing, teaching a 5/5 load (100 percent teaching) has a base salary of $49,000/year; this is an improvement from $30,000/year to teach a 4/4 load with service and professional development.

With voting representation in the department, our newly appointed representatives were able to voice their concerns on the biggest change: our new building move and renovation. At nearly every step of the process, our instructor representatives met with administration, architects, and planners to communicate how we operate in our office spaces and what we do there. These representatives worked tirelessly as a go-between for instructors and administration without extra compensation or course releases; instead, their service would mean they had a say in building design and office space. In August of 2017, we moved into our new offices, and most of the instructors were unhappy with our new spaces. We were placed into extremely open cubicle offices with little space to meet with students or store our belongings. Once again, our instructor representatives would serve as the unpaid go-between, communicating to administration (once again) how we use office space and how the designed space was inadequate. After listening, they bought locking cabinets for our things and gave us sole access to a handful of small-private meeting rooms. Finally, we all received an upgrade on our university-issued computers (some of us didn't own computers).

While these two positives, pay and representation, have made these positions better, large issues still persist. First, without instructors performing service roles in the department, our presence and our viewpoint on important issues has nearly vanished. Even with the representation at the department meeting, so many committees have either lost an instructor member or have disbanded all together because of lack of membership. In 2013–14 Writing Programs had seventeen standing committees that tackled issues as diverse as second language writing, and textbooks. Now only a handful of those committees remain, and they are run by lecturers, graduate students, and administration. Losing the majority of teaching faculty on these committees also means that the people most impacted by policies (teaching faculty) and people most connected to students (instructors teach approximately 250 students a year) actually lose a say in some of the day-to-day operations of faculty governance. For example, the Textbook Committee has completely disbanded, and as a result the move into application-driven textbooks like Pearson Revel has not been fully vetted by the department.

While the department offers $400/year for instructors to use on professional development, redefining the instructor job at 100 percent teaching has meant a sharp decline in professional development for all instructors. Anecdotally, a small handful still go to conferences, but many I talked to find the $400/year is not enough to pay the cost of attending a conference. While in the short term, this absence allows instructors to focus on the task of teaching five classes a semester, in the long term it sets a dangerous disciplinary precedent. Arizona State's is one of the largest writing programs in the nation, and should be leading on issues of faculty professionalization. By not making professional development a part of employment, ASU is contributing to deprofessionalization of instructors, eventually ensuring that the majority of its workforce will be out of step with the discipline they are teaching.

Another condition that has worsened is the difficult work of teaching five classes a semester at 125 students a semester, every semester. From personal experience, the workload is, at times, overwhelming. I'm beginning a research project where I discuss the burden of a 100 percent teaching workload with our instructors. So far, I have heard from seventeen of sixty-six instructors in small focus groups, and most everyone speaks to the emotional difficulty of trying to be their ideal educator under these conditions. Nearly everyone I spoke to says they have taken on the labor burden of increased course load, and they have not passed any of the burdens on to their students. One instructor discussed that the way she's made space for student conferences is by working one really long week, Monday–Friday 8 AM–6 PM (and some days later based on student availability). Other instructors mention giving up free time on the weekend to read five classes of student drafts or final projects. In terms of office hours, I heard from multiple Instructors that they just decided to give students their personal cell number and allow them to text with questions so that students would continue to feel supported by their instructor despite their instructor's increased workload. While these practices represent our instructors' commitment to their students, it actually falls under Anne Helen Peterson's explanation of the correlation between hard work and increased exploitation:

> Yet the more work we do, the more efficient we've proven ourselves to be, the worse our jobs become: lower pay, worse benefits, less job security. Our efficiency hasn't bucked wage stagnation; our steadfastness hasn't made us more valuable. If anything, our commitment to work, no matter how exploitative, has simply encouraged and facilitated our exploitation. We put up with companies treating us poorly because we don't see another option. We don't quit. We internalize that we're not striving hard enough. And we get a second gig. (n.p.)

And yes, some of us still have a second gig; the salary increases still do not completely secure our membership to the middle class. We take on community college classes or university overloads because a base salary of $50,000 just isn't enough to put our children in college, pay the daycare, afford a house, take care of an ailing dependent, or even just take a vacation. The work, the *increased* work, makes most of us work much more to provide the educational experience we know our students deserve.

Under this stress and strain, anecdotally more instructors have had to take short leaves mid-semester due to physical or mental health problems. What's worse is that the only people left to cover for them are fellow instructors, who themselves are asked to pick up the bits and pieces of a struggling colleague's course for a prorated portion of the $3,100 per class rate. In our old system, where service was a part of our job, two instructors received course release to be on-call as long-term subs for the semester, but now, nothing like that exists.

Finally, morale is at an all-time low. Instructors are often too busy to socialize with either other, except at the twice-a-year required convocation (an event that we should not have to attend because our jobs are defined as 100 percent teaching, but we do because fighting this technicality is harder). The evaluation structure feels unfair. Again, of the seventeen people I have interviewed, most say that think our evaluation system is unfair. We put together pages of documents attesting to our teaching that year, and we get back a half a page letter from our department chair that's basically a summary of our evaluation packet. Also, in the evaluation there are three scoring levels: 1, 2, or 3—3 means you're eligible for the merit raise pool (if we have money for raises that year), and 1 means you're in trouble. So, without ever stepping foot into our classrooms, we're evaluated by a new department chair many of us have not sat down with in a setting smaller than a lecture hall. It's another exploitative system that needs to be changed, yet without the time to work on it and meet with stakeholders, there's little appetite from instructors.

CONCLUSION: HOLD YOUR GROUND

While our story had a bit of a happy ending, the epilogue is sad. What we gained in pay, I believe we lost in dignity. Our campaign worked because in the end, the stories of our lives, our debts, and our struggle to make an honest living wouldn't travel—but they need to. Someone has to make parents, lawmakers, students, and administration listen to the poor conditions of contingent faculty members, and if I had to do it over again, I would have pushed more for it to be us. We would have found a way for those stories to travel.

So to those of you reading this for advice, here's what I have. Do all of the things that worked for us that apply to your situation. Run your labor fight like a political campaign—use social media, hold marches . . . maybe even make t-shirts, signs, and digital ads. More important, think about what kind of job and work environment you would like to go back to after this is over and advocate for that. For me, I wish we kept our service because fighting, even for the small stuff, without being in the "room where it happens" (i.e., committees and meetings) is an uphill battle.

REFERENCES

"ADE Guidelines for Class Size and Workload for College and University Instructors of English: A Statement of Policy." 1992. *Modern Language Association*. https://www.ade.mla.org/Resources/Policy-Statements/ADE-Guidelines-for-Class-Size-and-Workload-for-College-and-University-Teachers-of-English-A-Statement-of-Policy.
ASUAgainst55. 2014. *Asuagainst55*. https://asuagainst55.wordpress.com/links/.

College Composition and Communication. 2015. *Principles for the Postsecondary Teaching of Writing.* https://cccc.ncte.org/cccc/resources/positions/postsecondarywriting.

Dingo, Rebecca. 2012. *Networking Arguments: Rhetoric, Transnational Feminism, and Public Policy Writing.* 1st ed. University of Pittsburgh Press.

Flaherty, Colleen. 2019. "One Course without Pay." *Inside Higher Ed.* https://www.inside highered.com/news/2014/12/16/arizona-state-tells-non-tenure-track-writing-instruc tors-teach-extra-course-each.

Harding, Sandra. 1993. "Rethinking Standpoint Epistemology: What Is 'Strong Objectiv- ity'?" *Feminist Epistemologies,* edited by Linda Alcoff and Elizabeth Potter, 49–82. New York: Routledge.

Kahn, Seth, William B. Lalicker, and Amy Lynch-Biniek. 2017. *Contingency, Exploitation, and Solidarity: Labor and Action in English Composition.* Fort Collins, CO: WAC Clearinghouse.

Peterson, Anne Helen. 2019. "How Millennials Became the Burnout Generation." *BuzzFeed News.* https://www.buzzfeednews.com/article/annehelenpetersen/millennials-burn out-generation-debt-work.

Schell, Eileen. 2017. "Foreword: The New Faculty Majority in Writing Programs: Organiz- ing for Change." In *Contingency, Exploitation, and Solidarity: Labor and Action in English Composition,* edited by Seth Kahn, William B. Lalicker, and Amy Lynch-Biniek, ix–xx. Fort Collins, CO: WAC Clearinghouse.

Stuart, Elizabeth. 2015. "ASU Writing Instructors Balk over Pay Cuts | Phoenix New Times." *Phoenix New Times.* https://www.phoenixnewtimes.com/news/asu-writing-instructors -balk-over-pay-cuts-7401614.

Warner, John. 2014a. "ASU and the Non-tenured Human Shields." *Inside Higher Ed.* https:// www.insidehighered.com/blogs/just-visiting/asu-and-non-tenured-human-shields.

Warner, John. 2014b. "ASU English by the Numbers: It Ain't Pretty." *Inside Higher Ed.* https://www.insidehighered.com/blogs/just-visiting/asu-english-numbers-it-aint-pretty.

Warner, John. 2014c. "Yes, Small Class General Education Courses Do Make Money." *Inside Higher Ed.* https://www.insidehighered.com/blogs/just-visiting/yes-small-class-general -education-courses-do-make-money.

3

FROM "EXPENDABLE" TO CREDENTIALED

Transforming Working Conditions through the HLC's New Guidelines for Faculty Qualifications

Megan Schoen and Lori Ostergaard

In 1987, the Conference on College Composition and Communication (CCCC) voted to adopt "The Wyoming Conference Resolution Opposing Unfair Salaries and Working Conditions for Post-Secondary Teachers of Writing." At the time, John Trimbur and Barbara Cambridge (1987) described the resolution as composition-rhetoric's "declaration of independence" from a history of marginalization in the academy (14). More recently, James C. McDonald and Eileen E. Schell cite the resolution as the "beginning of the field's serious attention" to academic labor issues (2011, 360). Without doubt, we have expended considerable time addressing the labor crisis in the field; nevertheless, our field remains torn between these two seemingly contradictory impulses: to improve labor conditions for part-time and contingent faculty, many of whom possess few credentials in the field of composition, or to assert our (exclusive) disciplinary expertise.

More than three decades after the resolution, Elizabeth Wardle's (2013) program profile, "Intractable Writing Program Problems, *Kairos*, and Writing about Writing," demonstrates that we have heeded, but not yet enacted, the recommendations of the Wyoming Resolution. Wardle (2013) describes the "seemingly intractable set of problems" that WPAs encounter in their programs, and in particular, she decries the fact that the "macro-level knowledge and resolutions from the larger field of Writing Studies are frequently unable to inform the micro-level of individual composition classes, largely because of our field's infamous labor problems." Wardle (2013) suggests that the failures of programs to enact research and best practices in the field are owing, at least in part, to our inequitable labor practices:

https://doi.org/10.7330/9781646421428.c003

Writing program administrators often have no choice but to hire (sometimes at the last minute) teachers who know little about our field's research, to teach classes that are often too large, and to achieve outcomes that can vary wildly from classroom to classroom, program to program, state to state. In turn, these teachers are often treated as expendable, and institutions tend to invest very little in either their remuneration or professional development and advancement.

She opines that "no administrator would ever send untrained faculty members or graduate students from another discipline to staff an entire segment of courses in, say, biology or history or mathematics or economics" (Wardle 2013). Our disciplinary expertise is undermined by our labor practices, and our students may suffer as a result. But we also recognize that the field and our students are not the only ones who are hurt by these practices; thus, many WPAs and department chairs find themselves torn between championing our discipline and championing—standing in solidarity with, rather than further disenfranchising—our, sometimes inexpert, colleagues.

Composition faculty and writing program administrators may be torn between elevating our discipline (and its status in the university) and protecting our contingent colleagues, but these colleagues face similar contradictions. For example, contingent faculty must often choose between loyalty to our programs and the need to earn a living wage that forces them to seek work at multiple institutions. They may be identified as the instructor of record for their courses but lack the privileges of academic freedom and the right to provide input on curricular design. They may wish to engage in the work of the department, but most either have no seat at the table, or, if they do, they may not be compensated for that work. Finally, most have pursued careers in academia because they long for the professional status and privileges that their positions as contingent faculty render nearly impossible to achieve.

In a special issue of *WPA: Writing Program Administration*, Donald McQuade (1981) described part-time faculty as "migrants" who were hired, most often, because of "an accounting decision, not a professional decision based on clearly defined standards of how these part-timers should be selected, trained, and integrated into the intellectual communities of the college or the English department" (1981, 31). He outlined the conditions of employment that distinguish full- and part-time faculty, "that distinguish 'us' from 'them'":

At most colleges, adjunct faculty are denied a proportionate share of basic health insurance, or even time to recover from an illness . . .

adjuncts are rarely, if ever, granted paid leaves, despite literally years of consecutive service in many cases. Only a few colleges award research funds and travel grants to adjuncts. Curiously, most of the departments in which they serve require adjuncts to attend staff meetings but deny them a franchise . . . Many colleges do not extend to part-time faculty such routine professional courtesies as adequate office space, or in some cases, even mailboxes . . . Adjuncts are often casually bumped from one course to another to accommodate full-time faculty whose electives have failed to register. (31)

What we find most disturbing about McQuade's description of contingent faculty is that in the more than three decades since he wrote this article, the field has made little headway in improving the status and working conditions of these colleagues.

In this chapter, we suggest that professionalization and the credentialing of contingent faculty in the discipline of composition may help to resolve some of the conditions and contradictions described above, providing a means of further strengthening and legitimizing both the discipline and its practitioners. Our argument is not entirely new. In "Credentialing College Writing Teachers," Steve Lamos (2011) argued for the creation of a national credential for writing instructors as a means of achieving, among other outcomes, "an explicit set of guidelines articulating what college writing teachers know and do as professionals" (48). We argue that instead of developing a single, national credential for writing instructors, we may employ the faculty qualification guidelines handed down from higher education accreditation agencies to develop local, departmental standards for disciplinary expertise in the field. In the sections that follow, we draw on a formal departmental study we conducted using faculty interviews in order to outline our long-standing efforts to professionalize our contingent faculty and our previous successes in increasing their role in our departmental community to create ethical writing program labor practices. We then discuss a common threat to those efforts, and we describe how we are employing the new Higher Learning Commission (HLC) qualified faculty guidelines to counter that threat in order to further improve job security and increase professional status for our contingent faculty. We conclude this chapter by outlining some of the takeaways from our experiences with this process that we hope other programs and departments will find useful in their efforts to professionalize and protect both our discipline and our contingent colleagues.

PROFESSIONAL IDENTITY IN THE ACADEMY: OUR EFFORTS AND SUCCESSES AT INCREASING PROFESSIONALIZATION AND BUILDING COMMUNITY AMONG CONTINGENT FACULTY

In her article "Professional Identity in a Contingent-Labor Profession" Ann M. Penrose (2012) argues that a sense of professional identity and a sense of belonging in a professional community may impact more than our colleagues' "self-respect and job satisfaction" and also that research into secondary institutions suggests that there is a "relationship between coherent professional communities and the quality of student learning" (110). Penrose (2012) identifies three dimensions of professional communities: "(1) A specialized and dynamic knowledge base or body of expertise, (2) a distinctive array of rights and privileges accorded to members, and (3) an internal social structure based on shared goals and values" (112). While Penrose notes that much of our scholarship about contingent faculty centers around the second dimension, "rights and privileges," she also observes that these dimensions are "interrelated" (112). The rights and privileges afforded us within the profession are tied to our expertise and shared values.

For many years, our department has established successful practices to professionalize our contingent faculty members and enable their active participation in our department community. Our contingent faculty, who are designated as special lecturers (SLs) by the university, teach primarily Basic Writing, Composition I, and Composition II. The Basic Writing course was redesigned several years ago to introduce rhetoric and research to our at-risk students; Composition I provides students with a foundation in rhetoric and research as well, while emphasizing transfer and writing-about-writing; and Composition II provides students with an introduction to academic rhetoric and research practices. Instruction in each of these classes is dependent upon a workforce with both disciplinary knowledge and professional expertise. Thus, over the last decade, we have worked to professionalize our contingent faculty who teach writing classes at Oakland University (OU) by

- providing professional development to introduce our colleagues to, and engage them in, research, assessment, and best practices in the field;
- bestowing the few privileges our department was empowered to provide; and
- developing a community where mentoring, collaboration, and the sharing of instructional materials is common.

As documented in the 2015 *Composition Forum* profile of our first-year writing program, our midwestern doctoral research university has a large contingent of SLs: in our own department about 90 percent of our first-year writing classes are taught by forty SLs, most of whom have master's degrees in literature. Over the years, we've developed an "inclusive model for research and professional development, a model that seeks to empower the faculty to join disciplinary conversations about the teaching of writing" (Allan et al. 2015). In the sections that follow, we discuss our own efforts to incorporate the three dimensions of professionalism that Penrose identifies. We then examine external threats to these efforts and the impact one of those threats has had on our professional community.

A Specialized Knowledge Base or Expertise

Penrose's (2012) first dimension of a professional community is a "specialized and dynamic knowledge base or body of expertise" (112). Our writing program has worked to establish such a knowledge base through faculty professional development, which has proved to be vital to our program's development and success over the last ten years. The department requires that contingent faculty attend four professional development meetings and a daylong professional seminar every year, but our faculty are professionalized in other ways as well, including through their paid service on our department assessment committee, in individual and collaborative research projects, through department support for professional travel, and through our graduate-level course offerings. When Lori was the WPA, she invited contingent faculty to lead professional development meetings, showcasing some areas of their research or practice, and sharing their assignment descriptions, response techniques, and so forth. Megan has carried this approach further by including our contingent colleagues in the actual programming and planning of our four professional development (PD) meetings and annual seminar. Contingent faculty serve on the department's professional development committee and can determine session topics based on their own sense of what they and their fellow instructors may need. For example, our contingent faculty on the professional development committee have recently requested sessions on grading efficiency using the learning management system and on how to navigate difficult conversations with students. These faculty then sought out other members of the department they felt could lead these sessions effectively. In this way, our colleagues who know better the kinds of professional development they wish to have are responsible for planning those meetings. Because our colleagues are knowledgeable in the field of composition, even if some of them are not expert in the field, they are able to identify the areas of research and practice that they wish to learn more about. As Paulette Stevenson addresses in chapter 2 in this collection, when similar opportunities to participate in service opportunities and professional development were taken from non-tenure-track instructors at Arizona State University, many of those instructors experienced a significant sense of loss to their professional identity and a minimization of their role in the department. By offering our special lecturers opportunities for compensated departmental service and the chance to both plan and participate in professional development, we hoped to make our SLs feel like valued members of our professional community with the knowledge and expertise necessary to belong.

Professional Privileges

Penrose (2012) also suggests that central to the development of a professional community is the establishment of professional rights and privileges for members (112). Because OU faculty (both part time and full time) are in the OU faculty union, our contingent colleagues already enjoy a few rights and privileges associated with their status as teaching professionals. Union membership for our contingent colleagues means that our department and university are able to extend certain benefits to part-time faculty that would not be easily afforded or that might be impossible at institutions where contingent faculty are not represented by a union. For instance, we pay slightly more than other universities in the area, and our SLs, those colleagues who teach four or more sections per year, receive both annual and scheduled raises and have 65 percent of their medical, dental, and optical insurance paid by the university. They may also take up to eight credits per year for free, or they may share those credits with a family member. During their first five years, SLs receive one-year contracts, after which they work on two-year contracts. The contracts afford some limited protection, though a colleague who is originally scheduled to teach eight classes in one year may find that, because of enrollments, they are granted only four classes.

The university cannot bestow any additional privileges on our contingent colleagues, and the union has worked to limit the number of job-secure teaching positions that we might offer these faculty, but the department and the writing program are empowered to extend some professional privileges. For example, all of our colleagues have offices equipped with computers and printers where they may meet with students and prep their classes. Proceeds from the sales of our first-year writing guide, *Grizz Writes* (Schoen 2018), support contingent faculty's travel to regional and national conferences and fund two annual teaching awards that recognize the excellent work of our SLs. The guide costs students around $32 for a textbook that is used in our Basic Writing, Composition I, and Composition II courses, but it brings in about $8,000 in revenue each year, money that is designated for use only by the writing program administrators to support and enhance program quality. In addition, Lori has adjusted schedules for contingent faculty who were earning advanced degrees, caring for new babies, battling illnesses, or attending to family members who were ill. Flexible scheduling is generally a privilege reserved for full-time faculty only, but we believe it is important to ensure that our contingent faculty have fair schedules that allow them to meet their personal and professional obligations.

Finally, our first chair, Marshall Kitchens, established a special line for SLs in the department who wished to be more engaged in the work of the department, the 4/4/1 Special Lecturer. To be designated 4/4/1, our colleagues must have exceptional course evaluations and demonstrate active engagement in the department and the field. The department chair guarantees that these colleagues will be assigned 4/4/1 loads and that the 4/4 course load will be protected (low summer enrollments sometimes make guarantees for the one summer section impossible). Our 4/4/1 SLs are also asked to serve on department committees—*Grizz Writes* Editorial Board, the First-Year Writing Committee, the Assessment Committee, the Business Writing Committee, and others. Thus, they have an opportunity to shape the work of the first-year writing program and our department, and they are compensated for their work with $1000 annual stipends.

A Professional Community with Shared Values

In addition to specialized knowledge and professional privileges, Penrose (2012) observes that professional communities must also have "an internal social structure based on shared goals and values" (112), and she demonstrates the importance of the "social nature of professional expertise" in developing an individual's "professional identity," observing that "it is not simply accumulation of knowledge or even production of scholarship that marks one as a professional but participation in the community's knowledge building and self-definition" (118). Our Institutional Review Board (IRB) study, which included interviews with thirteen of our colleagues who have taught in the department for the past decade, seems to support Penrose's elevation of a social structure as a sine qua non for professionalization. These interviews demonstrate that over the past decade, our intentional professionalization efforts (PD, assessment, research) have been supported by the professional, supportive social structures that our faculty have developed. Indeed, our overt efforts to professionalize our colleagues pales by comparison to the covert work they have performed together and in collaboration with full-time faculty. While we were aware of the kinds of informal mentoring regularly happening in our contingent colleagues' offices, and we knew that they regularly shared pedagogical materials and assignment suggestions, it wasn't until we read the transcripts of these interviews that we learned of the full extent and success of these social structures. For example, Denny,[1] an experienced SL with an MA in the teaching of writing, noted that the change to her teaching over the last decade has been huge.

> You can't even name the differences. I feel much more confident. [This department's] given me form and language and, like, it's very clear for me what are the goals of the department and these courses I teach. I feel very confident in conveying these ideas to the students. I can't even say the differences.

As with Denny, our colleagues noted formal mentoring from the program administrators, faculty professional development meetings, professional travel, individual research, committee assignments, and program assessment as contributing factors in their development, but they also noted the importance of hallway conversations and idea sharing, of informal mentoring, and of the kinds of on-the-ground problem solving that occurred regularly in contingent faculty offices:

- Frank noted that he learned from the colleagues he shared an office with, describing their office as a "good place to just pick up things that people were saying about their teaching practice and stealing from them."
- Graham noted that he had become more comfortable and confident in his teaching, and some of this was attributed to his reliance on colleagues: "If I can get someone's ear, hey take a look at this. Is there anything here that's wildly out of place? . . . If I can catch somebody or buy someone a coffee."
- One of our most experienced SLs, Rhonda, noted that when she began teaching our composition I course "for the first time in eight years," she accessed the department's online practice classes, and she emailed colleagues who shared their materials with her.

Our efforts towards top-down professionalization, then, may have been surpassed by our colleagues' success in mentoring and supporting one another, in their office communities, and through their collegial relationships.

A COMMON THREAT TO PROFESSIONALIZATION

These efforts helped to establish equitable standards in the department and increase professionalization among contingent faculty in the early years of our department's development. However, our efforts toward professionalizing our contingent faculty and developing more ethical and compassionate administrative practices to support these colleagues were seriously undermined last fall when our college dean announced his intention to "re-appropriate" 65 percent of our contingent faculty offices to make room for the college's undergraduate advisors. When we protested, the dean recommended a "hotel" model where our forty-plus colleagues could reserve a desk—for the day—at one of several large offices around campus. Our contingent colleagues were demoralized, and we felt defeated by this change. This move to eliminate part-time faculty offices was precipitated by the college's need to accommodate a growing cadre of academic advisers and by a persistent shortage of office space that has plagued the college for the past decade. Nevertheless, we worried that the college had targeted our colleagues' offices in particular because we had somehow failed to demonstrate to upper-level administrators the unique expertise of our contingent faculty, their status as professionals in the department and the discipline, and the role they play in students' success. How else could we explain the elimination of professional space for our colleagues who are on the front lines of so many of the university's and college's pet initiatives: retention and completion, first-year experience, and undergraduate research. Fortunately, our protests of both the reappropriation and the "hotel" model did not go unanswered, and eventually the college arranged for our department to be given a large office in another building across campus. While this meant splitting the department between two buildings and increasing the number of faculty sharing each remaining office, at least our colleagues were not scattered to the winds, and, at the very least, all of our colleagues have a dedicated space to work.

This move caught us off guard as our dean has consistently advocated for and supported our department. We suspect that he respects the department as a whole, but like many upper-level administrators, he may also view our writing instructors as disposable employees, undeserving of space to work, "permanently impermanent" (Rysdam 2012, A14), "expendable" (Wardle 2013, para. 5), and easily replaced by "the next adjunct in line" (Lynch-Biniek 2012, A5). This perception, we now realize, was owing to both the status of contingent faculty around the country and to our failure to demonstrate what makes OU's writing faculty unique.

While offices represent a professional privilege, as Penrose (2012) notes, each of the three dimensions of professionalism is interconnected. In our interviews with colleagues, we learned of the greater impact, beyond morale, that limited office space may eventually have on the vital social structures of our program. For example, Rhonda reported missing the conversations about teaching that she had in her old office. Peggy suggested that "with the split in the office . . . people don't see each other," and this colleague who regularly mentored new faculty noted that "there are now some new people that I don't even know." This loss of office space also demonstrated that the work of our first-year writing program and instructors might not be fully valued by the administration. Indeed, Peggy reflected on the ways in which this loss emphasized the transient, anonymous nature of contingent work:

> Before the office move, you would have a space, and even though it was a shared space, it was still having some identity around it; and I think at this point we have had to move around so much and we have had so many people coming and going that I don't decorate anything anymore. None of my belongings are anywhere anymore. It feels anonymous to be in a space that you do not have any ownership over.

She added that "it makes a difference in how you interact with people when you own the space and when you don't." Other colleagues referred to the office move as "a trial," "a challenge," "difficult," and "hard" for the department. At present, we can't know what impact the loss of office space will have on the work our faculty do with students and with one another, but we suspect this loss of a professional privilege and this chipping away at the social structures of the department will have a significant effect on more than just morale.

FINDING SOLUTIONS: TURNING NEW
CHALLENGES INTO OPPORTUNITIES

Around the time that we lost the majority of our contingent faculty office space, we learned that our accrediting body, the HLC, was instituting new guidelines for determining "qualified faculty," essentially redefining what it means to be a professional in each discipline. Just as the college eliminated many of our contingent faculty offices, a privilege that they could remove because these colleagues are not considered professionals, we were required to demonstrate that these colleagues are experts in the teaching of writing, fully fledged members of our professional community.

The HLC's existing guidelines for qualified faculty included the provision that all "instructors are appropriately qualified" and that "the institution has processes and resources for assuring that instructors are current in their disciplines and adept in their teaching roles" (Higher Learning Commission 2016, 3). In March 2016, the HLC revised its guidelines specifically to stipulate that "if a faculty member holds a master's degree or higher in a discipline other than that in which he or she is teaching, that faculty member should have completed a minimum of 18 graduate credit hours in the discipline in which he or she is teaching." The new guidelines further offered that equivalent "tested experience" in a field could in relevant circumstances substitute for these earned credentials (Higher Learning Commission 2016, 3–4).[2]

The challenges to do more with less, while also having more stringent qualification guidelines, seemed at first like two sets of obstacles, but we began to see that the new HLC guidelines could, in fact, be leveraged to the benefit of our faculty in the long term. That is, we realized that if we could use the qualification standards as a way to set professional standards and then help our faculty meet those standards, our contingent faculty could become empowered as highly trained professionals within our discipline—specifically, the discipline of writing studies—and therefore more valuable and less disposable to the institution. Moreover, through further professionalization of our faculty, we could also elevate the status of the department and, by extension, the discipline of writing studies.

As an independent department of writing and rhetoric, we saw the new HLC guidelines as a chance to articulate our professional identity as writing specialists and help all our faculty attain the qualifications to be perceived as writing professionals. In order to find answers about how to interpret the new HLC rules, we turned to "CCCC Statement on Preparing Teachers of College Writing" (2015) for guidance. In the section on new and continuing faculty, the statement advises that "institutions must hire highly qualified writing faculty who hold at least a master's degree in Composition/Rhetoric, English, English Education, Linguistics, or a closely-related field." The statement further maintains that "graduate coursework must have included composition theory, research, and pedagogy; and rhetorical theory and research." These guidelines gave us the grounding in a professional mandate from our field to articulate our local goals for faculty credentials appropriate for our institutional identity.

Based upon these recommendations in this position statement, we created the following requirements for future hires and current faculty. To teach college-level courses in our department, faculty must have one of the following:

- a graduate degree in that subject area/field (e.g., an MA or MFA in composition and rhetoric, writing, creative writing, rhetoric, etc.);
- a graduate degree in another subject area/field, plus eighteen graduate credits in the subject area/field in which they teach (e.g., an MA in literature, communication, journalism, liberal studies, plus eighteen graduate credits in composition and rhetoric, writing, creative writing, rhetoric, etc.); or
- a degree in another subject area/field, plus "tested experience."

To implement these new requirements, we first determined who met the requirements and who needed to attain the appropriate credentials. All faculty shared their CVs and transcripts with Lori, who carefully vetted these documents to determine if the qualifications were held. She determined that the majority of department faculty met or exceeded the criteria either through graduate coursework in the teaching of writing or through tested experience in professional work as journalists, editors, marketing experts, copywriters, web developers, or similar positions.

The next step was to help faculty who had not met the requirements to develop a plan for doing so. Lori invited faculty affected by the new guidelines to meet with her about their individual qualifications and develop a plan for meeting the new criteria. Oakland University interpreted the HLC's guidelines as requiring that all faculty not meeting the criteria articulate a three-year plan for doing so. We believe these three-year plans helped to alleviate some of our colleagues' fears. Special lecturers who did not meet the requirements have been encouraged to take graduate writing courses in our department for credit toward the HLC requirements.[3]

INITIATIVES UNDERWAY, NEXT STEPS, AND ONGOING CHALLENGES

In terms of actual credentialing itself, we have discussed adding new graduate-level coursework to our current graduate course offerings. The department already offers a summer institute through our branch of the National Writing Project, which more than two dozen of our colleagues have taken for graduate credit. We also regularly offer our graduate courses in teaching writing and teaching writing with digital media. Last summer Megan taught a graduate course in writing center studies. Over the next year, we hope to develop a mentoring practicum course for new faculty to become oriented to the program and for current faculty who might not have the requisite coursework in writing studies to fully meet the HLC requirements. Because all of our classes in the department have partially and fully online options, we can run our graduate courses as hybrids or online classes to create flexible schedules for our busy new instructors. And in the coming years, we need to have conversations in the department among all faculty about what additional graduate-level courses we should begin to offer, adding to those already in our catalog, based on our own tenured/tenure-track faculty specializations and the most salient needs of our SLs.

Determining the most salient needs of our colleagues might come from discussions about what we value most in our teaching as well as a careful analysis of our contingent faculty's transcripts and CVs to find what areas of preparation are most needed. Further, we might consider putting together a writing certificate program awarded to faculty who complete a slate of such classes. And we believe we could do more to help educate SLs who might be interested in pursuing graduate degrees in writing studies at nearby institutions that offer MAs and PDs in the field to help them understand their options and know how to prepare applications effectively. Finally, we hope in the future to create opportunities for those SLs who are highly qualified and fully credentialed (i.e., those who hold PhDs in writing studies or a closely related field) to move into tenure-track or other positions with job security, in the ways that William Lalicker and Amy Lynch-Biniek (2017) advocate. Not only is this the ethical course for such highly qualified faculty, but it also offers incentive and motivation for those in the process of attaining the required credentials.

In addition to professionalizing through coursework to meet the new credentialing requirements, the SLs could use some new opportunities offered by the department to continue professionalizing in other ways, in further accordance with the HLC's mandate that institutions have "processes and resources for assuring that instructors are current in their disciplines and adept in their teaching roles" (Higher Learning Commission 2016, 3). For example, the department has accepted responsibility to host an upcoming regional conference, and five SLs are active members of the planning committee. Moreover, one of our tenure-track faculty members who specializes in service learning and community engagement has started a service learning committee composed of SLs to help develop systematic service learning curricula, programming, and community partnerships. We have also created a new mentoring committee, led by and created for SLs. This new committee is developing plans and resources for new as well as experienced SLs who are going up for review and contract renewal. These new activities continue our tradition of providing ongoing professional development and weaving SLs into the fabric of the department in meaningful ways.

Despite our efforts, we continue to face ongoing challenges to assist our faculty to meet the HLC accreditation standards and become fully credentialed by our department's definition. For example, while we offer graduate-level courses with tuition remission to SLs, and we offer such courses as partially or fully online, many instructors often have scheduling or workload conflicts that prevent them from taking such classes. In addition, we have worked to overcome the fears that SLs have about the HLC policies with mixed results. Despite our efforts to convince SLs that their jobs are not in danger and that this move presents an opportunity to professionalize and become more valuable to the institution, some might continue to see the policy as a threat to their careers or as a hurdle to surmount. Managing fears and encouraging people to perceive the benefits of these policies remain ongoing concerns that we continue to address.

SPECIAL LECTURER RESPONSES TO THE DEPARTMENT'S INTERPRETATION OF HLC GUIDELINES

In order to better understand how special lecturers perceived our new departmental interpretation of the HLC guidelines, we created a brief anonymous IRB-approved survey and distributed it to special lecturers. To help these part-time faculty remember the policy changes and our purposes in developing them, we shared a draft of this chapter and asked willing special lecturers to read the chapter before answering the survey. The two-question survey asked SLs about their thoughts on the department's adoption of the HLC guidelines and if those thoughts changed after reading the chapter draft. Although the response rate was small ($n = 4$), the data revealed how at least some of the SLs in the department viewed the new requirements.

While all respondents indicated that they were initially fearful about the new requirements (either for themselves or other part-time faculty these policies affected), most came to believe that the requirements were not overly stringent. For example, one respondent, after sharing initial fears, "felt a bit relieved when I learned unqualified colleagues just had to have a 'plan' to receive the qualifications within three years, and I know the department offers free graduate classes." Another stated, "After speaking with Lori soon after learning of these requirements, my concerns about it lessened considerably because I realized that my professional experience in writing would meet the requirement guidelines." Some special lecturers thus agreed with our assessment that the guidelines included flexible, reasonable pathways toward suitable credentials for those who did not yet meet the standards.

Moreover, respondents also indicated that despite their initial concerns, they eventually saw how the guidelines actually contained long-term benefits for contingent faculty, and they were persuaded by our argument about the importance of professionalization. One respondent noted:

> It seems like the HLC criteria was initially meant to punish unqualified colleagues; however, our department flipped the script and then created a plan to make everyone qualified. (Someone always has our back!) Now, based on reading the article, Lori and Megan want to use the HLC criteria to "professionalize" us within the eyes of the university—again flipping the script to not just protect us but to advocate for us.

Another respondent opined:

> I believe the HLC criteria will help Special Lecturers and the department as a whole. Special Lecturers will gain expertise in writing studies and pedagogy as a result of the individualized plans created to enhance their credentials. Although it will add to the workload of a 4/4 teaching schedule, it will . . . make contingent faculty less expendable or viewed as less expendable to upper-level administrators while giving department chairs and leaders more leverage over helping contingent faculty in their continued efforts to support them. (ellipsis added)

No respondent expressed that they felt the new qualification guidelines were either draconian or useless. While we cannot know if our survey response is representative of all our SLs' views, our survey at least reveals that some special lecturers could see the feasibility and benefits of the guidelines. Such knowledge can help us continue to craft our arguments to the department about the importance of faculty credentials and help us keep working to minimize fears about implementing the policies.

SUGGESTIONS AND APPLICATIONS FOR OTHER INSTITUTIONS

We believe these strategies can be adapted to the particular local conditions of other institutions by providing concrete examples of a strategic approach to concurrently improve labor conditions and elevate the professional status of a department's faculty. We further believe that similar efforts undertaken elsewhere can have the mutual benefits of improving contingent faculty working conditions while also raising the stature of writing instruction in higher education. The following are some guidelines that we think could prove useful to other departments undergoing similar credentialing efforts, based on our experiences:

- *Take a stand on what your discipline is and what counts as credentials:* This might look different for various kinds of departments. For our Department of Writing and Rhetoric, we took a firm stand that our faculty need coursework in writing studies or tested experience in some professional writing capacity. But this approach might not be the most practical for other departments, particularly traditional English departments with faculty who might be mostly literature specialists. Departments should have conversations about what they value in writing instruction and what they believe their faculty's qualifications should include. In any case, the department should set the standard for what constitutes a qualified teacher of their writing classes.

- *Articulate standards to the appropriate administrators such as associate deans, the dean, and the provost:* Make sure that the college or university's upper-level administration knows and understands those qualifications. Doing so ensures that your department is setting the standards for qualification rather than having them imposed upon the department from above, in accordance with someone else's interpretation of accreditation guidelines.

- *Set a high bar, but also commit to helping faculty reach it:* In order to continue to elevate the field of writing studies and offer our students writing instruction that is steeped in best practices, we need to maintain high standards for qualifications. But that doesn't mean leaving behind faculty who haven't yet attained those qualifications. Departments need to develop comprehensive plans to provide professionalizing opportunities for faculty and bring them into the field as experts themselves.

- *Dig deep for faculty "tested experience" and different kinds of expertise:* Because the HLC allows professional experience to demonstrate expertise in addition to coursework and degrees, department chairs and program administrators should look beyond contingent faculty members' CVs and transcripts for nonacademic work that counts. Provide examples of what this tested experience might be, and have face-to-face conversations with faculty about their previous work experience that might qualify as professional, civic, or public writing expertise. After all, while academic writing might be the primary outcome of many writing classes, many programs also have the goal of preparing students for writing that will take place beyond the academy after they graduate. With that in mind, it's beneficial to have nonacademic writing represented among faculty expertise, including workplace writing such as editing, publishing, copywriting, technical writing, business development, marketing, advertising, social media content development, and more. When students have contact with faculty who hold such experience, they have greater opportunities to see how their writing courses might have applications beyond the classroom.

- *Be transparent and manage fears/expectations*: Learning about new credentialing guidelines will inevitably cause fear and consternation among contingent faculty. Relaying information quickly and accurately is important to let them know what to expect. It's also important to reassure them that the department and university will help support them through the process of acquiring the required credentials when necessary. The HLC has a specific clause stipulating that no university should fire faculty deemed to not have met the credentialing requirements (Higher Learning Commission 2016, 7). Making sure that faculty understand that policy is important. Administrators should also understand that these guidelines make faculty feel even more precarious than ever. But departments can reassure them that by developing a plan to attain the credentials they may become more valued because they will have qualifications that others do not.

CONCLUSION

Initially the HLC guidelines seemed like another threat to both our program and our first-year writing faculty, one more top-down measure disrupting department morale and undoing our efforts to both support and recognize our contingent colleagues as professionals. But scholars like Steve Lamos and Amy Lynch-Biniek encourage us to be bold in our solutions to labor issues. In her editor's introduction to *Forum*, Lynch-Biniek (2016) notes that

> as we face the complicated web that is higher education's labor system in our research, advocacy, and curricula, teachers may feel overwhelmed, even powerless. But if we want to change higher education for the better, it is crucial that we find the strength in our growing body of knowledge and use our understanding of both the global and the local for scholarship and activism that make a positive difference in the lives of our teachers and our students. (A2)

In our department, we have embraced the HLC guidelines, recognizing them as an opportunity to establish the boundaries of our discipline, distinguish our work from the work of English, and raise the professional status of—and make irreplaceable—our contingent faculty. As Lamos (2011) notes, credentialing our contingent faculty may disrupt current labor practices that mark contingent colleagues as expendable or replaceable "by changing both the demand for and supply of professional college writing teachers" (49) and demonstrating the value of these colleagues while simultaneously demonstrating their scarcity.

An understanding of how to use accreditation guidelines to improve departmental/disciplinary and faculty status may prove essential to our field in the years to come. Recent trends indicate that regional accreditation bodies will continue to implement credentialing requirements and vet the qualifications of all faculty during review periods. As the number of contingent faculty has risen, so too have accreditation agencies' requirements that those faculty demonstrate appropriate credentials (Pham and Osland Paton 2017, 41). For universities and writing programs that have not yet been asked to consider faculty credentials for accreditation, we believe it best to assume that these requirements are forthcoming. That being the case, department chairs and writing program administrators should not delay in determining what qualifies a faculty member to teach in their departments and how best to support their colleagues who may not yet meet those requirements. Such proactive decision-making can also give departments time to get deans, provosts, and other administrators on board with the department's articulated qualification requirements and make it possible for programs to seek internal funding for additional professional development of inexperienced faculty. While these guidelines present a significant challenge to increase the professionalization of contingent instructors, they also present an important opportunity for the field to further define itself and to demonstrate the singular expertise of our faculty.

NOTES

1. The names of all participants in this study have been changed for the purpose of publication.
2. The HLC's guidelines for qualified faculty are similar to the "Faculty Credentials: Guidelines" published by the Southern Association of Colleges and Schools (SACS) in 2006. The HLC is the largest regional accrediting authority in the United States, and SACS is the second largest. Together, the HLC and SACS are responsible for accrediting not-for-profit and for-profit educational institutions in thirty states.
3. Contingent faculty, SLs, are members of our faculty union and, thus, receive tuition waivers for eight graduate credits a year (as mentioned earlier). While many of our colleagues have already met the HLC guidelines, those who haven't will be able to use their tuition waivers to enroll in our graduate-level pedagogy classes and in related classes (in education, communication and journalism, ESL) across the university.

REFERENCES

Allan, Elizabeth G., Dana Lynn Driscoll, David R. Hammontree, Marshall Kitchens, and Lori Ostergaard. 2015. "The Source of Our Ethos: Using Evidence-Based Practices to Affect a Program-Wide Shift from 'I Think' to 'We Know.'" *Composition Forum* 32. http://compositionforum.com/issue/32/oakland.php.

Conference on College Composition and Communication. 2015. "CCCC Statement on Preparing Teachers of College Writing." *National Council of Teachers of English.* http://ncte.org/cccc/resources/positions/statementonprep.

Higher Learning Commission. 2016. "Determining Qualified Faculty through HLC's Criteria for Accreditation and Assumed Practices: Guidelines for Institutions and Peer Reviewers." http://download.hlcommission.org/FacultyGuidelines_2016_OPB.pdf.

Lalicker, William B., and Amy Lynch-Biniek. 2017. "Contingency, Solidarity, and Community Building: Principles for Converting Contingent to Tenure Track." In *Contingency, Exploitation, and Solidarity: Labor and Action in English Composition,* edited by Seth Kahn, William B. Lalicker, and Amy Lynch-Biniek, 91–101. WAC Clearinghouse and University Press of Colorado. https://wac.colostate.edu/books/contingency.

Lamos, Steve. 2011. "Credentialing College Writing Teachers: WPAs and Labor Reform." *WPA: Writing Program Administration* 35.1: 45–73.

Lynch-Biniek, Amy. 2012. "Toward a Qualitative Study of Contingency and Teaching Practices." *Teaching English in the Two-Year College* 14.2: A3–A10.

Lynch-Biniek, Amy. 2016. "From the Editor: Growing the Argument." *Forum: Issues about Part-time and Contingent Faculty* 20.1: A1–A2.

McDonald, James C., and Eileen E. Schell. 2011. "The Spirit and Influence of the Wyoming Resolution: Looking Back to Look Forward." *College English* 73.4: 360–78.

McQuade, Donald A. 1981. "The Case of the Migrant Workers." *WPA: Writing Program Administration* 5.1: 29–34.

Penrose, Ann M. 2012. "Professional Identity in a Contingent-Labor Profession: Expertise, Autonomy, Community in Composition Teaching." *WPA Writing Program Administration* 35.2: 108–26.

Pham, Nhung, and Osland Paton, Valerie. 2017. "Regional Accreditation Standards and Contingent and Part-Time Faculty." *New Directions for Institutional Research* 176: 41–54. https://doi.org/10.1002/ir.20243.

Rysdam, Sheri. 2012. "The Political Economy of Contingency." *Teaching English in the Two-Year College* 14.22: A10–A15.

Schoen, Megan, ed. 2018. *Grizz Writes: A Guide to First-Year Writing at Oakland University.* 7th ed. Southlake, TX: Fountainhead.

Southern Association of Colleges and Schools. 2006. "Faculty Credentials: Guidelines." http://sacs.faytechcc.edu/Documents/SACSFacultyCredentialGuidelines.pdf.

Trimbur, John, and Barbara Cambridge. 1998. "The Wyoming Conference Resolution: A Beginning." *WPA: Writing Program Administration* 12.1–2: 13–18.

Wardle, Elizabeth. 2013. "Intractable Writing Program Problems, *Kairos*, and Writing about Writing: A Profile of the University of Central Florida's First-Year Composition Program." *Composition Forum* 27. http://compositionforum.com/issue/27/ucf.php.

4

ADVOCATING TOGETHER
Pros and Cons of Cross-Rank Collaboration as a Strategy for Advocacy

Rachel Hall Buck and Susan Miller-Cochran

It has been almost thirty years since James Sledd introduced the term "boss compositionist" to refer to those who coordinate and supervise writing programs (1991). In response, Joseph Harris described this new boss as one who is "able to interview, hire, and train a teaching staff, to fire teachers who don't work out, to establish curriculum, to set policies, and to represent the program as he or she sees best" (2000, 57). The description Harris offers is of a WPA who exerts singular control over a writing program, a model of centralized power and authority in one person. By contrast, Jeanne Gunner is critical of the centralized model of the WPA, one who is a "tenured leader in control of program policy and personnel" (1994, 8) and argues for a "decentered" model where power and authority are shared. Many feminist scholars have also called for revised ways of imagining leadership within writing programs as collaborative and grassroots (Ronald et al. 2010; Conti et al. 2017) and as nonhierarchical collaboration with shared leadership and authority (Goodburn and Leverenz 1998; Osorio, Fiscus-Cannaday, and Hutchison, chapter 1 in this collection). Revising current hierarchies, as John Trimbur and Barbara Cambridge suggest (1988), can be a messy challenge in academic work, much of which is bureaucratic in nature, as Richard Miller has noted (1998).

In this collaborative piece, we discuss the messiness of collaborative administration from two different perspectives: Susan as the writing program administrator at a large public university and Rachel, as a graduate student interim director of studio writing in the same program. Specifically, we explore our perspectives and cross-rank collaboration in the context of a project that Rachel was assigned as part of her administrative work: collecting data from students and instructors to be used to argue for keeping a lower course cap in those courses. In that capacity,

https://doi.org/10.7330/9781646421428.c004

she worked with the administrative team in the writing program and also with instructors of the courses to collect data and present the results of the data with the writing program director to institutional administration, arguing effectively to retain a low course cap in studio courses.

The end result of working together to argue for maintaining lower course sizes for basic writing was positive with regard to the course cap, far beyond our initial goal. Rachel shared her data in a meeting with the senior vice provost and other administrators interested in student success and retention. Following that meeting, upper administrators began conversations to discuss how to raise the university's rankings, and the senior vice provost shared the possibility of extending our lower course caps across all writing courses. In a series of conversations during the following summer, upper administration gave funding to the writing program to lower all course caps in first-year writing to nineteen for a two-year trial period to study impact. In essence, Rachel's data helped the writing program advocate for lower course caps across all first-year writing courses. By shifting hierarchies within the writing program and opening up an administrative position to a graduate student specializing in basic writing, Rachel and Susan were able to then transform the working conditions of instructors within the writing program.

While the argument was effective, the work itself presented several challenges. In a symposium on graduate student professionalization in *Rhetoric Review*, Roxanne Mountford suggests that graduate students have opportunities to reflect on the nature of power and authority in academia (2002). Following in the spirit of Mountford's call, we discuss the complications of giving graduate students opportunities to participate in administrative work, especially work that has high visibility at the institution. That work is even more complicated when the graduate student is placed in a position where they are expected to have authority but technically hold very little. Because the nature of hierarchies is multifaceted and complex, revising one hierarchical model does not dismantle all institutional hierarchies, and we argue that collaborative administration and shared leadership arrangements be entered into cautiously, intentionally, and with an eye toward protecting the interests and position of the graduate student.

A WPA'S PERSPECTIVE: DEVELOPING A GRADUATE ADMINISTRATIVE POSITION

During the 2016–17 academic year, the writing program at the University of Arizona was able to offer its first semester of research leave to a faculty member who was not on the tenure track. The first faculty member to take research leave was the course director for our studio writing course, ENGL 101A. ENGL 101A is a parallel course to our required first semester course (ENGL 101), but it adds a one-hour studio each week where the class is divided into two separate sections of nine to ten students. In these studio courses, students can receive additional support and feedback from the instructor (for more information about ENGL 101A and its development, see Hall and Minnix 2012, 59). Offering research leave was an exciting development for a program that was working toward more equity between tenure-track and non-tenure-track positions (the term that the university uses for contract positions off the tenure track), and I (Susan) needed to find a sustainable model for covering the duties of someone on leave so that the opportunity for leave could be offered to other faculty members.

Although all of the course directors and all but one of the assistant director positions were filled by faculty in the program and not by graduate students, the administrative team decided to offer the interim administrative position to an advanced graduate student who was studying basic writing. Our intention was both to provide a graduate student with helpful administrative experience and also to give a graduate student with interests in basic writing the opportunity to teach in and work in the studio writing program. Graduate students at the university are not currently able to teach our studio writing courses because there isn't an easy way to fit the course into their workloads without giving them a teaching overload. The writing program had just launched a new graduate assistant director position that same year, and the other administrators in the writing program wanted to provide additional administrative opportunities to interested graduate students when possible.

I immediately thought of Rachel for the position because she was writing a dissertation that explored connections between reading and writing in basic writing classrooms. Directing the course for a semester would give her the opportunity to teach a section of the course, and it would also give our instructors the benefit of learning from the research that Rachel was doing. When I spoke with Rachel about the possibility of filling the position, the interim assistant director of Studio writing had been tasked with two primary duties that were identical to other assistant directors who directed other courses and areas of the writing program:

- Provide teacher preparation and support in their area of administrative responsibility.
- Serve on the writing program advisory council representing their area of administrative responsibility. The first task, providing

teaching preparation and support, was broken down into specific
expectations:

- Organize and facilitate two professional development events per
  semester related to studio writing.
- Consult with instructors of the course when they have questions or
  concerns.
- Assist with responding to course-specific complaints and concerns.

While the writing program had some other requirements of assistant
directors (attending meetings and participating in other administrative support), the administrative team decided not to burden Rachel
with attending all of those meetings and doing other administrative
tasks in the program, because of concerns about having her work more
than twenty hours per week (her workload as a graduate teaching assistant [GTA]).

While the intention was to provide an opportunity through the
temporary administrative position, I was also aware of research exploring the complicated nature of graduate administrative positions and
the now twenty-year-old argument that Carrie Shively Leverenz and
Amy Goodburn made to "caution against an assumption that everyone
who teaches in a university writing program as a graduate student will
benefit—professionally—from involvement in the administration of
such a program" (1998, 23). My intention was to provide an opportunity
for a graduate student to contribute to the writing program as a collabo-
rator and not just a liaison or administrative assistant (Latterell 2003).
Such a proposal fit within the collaborative model of administration we
were trying to implement in the writing program (Gunner 1994), but
I was also aware that the power dynamics at work in the administrative
position would be challenging. Rachel would be a graduate student
directing a course taught exclusively by faculty. The writing program
administrators also felt, though, that Rachel's prior experience as an
adjunct faculty member at Arizona Western College and her experience
teaching and researching basic writing would provide ethos as she facilitated meetings and conversations with the ENGL 101A faculty.

At the same time that we created this position and invited Rachel to
fill it, we knew we would need to construct an argument for keeping the
caps in ENGL 101A at nineteen. Course caps had been at nineteen for
several years, but the writing program had to argue for funding every
year to keep the cap at nineteen instead of raising it to twenty-five (the
cap for other first-year writing classes). The funding had been provided
for several years from the Office of Student Success and Retention,
and we anticipated making the argument to that office again. Rachel's

leadership and assistance could help us gather data to make the argument more effectively.

A GRADUATE STUDENT'S PERSPECTIVE:
ADVOCATING AS A GRADUATE STUDENT

Discussing the experience of being a graduate student is a complicated act as the "urge to make oneself present is, paradoxically, to participate in one's own subjection" (Taylor and Holberg 1999, 698). Sharing experiences of conflicted graduate student identity(ies) does not simply reinscribe them, but also can also move us toward progress and opportunities for listening to competing narratives.

When Susan first approached me about the interim position, I was excited. As a PhD student in rhetoric and composition, I saw this administrative position as a "professionalizing" opportunity—one that would potentially help me when I entered the job market. By offering this position to a graduate student, Susan had shifted the writing program structures, but both of us were unaware of how this structural shift would also cause a shift in identity.

As a GTA, like many PhD students, I had been teaching in the writing program while also completing coursework. Many GTAs feel a struggle and tension as they navigate the roles of teacher and student. Many GTAs "find their writing confidence and competence undermined in one set of classrooms and faculty offices while being positioned (and positioning themselves) as writing experts in another set of classrooms and in their own offices" (Dryer 2012, 425). This feeling of unease was increased as I began the interim position where I was still teacher and graduate student; however, in this new administrative role, I was tasked with organizing meetings alongside lecturers who were teaching 101A, attending meetings with tenured and non-tenured faculty, and collecting data from the 101A instructors. This section is a reflection on the tasks assigned by the writing program, the shifting institutional structures, and the consequences for me as I negotiated these various roles.

Graduate Student WPA (GSWPA) positions are popular and are likely to continue due to "economic factors and other forces" in the field (Philipps et al. 2018, 78). But the labor of performing these transitory positions is often problematic for graduate students as they balance the intellectual work with other assigned "tasks." However, Sheryl Fontaine cautions, characterizing GSWPA work as tasks to be completed neglects the "part of administration that does not fit neatly into a list of guidelines or jobs, the intellectual work that requires the WPA to synthesize research and scholarship into a coherent philosophy" (1998, 87). Fontaine also states that administrative work "cannot be valued or rewarded as intellectual work as long as we continue to promote the idea that it can be reduced to a list of items to be checked off, parceled out, and accomplished by preprofessionals" (1998, 87). As a graduate student, I often moved back and forth between feeling like I had expertise in this position and feeling like a novice. Many of the other faculty members had taught Basic Writing longer than I had, but I also had some expertise that I brought to the position. Yet on the spectrum of professionalism, I felt clearly like more of a novice than many of the faculty teaching the course.

The highlight of this position for me was organizing the monthly collaborative meetings where I could draw on previous scholarship about the purpose of professional development as a way for teachers to transform "their knowledge into practice for the benefit of their students' growth" (Avalos 2011, 10). I sought and received feedback from all instructors about how they wanted to use the collaborative time and was also able to put together a time when all instructors could potentially participate. Teaching communities are valuable for teachers who may feel that teaching is sometimes a lonely calling. The intellectual work of this task was rewarding—drawing on disciplinary knowledge of writing studies and basic writing to find suitable readings and activities.

Organizing these collaboratives, however, was not without its challenges. As the only graduate student working with the twelve full-time, non-tenure-track faculty, I was acutely aware of my position as an outsider in this group. As a graduate student, I was arguably below the faculty in the academic hierarchy, but I was also given authority by the writing program to organize the collaborative meetings.

This shifting authority can be challenging for graduate students because a task can change depending on who assigns the task. For example, "Workshops offered by GSWPAs may not be as well attended as those offered by faculty WPAs, policies not as carefully adhered to, or daily procedures as adequately followed" (Fontaine 1998, 85). Although my position was not intended to be "supervisory" in nature (I was not asked to observe or evaluate faculty), the point that Fontaine makes about authority is certainly relevant. In the CWPA statement "Evaluating the Intellectual Work of Writing Program Administration," the authors discuss the intellectual work of faculty development, stating, "Instructors cannot simply be ordered and coerced, no matter how subordinate their position within the university. Thus faculty development, when it truly accomplishes its purpose of improving teaching and maintaining the highest classroom standards, is one of the most salient examples of intellectual work carried out within an administrative sphere" (1998, n.p.). Ann Penrose further elaborates on the need for acknowledging the expertise and autonomy of faculty off-the-tenure-track in professional development opportunities (2012). I was very careful about how I presented the collaborative to the instructors and how I shared authority within that space with the teachers, who all had teaching knowledge to share. For example, in the meetings, all participants sat at a round table demonstrating an equal share of authority. Activities during the meetings included a discussion on a short book chapter about basic writing; sharing of studio activities, which worked well; discussing how to revise activities to better meet the Writing Program Student Learning Outcomes. Notes and activities were sent out to all the 101A instructors.

Despite the faculty caring very deeply about their teaching and demonstrating thoughtful consideration about it, attendance at the collaborative meetings was low. One possible reason was the instructors' full-time workload and hectic semesters. Another reason was that they knew there was not an institutional incentive for attending and that in my position as a graduate student, I could not offer them an incentive other than a gathering place to create a community of teachers. In a busy semester, that is often not enough. There were also no negative institutional consequences for not attending the meetings. The academy is a hierarchical space, whether we like it or not, and "when a task that was once completed by a full-time faculty member is reassigned to a graduate student, the importance of the task has diminished in the minds of those who make the assignment" (Fontaine 1998, 84). Being in the position of assigning a certain task without having hierarchical authority was challenging, and it also led me to question the value of the work I was completing in the position.

This lack of authority was also apparent when I sent out the studio effectiveness survey to all the instructors. At the 101A course meeting at the beginning of the semester, the majority of the instructors volunteered to have their students participate in the survey, but when I sent the survey out after the semester had started, very few had their students complete it. Possible reasons might include the busyness of the semester, and also, as Fontaine suggests, the fact that I was the person sending out the email asking for participation and not really having institutional authority to require it. As a result, there were few participants.

Sending out the email was a prime example of how power and authority work in higher education. Roxanne Mountford suggests that because of the informality of many programs, "tenured and tenure-track faculty regularly share responsibilities with graduate students in a kind of apprenticeship model, all the while protecting them from the more difficult politics of the institution" (2002, 49). She further explains that this model is inadequate, and she describes how she felt ill prepared for the politics as she began a position as writing program administrator. Likewise, I felt ill prepared to gather data to support the studio component of 101A for a number of reasons. Although I had completed research training and participated in research projects in teams, this was the first research project I had completed on my own. I had participated in Susan's WPA course for graduate students, and while the readings and assignments were helpful in theorizing WPA work, I learned that the theory is often challenged by local contexts. Because of the nature of this transitory position and my position within the institutional hierarchy, I had not been a part of the conversations happening about the studio prior to that semester. I knew very little about what would be happening with 101A studio or who the participants in the conversation even were. When I sent out the email to the 101A instructors asking them for their participation in giving the survey, I told them the data would be useful to "upper administration" but did not have a clear understanding of who that was or how the data might be used to support the studio.

I was well aware of my lack of authority as a graduate student, so even being asked to participate in the discussions happening about 101A has potential setbacks and limitations. Similar to Mountford, Margaret Willard-Traub discusses her position as a graduate student on an assessment committee with other graduate students, tenured faculty, and nontenured faculty, and tenured-faculty administrators. Administrators were concerned that the assessment standards that were decided upon by the group needed to have faculty backing—the graduate students did not have enough authority on their own to convince other faculty members in the department to accept the results of the committee. Of this experience, Willard-Traub states, "I developed an understanding of the ways in which intellectual work in our field is bound up with institutional politics—and an understanding of how essential that knowledge is to the professionalization of graduate students generally" (2002, 62). In my position, the nature of institutional hierarchies and the temporary position I was in hindered developing a greater understanding of institutional politics.

Throughout the semester, I was aware of my position "in-between" various academic communities, and I experienced constant identity shifts. The temporary nature of the position also complicated the idea of my having any authority, as Willard-Traub suggests, to see myself as an "agent for institutional change" (2002, 68). In this "interim" position, I felt like I had a level of autonomy in fulfilling assigned duties, but this was also a lonely place to be—a graduate student separated from the faculty, an assistant director not invited to the meetings with the other assistant directors, a WPA isolated from the other WPAs. This sense of isolation led to a feeling of anxiety about roles, identity, and purposes within the writing program. What I learned through this position is that writing program administration is complicated, messy work bound up in politics, hierarchy, authority, and identity(ies). My position as interim assistant director of studio writing complicated these issues by placing me in precarious situations in which I questioned my own subjectivity as a graduate student, as a teacher of basic writing, and as a WPA.

CONCLUSIONS
Collaboratively Working toward Change

By shifting hierarchies within the writing program and opening up an administrative position to a graduate student specializing in basic writing, we were able to transform the working conditions of instructors within the writing program. However, shifting one hierarchy did not shift all institutional hierarchies. There are multiple hierarchies within the writing program, and the writing program exists within a complex network of institutional hierarchies. Because of this, we also advocate for caution about the possibilities and tensions in cross-rank collaboration. Rachel's position as assistant director had potential to allow her to see insights into the politics of basic writing at the university and how the institutional ideologies affect the classroom, but ultimately she was protected from those politics. She, like many basic writing instructors, existed on the periphery of the writing program (Horner 2011). She wanted to learn more about the institutional politics related to basic writing but could also see that involvement was complicated and possibly risky because of subject position.

As professionalization is becoming ever more important for graduate students, we are both enthusiastic and cautious about the experience Rachel had. Overall, the position was challenging, but as Stephen Jukuri states, it is important to "remain dutifully suspicious of ease, and respectful of the sort of unease" (2002, 78) graduate students may feel as they are given more responsibility within writing programs. Graduate students need to be prepared to "understand and work change in the material constraints of [their] local bureaucracies" (Duffey et al. 2002, 80). While we don't think that Rachel's role as a GSWPA has prepared her to undertake these responsibilities entirely, it did make her more aware of hierarchical structures within a writing program and the complicated nature of authority and the often precarious place of basic writing classes within a university. Being aware of academic bureaucratic structures is a first step to understanding how changes within these structures can be made. Rachel's realization, and even the collaboration we engaged in on writing this article, helped us brainstorm and enact the beginnings of hierarchical shifts within our own program.

Although we both agree that providing opportunities for graduate students to serve in administrative positions can be a valuable and successful site of collaboration and advocacy, these positions should not be provided without first focusing "more explicitly on *how* they should be conducted" (Rowan 2009, 13). As a starting point, Karen Rowan suggests three components of graduate student training: hands-on experience, reflection and analysis, and participation in professional communities. We add to these suggestions with our own in the following sections.

Mentoring

First, it is of the utmost importance that graduate student administrative positions be treated as mentoring opportunities; that there are ample opportunities to discuss issues of power, authority, and identity with a mentor; and that the range of challenges and complications that arise from doing administrative work from specific subject positions be an ongoing conversation and learning opportunity for both the mentor and mentee. In an "interim" position, mentoring seems especially important for graduate students, but perhaps it is harder to find because of the nature of an interim position as filling in for a person who might be the very person who offers mentorship. Rachel, like other graduate students, did not actively seek mentorship because she did not want to burden already-burdened faculty members (Phillips et al. 2018, 74).

We recognize that mentorship is also a problematic notion, as the labor invested by faculty mentoring is often not valued. Because of this, faculty do not always mentor as much, because it doesn't "count" on their annual evaluations in the same way a publication does. The mentoring that does happen is often done by women in the academy who take on the extra burden of this work. Theresa Enos discusses the gender disparities in mentoring, saying that women are primarily mentoring new members of the field (1997). These complicated issues are not only relevant to graduate students, of course, but also to junior faculty, women, minorities, faculty or staff off the tenure track, and others in administrative roles who may be marginalized in their institutional hierarchies, but we suggest that students not be given professionalization experiences without adequate mentorship as well.

Authority versus Accountability

In addition, we have found that it is important to understand the distinctions between sharing authority and sharing accountability. While WPAs can share authority in order to advocate for change, they can't always share the accountability of the consequences of the work graduate students complete. And academic hierarchies are persistent; no matter how hard we push against those hierarchical distinctions to share authority collaboratively, the academy is a modernist, hierarchical institution, and authority is prescribed and allocated according to that hierarchy. Others have also explored the complicated position that graduate students are put in when they are in a position of authority as a graduate student. As Latterell discusses, graduate student administrators often act as liaisons, administrative assistants, and/or policymakers, and there are important implications to consider in those positions to avoid putting them in the position of being surveillance in a writing program and isolating them from both their graduate student peers and other administrators.

This sense of isolation can come from the position being what Talinn Phillips et al. term "liminal" WPA positions; they are temporary positions. Because of this, a "liminal's work and initiatives are easily disregarded because the liminal 'won't be here next year,' 'is just a graduate student,' 'doesn't really know the field'" (2018, 70). These feelings of disregard may impact the liminal's own sense of value and worth since their work is not taken as seriously. This was true for Rachel. Her isolation and disregard often led her to devaluing the work she was doing in her interim position.

Because of the nature of liminal positions, the work that graduate students do in administrative roles needs to have ongoing support that is sustainable to create lasting change. Because the work often must be sustainable after the graduate student leaves the institution, administrative work must often be done collaboratively with a clear understanding of the implications of the work for both the graduate student and the WPA. These concerns raise questions such as: What kinds of responsibilities are ethical to ask a graduate student to take on, and what kinds of responsibilities are practical and sustainable? Collaborative work across ranks can provide a rich understanding of the potential implications and lived experiences of a range of stakeholders when working toward change in a writing program, but we must also consider the thorny complications and fuzzy boundaries between providing opportunities or engaging in exploitation, and between ensuring a place at the table versus requiring additional time/labor that is undercompensated. We must balance the desire to make manageable the time graduate students spend in administrative positions with the importance of making them and their work visible in order to truly share authority and collaborate.

REFERENCES

Avalos, Beatrice. 2011. "Teacher Professional Development in Teaching and Teacher Education over Ten Years." *Teacher and Teacher Education* 27: 10–20. http://citeseerx.ist.psu.edu/viewdoc/download?doi=10.1.1.466.6330&rep=rep1&type=pdf.

Conti, Maria, Rachel LaMance, and Susan Miller-Cochran. 2017. "Cultivating Change from the Ground Up: Developing a Grassroots Programmatic Assessment." *Composition Forum* (Fall) 37. https://compositionforum.com/issue/37/arizona.php.

Council of Writing Program Administrators. 1998. "Evaluating the Intellectual Work of Writing Program Administration." http://wpacouncil.org/aws/CWPA/pt/sd/news_article/242849/_PARENT/layout_details/false.

Dryer, Dylan B. 2012. "At a Mirror, Darkly: The Imagined Undergraduate Writers of Ten Novice Composition Instructors." *College Composition and Communication* 63, no. 3 (February): 420–52. http://cccc.ncte.org/library/NCTEFiles/Resources/Journals/CCC/0633-feb2012/CCC0633Mirror.pdf.

Duffey, Suellyn, Ben Feigert, Vic Mortimer, Jennifer Phegley, and Melinda Turnley. 2002. "Conflict, Collaboration, and Authority: Graduate Students and Writing Program Administration." *Rhetoric Review* 21.1: 79–87.

Enos, Theresa. 1997. "Mentoring—and (Wo)mentoring—in Composition Studies." In *Academic Advancement in Composition Studies: Scholarship, Publication, Promotion, Tenure*, edited by Richard C. Gebhardt and Barbara Genelle Smith Gebhardt, 129–45. Mahwah, NJ: Lawrence Erlbaum.

Fontaine, Sheryl. 1998. "Revising Administrative Models and Questioning the Value of Appointing Graduate Student WPAs." In *Foregrounding Ethical Awareness in Composition and English Studies*, edited by Sheryl Fontaine and Susan Hunter, 83–92. Portsmouth, NH: Boynton Cook.

Goodburn, Amy, and Carrie Shively Leverenz. 1998. "Feminist Writing Program Administration: Resisting the Bureaucrat Within." In *Feminism and Composition Studies: In Other Words*, edited by Susan C. Jarratt and Lynn Worsham, 276–90. New York: MLA.

Gunner, Jeanne. 1994. "Decentering the WPA." *WPA: Writing Program Administration* 18.1–2: 8–14.

Hall, Anne-Marie, and Christopher Minnix. 2012. "Beyond the Bridge Metaphor: Rethinking the Place of the Literacy Narrative in the Basic Writing Curriculum." *Journal of Basic Writing* 31.2: 57–82.

Harris, Joseph. 2000. "Meet the New Boss, Same as the Old Boss: Class Consciousness in Composition." *College Composition and Communication* 52.1: 43–68. https://www.jstor.org/stable/358543?seq=1#metadata_info_tab_contents.

Horner, Bruce. 2011. "Relocating Basic Writing." *Journal of Basic Writing* 30.2: 5–23.

Jukuri, Stephen. 2002. "Private Classrooms Made Public: Writing Program Administration and the Development of a Community of Scholar-Teacher Colleagues." *Rhetoric Review* 21.1: 70–79.

Latterell, Catherine. 2003. "Defining Roles as Graduate Students in Writing Program Administration: Balancing Pragmatic Needs with a Postmodern Ethics of Action." *WPA: Writing Program Administration* 27.1–2: 23–39.

Leverenz, Carrie Shively, and Amy Goodburn. 1998. "Professionalizing TA Training: Commitment to Teaching or Rhetorical Response to Market Crisis?" *WPA: Writing Program Administration* 22.1–2: 9–32.

Miller, Richard. 1998. *As If Learning Mattered: Reforming Higher Education.* Ithaca, NY: Cornell University Press.

Mountford, Roxanne. 2002. "From Labor to Middle Management: Graduate Students in Writing Program Administration." *Rhetoric Review* 21.1: 41–53.

Penrose, Ann M. 2012. "Professional Identity in a Contingent-Labor Profession: Expertise, Autonomy, Community in Composition Teaching." *WPA: Writing Program Administration* 35.2: 108–26.

Phillips, Talinn, Paul Shovlin, and Megan L. Titus. 2018. " 'An Exercise in Cognitive Dissonance': Liminal WPA Transitions." In *WPAs in Transition: Navigating Educational Leadership Positions,* edited by Courtney Adams Wooten, Jacob Babb, and Brian Ray, 70–84. Boulder: University Press of Colorado.

Ronald, Kate, Cristy Beemer, and Lisa Shaver. 2010. " 'Where Else Should Feminist Rhetoricians Be?': Leading a WAC Initiative in a School of Business." In *Performing Feminism and Administration in Rhetoric and Composition,* edited by Krista Ratcliffe and Rebecca Rickly, 159–69. New York: Hampton Press.

Rowan, Karen. 2009. "All the Best Intentions: Graduate Student Administrative Professional Development in Practice." *Writing Center Journal* 29, no. 1 (Spring): 11–48.

Sledd, James. 1991. "Why the Wyoming Resolution Had to Be Emasculated: A History and a Quixotism." *Journal of Advanced Composition* 11, no. 2 (Fall): 269–81. http://www.jstor.org/stable/20865795.

Taylor, Marcy, and Jennifer L. Holberg. 1999. " 'Tales of Neglect and Sadism': Disciplinarity and the Figuring of Graduate Students in Composition." *College Composition and Communication* 50.4: 607–25.

Trimbur, John, and Barbara Cambridge. 1988. "The Wyoming Conference Resolution: A Beginning." *WPA: Writing Program Administration* 12.1–2: 13–17.

Willard-Traub, Margaret. 2002. "Professionalization and the Politics of Subjectivity." *Rhetoric Review* 21.1: 61–70.

PART 2

Transforming Institutions

Authors in this section direct our attention to the sometimes ignored, and often confusing, institutional practices that composition and rhetoric professionals must navigate to do the work required to maintain and advance writing programs. In transitioning from thinking about our labor practices, part 2 opens with a meditation on care work. A long-standing concern in a field that has historically been categorized as feminized, one that relies on graduate- and non-tenure-track labor, care work is a part of the everyday reality of all writing instructors but tends to be labor taken on more by white women and faculty of color (well documented in research and reporting on faculty labor; see Caron 2018; June 2015; Kafka 2018).[1] By emphasizing care work as a part of our institutional practice, this section focuses on common institutional writing program models that include Writing Across the Curriculum, Accelerated Learning Programs, developmental writing courses, and digitally mediated or online courses.

What sets these chapters apart is that while there is a great deal of scholarship dedicated to each component of our institutional practices—problematizing them, exploring them, offering best practice models for them—few of our long-standing discussions posit these as places where productive change is always already happening. When thinking about the role that WAC, dual-credit or developmental writing, and online writing courses have played in composition and rhetoric, we tend to use scholarship to make arguments about whether or not these programs should exist or be sustained. In this section, authors move beyond that paradigm and instead offer strategies for how to navigate institutional hierarchy, politics, and budgetary priorities to maximize investment in writing programs. In fact, in the final chapter of this section, the authors provide a template for how to work across the different units across campus in order to tap into the commitment of stakeholders who are invested in the work of writing programs.

https://doi.org/10.7330/9781646421428.p002

REFERENCES

Caron, Paul. 2018. " 'Dancing Backwards in High Heels': Study Finds Female Professors Experience More Work Demands and Special Favor Requests, Particularly from Academically 'Entitled' students." *Inside Higher Ed.* January 11. https://taxprof.typepad. com/taxprof_blog/2018/01/dancing-backwards-in-high-heels-study-finds-students-set -higher-standards-for-female-profs.html.

June, Audrey Williams. 2015. "The Invisible Labor of Minority Professors" *Chronicle of Higher Education.* November 8. https://www.chronicle.com/article/the-invisible -labor-of-minority-professors/.

Kafka, Alexander. 2018. "Instructors Spend 'Emotional Labor' in Diversity Courses, and Deserve Credit for It." *Chronicle of Higher Education.* November 15. https://www.chro nicle.com/article/instructors-spend-emotional-labor-in-diversity-courses-and-deserve -credit-for-it/.

5

TIME, CARE, AND FACULTY WORKING CONDITIONS

Heather M. Robinson

> *To seize the agenda requires an alternative semantics of accountability and a knowledge of power.*
> —Cris Shore and Susan Wright (1999, 572)

As many scholars have pointed out, the expectation of significant affective labor in composition classrooms is at the core of the issues with working conditions that are endemic in staffing and teaching composition classes (e.g., Schell 1992; S. Miller 1993; Ritter 2012). Furthermore, these issues extend beyond composition into working conditions of those teaching in our institutions' general education curricula. I argue that in order to transform our working conditions, we not only need to center care work as what academics *do*, but also change the discourses which we build around care, and by extension, feminized work. Care work, in the way I am conceiving of it here, builds on the idea of "academic housework" in T. M. Heijstra et al. 2017 (764), who use this term to describe "All the academic service work within the institution that is performed by all academic staff, both women and men, but that receives little recognition within the process of academic career making or within the definition of academic excellence" (765). More specifically, care work is the activities that academic staff undertake to support students' learning, and to support students' and other colleagues' emotional health and academic advancement. Care work focuses on the affective parts of teaching, service, and research, rather than the content of what we teach and do in our academic work.

Many discussions of how the working conditions of writing instructors might be improved focus on what I consider to be "masculinizing" strategies: make all writing courses electives (Crowley 1998); create a department of writing studies with tenure-track faculty doing writing

https://doi.org/10.7330/9781646421428.c005

research and teaching graduate students (Lalicker 2016), get rid of writing programs altogether (Bousquet 2003), and value writing program administration (WPA) as scholarship (Council of Writing Program Administrators 1998). These strategies are masculinizing because rather than contending with the cultural devaluation of the "feminine," they instead embrace existing academic hierarchies that are well known to favor white, heterosexual men even when women play by "the rules" by rejecting care work in most if not all aspects of their work lives (Bird 2004; Winslow 2010; O'Meara et al. 2017). Furthermore, such proposals do nothing to address the structural inequalities that are inherent in academic work, where most composition and general education classes are taught by contingent faculty; indeed, many of these proposals predate US universities' shift to a massive reliance on contingent and non-tenure-track faculty.[1] Instead, I suggest that we can change the system on the ground by looking at what we have control over. These things might include changing how workloads are distributed among courses; how we make care visible and count in professional evaluation; and how we describe care work in our reappointment, tenure, and promotion documents and narratives. That is, I am proposing that in order to change working conditions in writing programs, we need to change our institutional and professional discourses of what counts as success, and value as primary the work that is predominantly done by women and faculty of color: teaching general education courses and providing care to students and colleagues in our teaching, mentoring, and institutional service.

In developing my discussion, I draw from the slow scholarship movement to argue that in order to value care work appropriately in our institutions, we must move away from understanding of academic success based on individual "productivity." The slow scholarship movement, which builds on other "slow" movements (e.g., slow food, Andrews [2008]), resists "the accelerated timelines of the neoliberal university" (Mountz et al. 2015) by focusing on a commitment to thorough and thoughtful scholarship, and an embrace of an ethic of care in our academic work, as explored, for instance, in Luke Martell (2014), Daniel McCabe (2012), Maggie O'Neill (2014) and Maggie Berg and Barbara K. Seeber (2016). In particular, I follow Alison Mountz et al. (2015) in making collectivity central to my version of slow scholarship, along with its attention to structures of power and (in)equality, in order to (among other things) foster student success and enable faculty to lead healthy lives (see also Berg and Seeber 2016; Hogan 2017).

The questions with which I will frame the next part of this discussion are the following:

- What conditions would best enable faculty to make determinations about where we invest our nurturance energies (rather than having them determined or imposed upon us)?
- "How can we demand, foster, and sustain these conditions as a matter of course so that we are not forced to set our humanity aside in the workplace?" (Inayatulla and Robinson 2019).

These questions, which challenge us to think about ways in which we can center and foster our humanity in the workplace, are at the core of the slow scholarship movement. This movement sets up an expectation that there is a place for our nurturance time and energy to "count" in our institutions. It opposes "neoliberal temporal regimes" (Mountz et al. 2015), which are those that govern the high-productivity "ideal worker" model first named by Joan Williams (1999). The attitudes toward care work that currently prevail in our institutions and profession are at the center of these neoliberal temporal regimes because, culturally, time devoted to care is wasted, "unproductive" time (Mountz et al. 2015), and, in academic contexts should instead be dedicated to the production of products: articles, books, funded grants, and also possibly graduates. In other words, care doesn't count according to the standard metrics that we use to measure success. But not counting the time we spend on care has the effect of dehumanizing faculty and students in the academic workplace. If our only value as academic workers is our "productivity," then there will always be people on campus who are less valuable than others because our research *and* our teaching is labeled as less productive or unproductive. So what does count on campus? And where does care fit into this system?

I look to my university's governance documents to establish how to count academic labor. The bylaws and collective bargaining agreements of the City University of New York (CUNY) establish how many hours faculty in each title and at each of the colleges that make up CUNY must teach: our number of teaching hours are clearly quantified. Department chairs, according to the bylaws, break that workload down into class schedules; the number of classes that faculty must teach depends on the workload hours allotted to each class. These decisions about workload hours per class are made locally, as are the numbers of students who may enroll in each class section. These are student-facing numbers and so must be published, though they are negotiable from semester to semester and, with governance approval, from course to course.

Our contract also states that faculty must undertake "research"; "scholarly writing" and/or "creative works in individual's discipline," alongside "departmental, college and university assignments," "student guidance," and "course and curricula development" (PSC-CUNY n.d.-b). These duties, however, are articulated in existential statements, and my college, like many others in the United States, has been reluctant to precisely quantify the amounts of each which faculty are expected to engage. However, we do find ways on campus to articulate a general sense of how much scholarship and research is enough, whereas we determine sufficiency of service, student advising and mentoring, and other nonteaching, nonresearch labor on a case-by-case basis by looking at what individuals are doing. As Joya Misra et al. (2011), and Gabriella Gutiérrez y Muhs et al. (2012) have shown, however, the amount of service, mentoring, and student guidance undertaken by white women and faculty of color tends to be much higher than for white men. This has the effect of taking members of these care-work-providing groups away from the work that unequivocally counts: research and scholarship. For instance, Misra et al. (2011) show that at the associate professor level, women faculty report spending 27 percent of their time on service and 25 percent on research; associate professors who identify as men report spending 20 percent of their time on service and 37 percent of their time on research.

Furthermore, my university has recently taken a problematic step in the realignment of expectations of faculty work, a much celebrated "teaching load reduction agreement." The agreement is celebrated because the contractually mandated teaching load of 21 hours or 27 hours annual for 4-year college and 2-year college professorial-line faculty respectively was seen as incompatible with the goal of having CUNY faculty's research output increase at a time when the university is trying to build its reputation as a nationally recognized research institution. The teaching load reduction agreement reduces faculty's teaching load by three hours over a three-year period and is often described as a workload reduction agreement, but the language of the agreement makes it clear that it is explicitly not that. Beneath the calculation of how the teaching load reduction should be handled administratively, the agreement states:

> The parties agree that the additional time resulting from the reduction in the undergraduate contact teaching hour workload specified above will be devoted to such activities as *student and academic advisement, office hours, academic research and such other activities that allow the University to improve our students' success and outcomes.* (PSC-CUNY n.d.-c, n.p.; emphasis mine)

In fact, this agreement provides a clear example of the clash between counted and uncounted time that governs the lives of many full-time faculty. The parts of the agreement that I have emphasized in italics articulate an expectation that in lieu of counted teaching hours, faculty will be expected to engage in other activities that "allow the University to improve [its] students' success and outcomes" (n.p.). With the exception of the phrase "academic research," this language implies that the university will be increasing its expectations of care work of the faculty. The teaching load reduction agreement shifts our care work from the classroom, in which space care work is at least counted in a rudimentary way, to a fuzzy, uncounted space. This space, this work, will remain uncountable *unless* the university decides to find a way to quantify it, to make it part of our productivity as faculty, which the last clause suggests it could, by tying these things directly to "student success and outcomes." If this shift in labor practices from the classroom to other service/advising/mentoring contexts could be distributed equally, then perhaps the language of the teaching load reduction would be fair. However, the language of the teaching load reduction agreement is highly problematic. To understand why, we must look in more detail at who does the care work on campus, and how such work is and is not rewarded and/or how much it "costs" the carers.

CARE WORK ON CAMPUS

It is commonly accepted that teaching, service, and student mentoring is care work, and as such these aspects of faculty work are often under-compensated, institutionally devalued, and dissociated from metrics of "productivity" (e.g., Ritter 2012; Schell 1992; Holbrook 1991 for teaching; Bird et al. 2004; Misra et al. 2011; Massé and Hogan 2010; Hogan 2010 for service). This undervaluing is not accidental but, rather, is connected with the long western tradition of treating care work as the work of women and people of color. These groups have often been culturally deprecated. Paula England (2005) explains the effects of such deprecation on not only women but also the work done by women:

> Cultural ideas deprecate women and thus, by cognitive association, devalue work typically done by women. This association leads to cognitive errors in which decision makers underestimate the contribution of female jobs to organizational goals, including profits. It may also lead to normative beliefs that those doing male jobs deserve higher pay. (382)

Brittney Cooper (2017), in a related vein, explores how the time of Black people has been devalued, resulting in a cultural idea that the work that Black people do cannot be worth as much as the work—and the time—of white people: "White people own time. Those in power dictate the pace of the work day. They dictate how much money our

time is worth" (5:56–6:03) and "We black people have always been out
of time. Time does not belong to us" (11:02–11:06). Women and people
of color have been historically and culturally assigned to care work in
US academic culture, doing the domestic labor that has enabled white
men and, increasingly, white women, to go out into the workforce and
engage in what we have traditionally seen as productive labor. The care
work that supports paid work has been termed reproductive labor by
feminist scholars (e.g., Hansen and Philipson 1990; Nakano Glenn 1992;
Laslett and Brenner 1989), and is invisible in our cultural accountings
of productivity. Mignon Duffy explains:

> Although feminists have argued that reproductive labor produces value,
> and that the sustainability of productive labor and of society itself depends
> on it, domestic activities remain largely defined in contrast to work. And
> when those domestic activities are performed by paid workers, they seem
> to retain their invisibility as labor. (2007, 316)

Duffy's observation explains why the language of the CUNY teaching load reduction in particular, and the ways in which we treat care
work on campus more generally, are problematic because they make
"reproductive labor" involved in supporting student success and outcomes invisible and therefore uncountable. Reproductive labor, in this
sense, is the opposite of work. This means that the labor of a certain
sector of our workforce becomes invisible and therefore is seen as not
contributing to the productivity of our organizations. And the fact that
it is care work—women's work, people of color's work—means that it
is devalued as important labor. The teaching load reduction language
makes this devaluation clear; it makes reproductive labor involved in
supporting student success and outcomes invisible. This invisibility, in
turn, means the labor of a certain sector of our workforce becomes invisible and therefore is seen as not contributing to the productivity of our
organizations. In other words, care work on campus has a low exchange
value, where we understand exchange value as the "quantified worth
of one good or service expressed in terms of the worth of another"
("Exchange Value").

Sharon Bird et al. argue that "service work carries little if any exchange
value for those who do it" (2004, 201) and offer suggestions as to ways in
which our institutions can change our exchange value equations when
considering institutional service. They suggest that remedies must come
from institutions, rather than by encouraging women to set their own
limits of what they will agree to. This latter kind of approach, which
Sharon Bird calls "women-centered" (Bird 2004, 202), is necessarily limited because it requires women to resist culturally enforced behaviors in

the workplace. While doing so is not necessarily a negative approach to take to expectations of nurturance (see Inayatulla and Robinson 2019), to navigate such an approach successfully is difficult because expectations of the degree of resistance will change from context to context, and women and faculty of color may be punished as uncollegial if they reject the kinds of institutional care work that is usually expected of members of these groups. Relying on women and people of color, on an individual level, to solve the gender problems that inhere in our institutions also shifts the burden of responsibility onto individuals rather than creating systems of collective accountability and forcing our institutions to change. Bird et al. (2004), Michelle Massé and Katie Hogan (2010), Misra et al. (2011), and Gutiérrez y Muhs et al. (2012) have shown convincingly that faculty who are women and/or people of color are expected to do more service on our campuses than their white, male counterparts: there is an assumption that they will take care of the "institutional housekeeping" (Bird et al. 2004, 194) that keeps our universities and colleges running. However, this care work tends not to show up, beyond existential statements, in evaluations of professional work—reappointment and tenure and promotion discussions—often only to focus on the details of a faculty member's service work when they have been deemed to be doing too much.

Alongside the hierarchy of people that this view of care perpetuates, it also perpetuates a hierarchy of teaching, where certain kinds of teaching are more valued in our institutions than other kinds. Low-care teaching—the kind of teaching that involves less nurturance of students as people and can focus more on the delivery of and engagement with content—is more prestigious and more sought after than high-care teaching; such low-care teaching includes upper-division disciplinary courses, graduate courses, and lecture-based courses. This low-care teaching also tends to carry a higher exchange value; that is, it is worth more in our reappointment, tenure, and promotion decisions because it tends to be a site in which instructors demonstrate disciplinary prowess. This higher exchange value is also directly related to the material conditions under which instructors tend to operate in these courses: low student numbers, high levels of intrinsic student motivation, connection with our own research programs, and potential for visible productivity in terms of collaborative publications with students. By contrast, general education courses, including but not limited to first-year writing courses, and other courses that students take primarily to fulfill graduation requirements, are associated with lower exchange value and thus worse working conditions. The nature of these courses is such that levels of background knowledge and intrinsic motivation for taking these courses is potentially low, while enrollments tend to be high. These courses also tend to be taught by part-time, contingent and pretenure faculty, who often cost less to employ than full-time and tenured faculty. And, perhaps most significant for care work, these courses come with increased administrative expectations, including more regular and standardized assessment to ensure alignment with institutional learning goals, requests for information about student progress, coordination with student support services across campus, and so on. Furthermore, at least in composition and writing intensive courses, there is an expectation of using process pedagogy, which is inherently labor intensive, even as the benefits of this labor for students remain unclear (Ritter 2012; Sommers 1982), as well as a full embrace of "active-" and "student-centered" learning, which are also labor intensive to set up.[2]

The contrast between these types of teaching is striking, not just when written out but also in many instructors' lived experiences. In drawing this contrast, I do not mean to suggest that all faculty are not engaged in care work to some extent: at an institution like mine, for instance, where the president is committed to a "small college feel," enacted by maintaining relatively small class sizes (i.e., we have no large-enrollment lectures and no teaching assistants running recitations), the relatively low instructor to student ratio means that students are individually visible to instructors, and thus instructors are likely to understand what it is that each student in their class might need, in terms of instructor attention, to succeed. Furthermore, there is no less potential for care work in graduate courses and the supervision of graduate students. However, institutional expectations do not *require* care as part of those teaching arrangements, as attested to the long history of terrible, care-less graduate instruction that any conversation among academics could bring out. My point is, rather, that in these low exchange value courses, our institutions *expect* and *require* instructor care work and *because* of this, teaching these classes brings less compensation for time and less professional reward to their instructors. One institutional response has thus been to assign such courses to instructors with lower professional status; these instructors are, of course, those with lower social status, too, as is made clear by the well-known small of numbers of women and people of color in among the ranks of full professors, and the fact that the majority of adjunct faculty are white women and/or people of color (Finkelstein et al. 2016).

Our institutions, and, indeed, our very system of higher education, participate in and maintain this hierarchy between types of teaching, in effect asking faculty to choose between professional advancement and doing care work in their classes. Those institutions whose goal is to have nationally recognized research outputs keep their full-time faculty out of the classroom, and certainly out of the introductory classroom, as much as possible. Institutions like mine, on the other hand, not only require full-time faculty to teach more, but the implicit requirement is that all faculty will teach general education courses, which require more care work. But even at institutions like mine, the costs of care work on professional advancement and working conditions are well understood by the faculty: for instance, one faculty member in my department on the tenure track has asked not to teach general education classes for two years not because the subject matter is not important, but because all the management of requirements for the course, linked to institutional goals and assessment, and all the attendant care for students, is just exhausting. Another, tenured faculty member, planning to go up for promotion to full professor in the next few years, has asked to be assigned to our 300-level research writing course, rather than first-year composition, because the latter "has too many requirements." These faculty members, in their assessment of the toll that the required care work for our composition courses will take on their own working conditions and ability to fulfill other requirements of our job, are absolutely correct: teaching introductory writing courses requires care work of us, so that our students can succeed in our introductory classes and beyond.

It is worth noting again and again that this hierarchy is detrimental to faculty who are women and people of color, as well, to an extent, for everyone in feminized disciplines. And it's certainly detrimental for our adjuncts, who teach most of our general education courses (National Census of Writing n.d.). The current climate around funding higher education, in the United States and internationally, makes it unlikely that proposals to improve the working conditions of teachers of writing will come to fruition (e.g., Bousquet 2003; Lalicker 2016; Crowley 1998). Other proposals to increase the exchange value of the discipline of composition, and thus value the time of composition faculty, rely on the perpetuation of a divide between those researching composition and those teaching it, since it is unlikely that all composition teaching jobs will be held by full-time, tenure-track faculty, as noted by critics of such proposals such as Jeanne Gunner (1998). So, rather than repeating proposals that do nothing to change the feminized, racialized position in which composition teaching persists, I call for a bigger shift in the ways we articulate and value what is considered feminized and racialized on campus. I propose radically recentering what we value and compensate. The care work that we do at our institutions is known to be vital to student success (Noddings 2012). Therefore, rather than considering teaching our introductory courses fringe elements of the real work that faculty do, I suggest that faculty care work should be at the center of our narratives of success and our considerations about compensation, thus resisting the tendency, described by Duffy, of rendering care work invisible as work, even when it is done by paid employees. Mountz et al. write:

> Care work is work. It is not self-indulgent; it is radical and necessary (Federici 2012; Ahmed 2014). Care, moreover, is risky, imposing a burden on those who undertake care work (Tronto, 1989). Systematically marginalizing care "furthers the myth that our successes are achieved as autonomous individuals and, as such, we have no responsibility to share the fruits of our success with others or to dedicate public resources to the work of care" (Lawson 2007, 5). (2015, 1238–9)

I adapt Mountz et al.'s description above, from their discussion of a "slow" approach to academic work, to claim that "care work *is* our work." As such, therefore, it should be made visible *as* work in our workload calculations and in our narratives of what successful academic workers do. Enacting this revaluing of care requires a systematic reconsideration of how care work fits in with our professional expertise, especially because of the positive role that it plays in students experiences, as suggested in Scott Carlson (2014), describing the results of a Gallup-Purdue poll. The poll found that

> college graduates, whether they went to a hoity-toity private college or a midtier public, had double the chances of being engaged in their work and were three times as likely to be thriving in their well-being if they connected with a professor on the campus who stimulated them, cared about them, and encouraged their hopes and dreams. (n.p.)

Several authors have described a dichotomy in which instructors are asked to choose between care work and their classes because it is not possible to do both adequately, despite the fact that we are asked to do it: content instruction and what Kelly Ritter calls "maternal-ethical care." She writes,

> It should not be, in my view, professionally acceptable to see first-year composition as the site of maternal-ethical student care. Writing teachers are increasingly pressured to be agents of literacy instruction and agents of personal care. We may need to decide which of these roles we want to prioritize if we expect to have reasonable working conditions for our already-undervalued writing faculty. (2012, 412)

Ritter frames the choice between instruction and care work as a site of exploitation in our working conditions and calls upon writing programs to decide what it really is that they want their faculty to do. I suggest that our current educational conditions indicate that we do really want our general education instructors to do both of these things. In order to improve faculty working conditions, our institutions need to find ways in which we can compensate instructors for doing both, rather than expecting a feminist ethic of care in the ways instructors teach their courses, without providing the necessary time to do so. In other words, we have an opportunity to refuse to use feminist principles to "aid the 'surface amelioration of the unacceptable'" (Ozga and Deem 2000, 152, quoted in Snyder 2009, 29), by, first of all, making this care work visible, and, second, being explicit about the resources that this care work requires to be sustained. We can show, through how we count time "spent," that this is what we value including creating discourses and narratives that center our care work, rather than hiding because we work in a system where providing care in the classroom detracts from our professional status. As researchers into other kinds of care work have shown, having skilled carers increases the benefits that accrue not just to the people being cared for, but also to the public good (e.g., England 2005). Care work in the classroom benefits more than just the students; it benefits our institutions because it supports student retention and graduation through the connections with and integration into the institution that it facilitates, which has been shown to be a crucial element of students' academic success (see Tinto 1993: Umbach and Wawrzynski 2005). Therefore, I reject the dichotomy that Ritter presents, but in doing so I reject the zero sum economic game in which our institutions exist. Ritter is right that the current system is unsustainable. But rather than choose, we need to find ways to explicitly value care as a means to the achievement of our institutional and personal goals.

CARE AND AUDIT CULTURE

Many authors have contested the inevitability and the success of the neoliberal, corporate university. By definition, in fact, the neoliberal university can never be successful, because successful performance is framed as improvement, as Cris Shore and Susan Wright argue: "Central to this process [of auditing academic institutions] has been the re-invention of professionals themselves as units of resource whose performance and productivity must constantly be audited so that it can be enhanced" (1999, 559). Katie Hogan, citing Tim Jackson, writes, "Education . . . it is a low-productivity sector 'where chasing productivity growth doesn't make sense'" (2017, 247). Working in education often means balancing productivity and reproductivity. Traditionally, we have considered our research and scholarship to be productive labor; teaching and service, on the other hand, are reproductive labor. Even though the neoliberal university is focused on measuring improvement, we have devised no direct metrics for measuring the care work that faculty do, because we do not really consider it as work that should be rewarded, and our conversations about doing it better are local and often perfunctory. Furthermore, these efforts are often directed toward those with the least capital in our systems: teaching assistants and adjuncts, as evidenced by, for instance, the strong programs in graduate student training and adjunct professional development that we read about (e.g., Cripps et al. 2016; Pytlik and Liggett 2002; WPA listserv discussion, November 2–5, 2018).

Richard E. Miller (2001) suggests a way in which care and service can be valued as part of what he facetiously calls "university of excellence" model, making the work of composition programs central to the measures of excellence in the institution. I take his facetious description seriously: after all, the neoliberal university's focus on quantifying productivity is part of a narrative of movement toward excellence and continuous improvement. All faculty and all departments—indeed, all operating units—are required to produce "outcomes" and account for these outcomes for audit purposes. However, all research will not be counted equally: so-called frontier research, which tends to be understood as scientific research that expands the boundaries of human knowledge or human invention, is commonly understood to be more valuable to our institutions because of the revenue, either through grants or patents or licenses, that it can bring to our institutions. Therefore, as Miller suggests, a service ethic might be what distinguishes those departments and individuals who are not doing this kind of frontier scientific research. He writes, of Writing Programs, that

> it is a mistake to abandon the ethic of service that defines [Composition] in the hope that doing so will bring about a broader respect for the intellectual work done in the discipline . . . all research projects, from the use of the comma to the makeup of subatomic particles, are increasingly scrutinized, assessed, and frequently funded on the basis of their utility—on the basis, in other words, of the service they perform for society. Bereft of its service ethic, committed only to the project of researching the production of writing and the history of rhetoric, composition will be left to compete for resources in a game that it can never win. (R. E. Miller 2001, 103–4)

One of the meanings of audit is "rendering visible" (Shore and Wright 1999, 559). Care is auditable, if we have the will to find ways to make it visible as labor. While I am not arguing for a total quality management approach to academic care work, where our care work is documented down to the minute, I *am* arguing for the creation of a discourse of care's value on campus, and on its own terms. Creating this discourse means making care visible. This approach is in contrast to other attempts to articulate the value of administration and mentoring, such as the Council of Writing Program Administrators' position statement on the Intellectual Work of Writing Program Administration does. This statement describes the value of WPA in terms of how we value scholarship, in fact equating WPA *to* scholarship. As Laura Bartlett Snyder argues, such a strategy reinforces masculinist hierarchies by translating one articulation of productivity into another realm, while leaving in place the gendered divisions of labor between administration and instruction, scholarship and teaching (Snyder 2009). Therefore, I offer some suggestions for how we can center care in our workloads and narratives and so reject the idea that care work should not be counted, compensated, and rewarded.[3]

- Compensate composition and general education course teaching with fewer undergraduate students, and with more "counted" time per student.
- Articulate, on the institutional level, the exchange value of various kinds of service and teaching so that faculty can make strategic decisions about where to spend their energy.
- Articulate and implement workload tariffs frameworks and methods such as Workload Planning Frameworks, as discussed below (e.g., "University Workload Planning Framework"; see also Perks 2013).[4]
- Articulate and value faculty's care work in reappointment, tenure, and promotion processes and guidelines.
- Articulate local care work as service work for our institutions, professions, and disciplines.

Through these measures, we can reward faculty for care work well done, talk about care on campus, and count the care work that faculty are doing, and thus involve supervisors when faculty are taking on too much or doing too little. For instance, workload tariffs are an example of vertical involvement in the care work assigned to and undertaken by faculty members. In a workload tariff framework, such as that set out by Oxford Brookes University in the United Kingdom, all activities are named and accounted for within a 1,600-hour yearly workload allocation. While, as in US institutions, only formal teaching activities are counted in contractual terms, the workload tariffs—as established and negotiated by a committee chaired by a high-level administrator—allow individual faculty members to account for their activities in the context of their academic job and to include not only hours spent on research, but also those spent on, for instance, student advising (2 hours per student per year), research supervision (10–75 hours per year, depending on the level of the student), course preparation (1.5 hours per formally scheduled teaching hour), and grading and student assessment (hours vary depending on class size and "nature and complexity of assessment requirements") ("Workload Planning Framework 2018–19," 2). In models such as this, care work can become central to the stories that department chairs and deans tell about full-time faculty in reappointment, tenure, and promotion processes, and WPAs and chairs can advocate for their programs in terms of the care that they provide to students. This articulated approach disproportionately benefits faculty who are women and people of color because these academic workers are known to do the preponderance of care work on campus. Furthermore, the approach takes the important steps of centering and "normalizing" the lived experiences of faculty who are women and/or people of color and set their narratives as the baseline against which all other faculty are compared.

Another more local example of how care work can be counted in CUNY's 2019 Collective Bargaining Agreement. For the first time, adjunct faculty will be paid to conduct one paid office hour per week per course that they are teaching. Previously only adjunct faculty teaching six or more workload hours per week were eligible for paid office hours, and they were only paid for one hour per week (PSC-CUNY Memorandum Agreement). These paid office hours are a direct acknowledgment of and compensation for care work, since most CUNY adjunct faculty teach general education courses, which, as I argue above, require more care work in terms of student support and managing administrative details. And in another CUNY example, the English Department at Hostos Community College recently succeeded in changing their required second-semester composition course from three- to four-contact hours, while remaining a three-credit course. This action brought this course in line with other second-semester composition courses across CUNY, and it acknowledges the care work involved in the teaching of writing.

And, finally, Raritan Valley Community College (RVCC), in north-central New Jersey, pays faculty, on an hourly basis, to advise students. The full-time faculty's collective bargaining agreement at RVCC indicates that while advising is "additional to their normal teaching responsibilities," "faculty members have a responsibility to advise students, to the best of their ability, as to courses, schedules, sequencing, transfer and other educational issues" (RVCC Faculty Federation 2015); the contract furthermore specifies how much compensation faculty members will receive and how much time is expected to be allocated per students. This codification of compensation for advising in the Collective Bargaining Agreement indicates, to me, that RVCC acknowledges that this care work has value and that while it is a faculty responsibility, it is also above the faculty's regular fifteen-hour per semester teaching workload.

CONCLUSION

It is time that we started compensating faculty for all the things that help students succeed, rather than shifting them into an uncompensated, undervalued invisible labor space. Re-placing care in our narratives of success is an example of "political reflexivity," which Shore and Wright describe as a form of resistance to audit culture in UK higher education. They define political reflexivity as

> neither navel-gazing nor "rendering the implicit explicit" by revealing the inside to the outside (Strathern 1997, 314). Rather, as Okely (1992) argues, it is a political activity. It is about understanding critically the way individuals, as social persons, are positioned within systems of governance and how concepts, categories, boundaries, hierarchies and processes of subjectification are experienced and culturally reproduced. (1999, 572)

In our current climate of "doing more with less," it seems more plausible to focus on what we can do locally and to make the case for allocating more time to teaching, and for counting our workloads differently. However, universities and colleges in the United States are similar enough to each other such that a national discourse about best practices for valuing care work on campus is very possible, especially as led by our professional organizations. Indeed, if our accreditors valued care work, our institutions would too. Because, as R. E. Miller (2004) puts it in "Our Future Donors," our students, who benefit from this care work, are our future donors or, in the case of a college like mine, our future graduates. Faculty administrators may not, on the individual level, have the institutional power to change course caps and workloads, but we can shape institutional and professional discourses and practices.

NOTES

1. Thanks to Kirsti Cole for this observation.
2. Thanks to Rochelle Rodrigo for pointing this out.
3. I note that various writing programs have put in place some of these strategies for valuing care work but often in contexts where writing faculty are non-tenure-track

(e.g., Princeton, Duke, Harvard). It is at institutions where composition is taught by full-time faculty that we see the push to "compensate" writing faculty via making composition a more traditional academic discipline (e.g., Lalicker 2016), so maintaining gendered, classist academic hierarchies.

4.   Thanks to Andie Silva for bringing workload tariffs to my attention.

REFERENCES

Andrews, Geoff. 2008. *The Slow Food Story: Politics and Pleasure.* London: Pluto Press.

Berg, Maggie, and Barbara K. Seeber. 2016. *The Slow Professor: Challenging the Culture of Speed in the Academy.* Toronto: University of Toronto Press.

Bird, Sharon. 2004. "Unsettling Universities' Incongruous, Gendered Bureaucratic Structures: A Case-Study Approach." *Gender, Work and Organization* 18.2: 202–30.

Bird, Sharon, Jacquelyn Litt, and Yong Wang. 2004. "Creating Status of Women Reports: Institutional Housekeeping as 'Women's Work.'" *NWSA Journal* 16.1: 194–206.

Bousquet, Marc. 2003. "Composition as Management Science." *Works and Days* 41/42: 189–218. http://www.worksanddays.net/W&D%202003.html.

Carlson, Scott. 2014. "A Caring Professor May Be Key in How a Graduate Thrives." *Chronicle of Higher Education.* May 6. https://www.chronicle.com/article/A-Caring-Professor-May-Be-Key/146409.

Cooper, Brittney. 2017. "The Racial Politics of Time." *TEDWomen.* from TED.com. https://www.ted.com/talks/brittney_cooper_the_racial_politics_of_time.

Council of Writing Program Administrators. 1998. *Evaluating the Intellectual Work of Writing Program Administration.* http://wpacouncil.org/aws/CWPA/pt/sd/news_article/242849/_PARENT/layout_details/false.

Cripps, Michael J., Hall, Jonathan, and Robinson, Heather M. 2016. "'A Way to Talk about the Institution as Opposed to Just My Field': WAC Fellowships and Graduate Student Professional Development." *TAs and the Teaching of Writing Across the Curriculum,* special issue of *Across the Disciplines* 13.3. https://wac.colostate.edu/docs/atd/wacta/cripps etal2016.pdf.

Crowley, Sharon. 1998. *Composition in the University: Historical and Polemical Essays.* Pittsburgh: University of Pittsburgh Press.

Duffy, Mignon. 2007. "Doing the Dirty Work: Gender, Race, and Reproductive Labor in Historical Perspective." *Gender and Society* 21.3: 313–36.

England, Paula. 2005. "Emerging Theories of Care Work." *Annual Review of Sociology* 31: 381–99.

"Exchange Value." *Business Dictionary.* Accessed October 12, 2018. http://www.business dictionary.com/definition/exchange-value.html.

Finkelstein, Martin J, Valerie Martin Conley, and Jack H. Schuster. 2016. "Taking the Measure of Faculty Diversity." TIAA Institute. https://www.tiaainstitute.org/publication/taking-measure-faculty-diversity.

Gunner, Jeanne. 1998. "Among the Composition People: The WPA as English Department Agent." *JAC* 18.1: 153–65.

Gutiérrez y Muhs, Gabriella, Yolanda Flores Niemann, Carmen G. González, and Angela P. Harris. 2012. *Presumed Incompetent: The Intersections of Race and Class for Women in Academia.* Logan: Utah State University Press.

Hansen, Karen V., and Ilene J. Philipson. 1990. *Women, Class, and the Feminist Imagination: A Socialist-Feminist Reader.* Philadelphia: Temple University.

Heijstra, T. M., F. S. Steinthorsdóttir, and T. Einarsdóttir. 2017. "Academic Career Making and the Double-Edged Role of Academic Housework." *Gender and Education* 29.6: 764–80.

Hogan, Katie J. 2010. "Superserviceable Feminism." In *Over Ten Million Served: Gendered Service in Language and Literature Workplaces*, edited by Michelle Massé and Katie J. Hogan, 55–72. New York: SUNY Press.

Hogan, Katie J. 2017. "The Academic Slow Lane." In *Staging Women's Lives in Academia: Gendered Life Stages in Language and Literature Workplaces*, edited by Michelle Massé and Nan Bauer-Maglin, 247–60. Albany: SUNY Press.

Holbrook, Sue Ellen. 1991. "Women's Work: The Feminizing of Composition." *Rhetoric Review* 9.2: 201–29.

Inayatulla, Shereen, and Heather Robinson. 2019. "Backwards and in High Heels": The Invisibility and Underrepresentation of Femme(inist) Administrative Labor in Academia. *Administrative Theory & Praxis*. https://doi.org/10.1080/10841806.2019.1659045.

Lalicker, William B. 2016. "The Five Equities: How To Achieve a Progressive Writing Program within a Department of English." In *Minefield of Dreams: Triumphs and Travails of Independent Writing Programs*, edited by Justin Everett and Cristina Hanganau-Bresch, 293–329. Fort Collins, CO: WAC Clearinghouse and University Press of Colorado.

Laslett, Barbara, and Johanna Brenner. 1989. "Gender and Social Reproduction: Historical Perspectives." *Annual Review of Sociology* 15.38: 1–404.

Martell, Luke. 2014. "The Slow University: Inequality, Power and Alternatives." *Forum: Qualitative Social Research* 15.3. http://www.qualitative-research.net/index.php/fqs/article/view/2223/3692.

Massé, Michelle A., and Katie J. Hogan, eds. 2010. *Over Ten Million Served: Gendered Service in Language and Literature Workplaces*. New York: SUNY Press.

McCabe, Daniel. 2012. "The Slow Science Movement." https://www.universityaffairs.ca/features/feature-article/the-slow-science-movement/.

Miller, Richard E. 2001. "From Intellectual Wasteland to Resource-Rich Colony: Capitalizing on the Role of Writing Instruction in Higher Education." *WPA: Writing Program Administration* 24.3: 25–40.

Miller, Richard E. 2004. "Our Future Donors." *College English* 66.4: 365–79.

Miller, Susan. 1993. *Textual Carnivals: The Politics of Composition*. Carbondale: Southern Illinois University Press.

Misra, Joya, Jennifer Lundquist, Elissa Dahlberg Holmes, and Stephanie Agiomavritis. 2011. "The Ivory Ceiling of Service Work." *Academe* 97.1: 22. https://www.aaup.org/article/ivory-ceiling-service-work#.XY65UkZKhPY.

Mountz, Alison, et al. 2015. "For Slow Scholarship: A Feminist Politics of Resistance through Collective Action in the Neoliberal University." *ACME: an International E-journal for Critical Geographies* 14.4: 1236–59.

Nakano Glenn, Evelyn. 1992. "From Servitude to Service Work: Historical Continuities in the Racial Division of Paid Reproductive Labor." *Signs: Journal of Women in Culture and Society* 18.1 (Autumn): 1–43.

National Census of Writing. n.d. Accessed June 22, 2018. writingcensus.swarthmore.edu.

Noddings, Nel. 2012. "The Caring Relation in Teaching." *Oxford Review of Education* 38.6: 771–81.

O'Meara, KerryAnn, Alexandra Kuvaeva, Gudrun Nyunt, Chelsea Waugaman, and Rose Jackson. 2017. "Asked More Often: Gender Differences in Faculty Workload in Research Universities and the Work Interactions That Shape Them." *American Educational Research Journal* 54.6: 1154–86. https://doi.org/10.3102/0002831217716767.

O'Neill, Maggie. 2014. "The Slow University—Work, Time, and Well-being." https://www.qualitative-research.net/index.php/fqs/article/view/2226/3696.

Perks, Simon. 2013. "Academic Workload: A Model Approach." *Guardian*, April 15. Accessed November 9, 2018. https://www.theguardian.com/higher-education-network/blog/2013/apr/15/academic-workload-modelling-management.

PSC-CUNY. n.d.-a "Memorandum of Agreement 2019." Accessed February 12, 2020. https://psc-cuny.org/contract/memorandum-agreement-2019.

PSC-CUNY. n.d.-b "Professional Evaluation." October 15, 2018. https://psc-cuny.org/con tract/article-18-professional-evaluation.

PSC-CUNY. n.d.-c "Teaching Load Reduction Agreement." Accessed September 15, 2018. http://psc-cuny.org/sites/default/files/TeachingLoadReduction_Web.pdf.

Pytlik, Betty Parsons, and Sarah Liggett, eds. 2002. *Preparing College Teachers of Writing: Histories, Theories, Programs, Practices.* Oxford: Oxford University Press.

Ritter, Kelly. 2012. " 'Ladies Who Don't Know Us Correct Our Papers': Postwar Lay Reader Programs and Twenty-First Century Contingent Labor in First-Year Writing." *College Composition and Communication* 63.3: 387–419.

RVCC Faculty Federation. 2015. "Federation Full-Time Faculty Contract 2015–2019." https://aft2375.files.wordpress.com/2013/09/federation-full-time-faculty-contract-2015-19.pdf.

Schell, Eileen E. 1992. "The Feminization of Composition: Questioning the Metaphors That Bind Women Teachers." *Composition Studies* 20.1: 55–61.

Shore, Cris, and Susan Wright. 1999. "Audit Culture and Anthropology: Neo-liberalism in British Higher Education." *Journal of the Royal Anthropological Institute* 5.4: 557–75.

Sommers, Nancy. 1982. "Responding to Student Writing." *College Composition and Communication* 33.2: 148–56.

Snyder, Laura Bartlett. 2009. "Feminisms and the Problem of Complicity in Writing Program Administrator Work." In *The Writing Program Interrupted: Making Space for Critical Discourse,* edited by Donna Strickland and Jeanne Gunner, 28–40. New York: Boynton/Cook Publishers.

Tinto, V. 1993. *Rethinking the Causes and Cures of Student Attrition.* Chicago: University of Chicago Press.

Umbach, Paul D., and Matthew R. Wawrzynski. 2005. "Faculty Do Matter: The Role of College Faculty in Student Learning and Engagement." *Research in Higher Education* 46.2: 153–84. https://files.eric.ed.gov/fulltext/ED491002.pdf.

University Workload Planning Framework: Tariffs for 2018–19. *Oxford Brookes University.* Accessed November 9, 2018. https://www.brookes.ac.uk/services/hr/handbook/work inghours/WLP_tariffs_for_2018-19_approved_by_VCG.doc.pdf.

Williams, Joan. 1999. *Unbending Gender: Why Family and Work Conflict and What to Do About It.* Oxford: Oxford University Press.

Winslow, Sarah. 2010. "Gender Inequality and Time Allocations among Academic Faculty." *Gender and Society* 24.6: 769–93.

6

EVERYONE WRITES
Expanding Writing across the Curriculum to Change a Culture of Writing

Tiffany Rousculp

All people in the SLCC community will respectfully support those who want to produce high quality, effective writing.

—WAC Vision Statement

This statement offers a vision of a WAC program that fosters a culture of writing based on empathy and compassion for all writers within a college community, one based in respect not only for students but for staff members, faculty, and administrators alike. This vision, and the program that has been attempting to enact it for the past five years, hybridizes the well-established Writing Across the Curriculum educational reform movement with more recent theory and praxis that have emerged from community writing work. This chapter situates this program, located at an urban community college, within the broader field of WAC/WID and the history of WAC at this particular institution, and shares how it has built a sustainable program by approaching its development from a community writing foundation.

WAC AS ESTABLISHED REFORM

Writing Across the Curriculum (WAC) programs are, and have always been, centered on change. As "one of the longest running educational reform movements in higher education in the U.S" (INWAC 2014), Writing Across the Curriculum began in response to increasing and diversifying student populations and was based upon knowledges of writing and learning that were developing in the early 1970s (Russell 1990). For decades, this educational reform movement has been led by dedicated faculty, whom, thirty years ago, WAC advocate Susan McLeod

https://doi.org/10.7330/9781646421428.c006

(1988) unflinchingly named "agents of change" (5). This identity has held up over time, and appears in William Condon and Carol Rutz's taxonomy, which provides myriad and diverse WAC programs a developmental stage within which to locate themselves: "Foundational," "Established," "Integrated," and "Institutional Change Agents" (Condon and Rutz 2012). According to Condon and Rutz, Institutional Change Agent WAC programs are the most fully developed, those that are "seamlessly incorporated into an institution's approach to teaching and learning" (374).

Across the country, WAC programs, whether they are in a "Foundational" stage or further along in their development, seek to influence change across multiple contexts. The International Network of Writing Across the College (INWAC) "Statement of Principles and Practices" notes that WAC programs work toward increasing the "amount and frequency of student writing"; fostering "sustained instruction in writing, in more courses, spread out over [students'] academic careers"; creating "a community of faculty around teaching and student writing"; and "promot[ing] a cultural shift on campus in how writing is perceived and valued" (INWAC 2014). These change efforts have most recently been theorized by Michelle Cox, Jeffrey R. Galin, and Dan Melzer in their work on creating sustainable WAC programs (Cox et al. 2018). They argue that WAC programs should undertake a "whole systems approach for transformational change," which includes "a methodology, and a set of principles, strategies, and tactics for making change to campus cultures of writing and for building programs that are integrated, highly visible, and sustainable" (17). WAC programs and their "agents" increase, foster, create, promote, transform, and make change; they do not stand still nor do they accept the status quo of writing at a given institution.

Nearing its half-century mark, the Writing Across the Curriculum movement and its sister movement, Writing in the Disciplines (WID), have become well-recognized components of writing instruction in higher education. Hundreds of colleges and universities have WAC/WID programs, a professional organization and national conference support this work, and the open-access WAC Clearinghouse provides ready access to networking, research, and other resources. The successes of WAC/WID at making change and becoming sustainable within the localities of specific institutions, however, have varied significantly. Chris Thaiss and Tara Porter illustrate this national/local inconsistency in the results of their "US Survey of the International WAC/WID Mapping Project," which analyzes their own survey in relation to McLeod and

Shirley's 1988 "National Survey of Writing Across the Curriculum Programs" (Thaiss and Porter 2010). Thaiss and Porter use these data to identify markers of long-lasting WAC programs, including the academic rank of the WAC leader, reporting lines, the director's length of service, partnerships with other college entities, faculty development workshops, and upper-division writing intensive courses (558–62). In their findings, they show that, nationally, the percentage of WAC programs in higher education has increased, appearing in "51 percent of 1,126 reporting institutions" up from "38 percent of 1,113" in 1987 (563). That said, "well over half" of the WAC programs from the 1987 survey "either no longer exist or have been 'restarted' in the years since" (558). Cox and colleagues' 2018 theoretical framework and methodology for sustainable WAC programs have been a laudable response to this variability (8–14).

Regardless of the tenacity and growth of the WAC movement as a whole, becoming sustainable within a specific location, or reaching the stage of an Institutional Change Agent, remains difficult. In fact, William Condon and Carol Rutz (2012) identify only a handful WAC programs that have reached—or are near to reaching—this stage, which they describe as "simply viewed as a part of the team, and others [in the institution] feel entitled to engage WAC in their own efforts" (374–79). The WAC Institutional Change Agent, which exists within Barbara Walvoord's 1996 "macro-levels" of operation at an institution, is one that may be able to actually make a change to "campus cultures of writing" and effect a "cultural shift on campus" that Michelle Cox et al. (2018) and INWAC (2014), respectively, claim is the goal. This change is difficult to attain, however. In fact, Sherry Lee Linkon and Matthew Pavesich (2015) recognize that "creat[ing] institutional change . . . remains one of the central puzzles for writing program administrators, especially for those working on writing across the curriculum and/or writing in the disciplines" (22). Traveling from a national education reform movement to effecting actual and sustainable cultural change within an institution is a road fraught with delays, diversions, and barriers.

WAC AT COMMUNITY COLLEGES

The WAC movement discussed so far includes programs across all types of higher education institutions in the United States. When we turn to WAC programs at community colleges, the likelihood of sustainable cultural change becomes much more limited. Thaiss and Porter (2010) note the "markedly lower percentage of community colleges reporting

[WAC] programs" than PhD-, MA/MS-, and BA/BS-granting institutions (541). Only 33 percent of community college respondents indicated any type of WAC programming, between 22 to 32 percentage points lower than the other types of institutions (541). Their findings are much higher, however, than those found in Leslie Roberts's 2008 "National Research Initiative Survey Section IV: Writing Across the Curriculum and Writing Centers in Two-Year College English Programs," which showed that only 18 percent of 342 responding institutions had a WAC program (141).[1] Even so, Roberts's TYCA study found that of the 18 percent of institutions who did report a WAC program, only 7 percent of 332 respondents reported "being very satisfied with their college's approach to WAC" (146).

Most community colleges provide lower-division undergraduate courses, taught by faculty carrying huge loads, within an administrative culture not terribly attuned to faculty serving in program leadership roles. Clint Gardner, the founding director of the Salt Lake Community College Student Writing and Reading Center, sums up the community-college-specific conditions we faced in his introduction to a guest-edited issue of *Across the Disciplines*: "There are various factors at play: the 'grade level' of students; the working conditions of faculty; the relationship of faculty to administration; and an unclear notion of what WAC/WID programs are" (Gardner 2010, 2). With some exceptions, most notably Metropolitan Community College-Longview where the WAC program has long been shepherded by Mary McMullen-Light (2010), the University of Hawai'i, Kapi'olani Community College, community colleges have not proven to be very fertile ground to sustain WAC programs, much less programs that make institutional change.

WAC AT SALT LAKE COMMUNITY COLLEGE

It was within these grim realities that the third version of the Salt Lake Community College (SLCC) Writing Across the Curriculum program was launched in the summer of 2014. But, it wasn't the first time.

SLCC WAC Version 1.0

The first time was in 1996. Following Walvoord's 1996 "micro-level" approach that many institutions start with, Stephen Ruffus (then writing program coordinator) and I had received a small internal development grant to implement a WAC workshop for twenty faculty from across the college. Ruffus already had been meeting regularly with a small, informal, but dedicated group of faculty (two from composition, two from business, one from psychology, two from developmental education) to talk about writing pedagogy. I had newly joined the department, and my youthful enthusiasm and energy (i.e., first job, new-to-town, mid-twenties, single, no kids) motivated Ruffus to move beyond these informal gatherings towards an institutionally supported program.

The grant allowed us to pay the participating faculty to read and discuss scholarship on writing pedagogy, revise assignments, and practice feedback and assessment. Faculty from many different academic and career/technical areas of the college participated: ESL, electronics, history, accounting, mechanical technology, humanities, languages, environmental hazardous materials, physical therapy, and more. The group met throughout the academic year, identifying departmental writing expectations and evaluation strategies, developing assignments and a set of writing resources for the Student Writing and Reading Center and the Faculty Teaching and Learning Center. The workshop series was well received, and the participants were as enthusiastic as we were about making changes to their curriculum.

That enthusiasm didn't last, however, once the grant was finished. While individuals made changes to their own curriculum, none were interested in serving on a committee to develop a WAC program, because there was no institutional support for it. Moving beyond Condon and Rutz's (2012) "Type 1: Foundational" level seemed impossible. Sustainable institutional change cannot be built on faculty enthusiasm. Change may be recognized or revealed from effort and motivation, but sustaining change (i.e., institutionalizing) requires whole systems of support and priority (Cox et al. 2018).

SLCC WAC Version 2.0

Flash forward a decade. Salt Lake Community College was undergoing significant changes based on an "Executive Dean" administrative model in which deans oversaw individual campuses developing a site-specific academic or occupational focus (e.g., creative arts and media, health sciences) yet also provided general education and career exploration for all students. This shift highlighted a need to coordinate writing program efforts across the different campuses, while each worked to establish their specific identities. The Writing Program Council was established by Ruffus, who was then the English Department chair. The council consisted of representatives from the composition program, the developmental reading and writing program, the Student Writing and

Reading Center, and the Community Writing Center (CWC) (of which I was the director at the time). Given the circumstances, the council was successful in securing a half-time reassigned faculty position to direct a WAC program and a small budget for expenses.

A faculty member from developmental education (reading and writing) was appointed to the WAC coordinator position. For the next two years, she held occasional workshops on writing pedagogies and met individually with faculty members across different departments who wanted to infuse writing pedagogies into their curriculum. Sadly, the initiative was never able to build momentum beyond this. Even though the program was following WAC development practices that were often successful at four-year colleges, it was not enough to gain a solid footing at the community college. Further, major changes in college administration and its reporting structure meant that the Writing Program Council lost its executive administrative sponsorship, and, subsequently, the WAC coordinator lost motivation to continue the work on her own. Again, WAC at SLCC came and went. Again, we joined the "well over half" of WAC programs that ceased to exist, restart, and/or cease to exist again (Thaiss and Porter 2010).

SLCC WAC Version 3.0

Another decade passed.

Then, in 2014, circumstances arose that encouraged Ruffus to try one more time to establish a WAC program. He worked with the dean of humanities and social sciences, John McCormick, and together they gained the support of the academic vice president, Chris Picard, to create a hard-funded WAC director position. This faculty position would receive 80 percent reassigned time to "build on and enhance the existing objectives of the six-hour composition requirement by promoting proven writing across the curriculum concepts" and "[develop] writing intensive courses . . . or [link] courses in various departments . . . with composition courses" ("SLCC Writing Across the Curriculum Call for Applications" 2014). The position successfully made its way through the college's Informed Budget Process and a call went out for applicants.

Three years earlier, I had stepped away from directing the SLCC Community Writing Center. I was itching for something new to explore, but when the position posted, I was not sure that I wanted to take on WAC. As I applied for the position, I didn't really believe the aspirations I presented because the position description was based on a four-year institution WAC model, and, based on our history, I knew this would not work at SLCC. Still, Ruffus and I had founded the Community Writing Center together, so I hoped he would be open to alternative approaches.

I was offered the position. As I prepared my first work plan for my supervisors, I dove into WAC scholarship and, in doing so, discovered Mary McMullen-Light's 2010 "Great Expectations: The Culture of WAC and the Community College Context." After reviewing the poor success rates of WAC programs in community colleges, McMullen-Light notes a respondent's comment within Roberts's 2008 analysis: "a culture of writing" (3). McMullen-Light went on to argue that "viewing WAC as the primary mechanism through which to create a true culture of writing may well be the best cornerstone in the foundation of any version or model of WAC or CAC in any community college" (3).

"A true culture of writing."

My mind opened. The impossibility of creating a WAC program at a community college dissolved as my experience with the CWC flooded forward. The CWC had impacted Salt Lake City's "culture of writing" in multiple ways (which I articulate in *Rhetoric of Respect* [Rousculp 2014]). If this was possible in a metropolitan area, then surely there were opportunities to do the same in a community college; however, I believed I would have to make a major alteration to the primary purpose of WAC in order to do so. At SLCC, WAC would have to become about the entire community, not just students.

Four of the five "Typical Goals of US WAC Programs" directly name students, and student writing, as the target of their efforts (INWAC 2014, 2). Chris Thaiss and Tara Porter (2010) conclude their findings of the WAC/WID Mapping Project with a "consensus definition" of Writing Across the Curriculum programs as those that "[strive] to improve student learning and critical thinking and to help students learn the writing conventions of their disciplines" (562). This focus on students is, of course, natural, appropriate, and expected: education reforms are supposed to improve learning opportunities and outcomes for students.

To change a culture of writing at a given institution or locale, however, I believed that all stakeholders must have a connection to it. The writing culture of Salt Lake Community College lives within student writing and learning experiences; it also resides within staff member's job tasks and emails, in faculty drafts of syllabi and sabbatical applications, and within administrators' reports and requests for proposals. While student writing would need to remain central to the WAC program—after all, the college's primary purpose is education of students—all writing at the college needed to be addressed. If not, WAC could always remain an "add-on" to the culture of the college, something optional, and only for those who were enthusiastic about it. Or, worse, it could be relegated to what Barbara Walvoord (1996) calls "the 'they' side of faculty backlash . . . if faculty see it as a way of making them do more work for the same money within the same constraints" (71). If the object of WAC work is solely student writing, faculty, staff, and administrators do not have to empathize with, relate to, or face the cognitive, social, and emotional work that goes into writing—neither their own, or by extension, student writing. How can a "true culture of writing" be built when those who hold the social capital and discursive power within that culture do not see themselves as belonging to it?

I was enthusiastic. I had ten days to submit a work plan to Ruffus and McCormick, and I knew it had to present a compelling case for change. Fortunately, I brought significant affordances to the situation (Linkon and Pavesich 2015). Cox et al. (2018) and Thaiss and Porter (2010) advocate for WAC program leadership to be held by senior, established faculty. I had been at the college for twenty-one years, had founded and directed the SLCC Community Writing Center, served in leadership roles, published work, and received numerous awards. These affordances allowed me the chance to try something different, but afterward, I had to meet all of the same expectations and assessments of any new program at the college. On my first day as director, I presented Ruffus and McCormick with a proposal. In it, I wrote:

> In order to build a sustainable WAC program, the WAC Director plans to follow a similar path to that of the development of the SLCC Community Writing Center, one based in community literacy praxis and within a rhetoric of respect for all stakeholders. This approach is predicated upon collaboration with sustainable resources already in place at SLCC and recognition of boundaries and limitations that are present as well.
>
> For a WAC program to succeed at SLCC, cultivating broad-scale relevance and ownership is necessary. In fact, the WAC program should see itself as a "college"—and not just "curriculum"—program; as such, the program should ideally provide opportunities to "learn to write and write to learn" for all members of the SLCC community: students, faculty, staff, and administrators.

In this proposal, I reframed the Writing Across the Curriculum program into "Writing Across the College" within which every person who belonged to the SLCC community—students, faculty, staff, and administrators—was to count, and their writing was to have worth and be supported. Ruffus and McCormick approved this new direction, and a few days later, the provost did as well. The Community Writing Center's tagline "Everyone Can Write!," which had kept us on course for a decade, was remixed to do the same for Writing Across the College: "Everyone Writes."

STARTING OUT

Standard practice for any WAC program is to first "learn the lay of the land" (INWAC 2014, 3). Cox et al. (2018) name this stage "Understanding the Institutional Landscape" (77), while Martha Townsend (2008) notes the "axiom within WAC initiatives that . . . it must respond to the exigencies of each institution" (47), and Linkon and Pavesich (2015) write, "Long before we could act on the local environment, we had to act in it" (24). Given the previous failed starts of WAC at SLCC, I knew that this was a precarious stage and I had to be completely receptive to what I might find. I turned to the processes we had followed at the CWC when entering into partnership with a community organization or individual: "[Be] sure you go into planning meetings and discussions 'blank.' This means that you may have researched working with a particular population, or may have ideas, but this knowledge and these ideas stay in the background, only to be brought up as suggestions or ideas in response to questions" (Rousculp 2014, 27).

My goal was to understand the culture of writing at SLCC as it was, not with an intent to change it to what I thought it should be.

To do this, I spent the first six months conducting a Writing Inventory and Climate Assessment to answer the following questions: (1) Where does writing take place at SLCC?, (2) What kinds of writing takes place at SLCC?, (3) What support exists for writing?, and (4) What attitudes circulate around writing? Along with Institutional Research staff and administrators, I collected local survey data and performed meta-analysis of seven institutional and national assessments and reports. I conducted eighty structured interviews with students, faculty, academic and student services staff, and administrators. Interview notes were analyzed for both the Inventory and the Climate Assessment. For the Writing Inventory, distinct types of writing were noted and counted. For the Writing Climate Assessment, sixty-one distinct comment areas were determined. The data were then reviewed for these comment areas and coded. The coded data were then quantified and ranked.

This research resulted in a report, "The State of Writing at SLCC: An Inventory and Climate Assessment," which was shared with all academic administrators, faculty leaders, student service administrators, student leaders, and upper administration (Rousculp 2015). The climate assessment began, "Overall findings suggest that the ability to write well is highly valued amongst all stakeholders at Salt Lake Community College. At the same time, writing at SLCC is an act surrounded by attitudes (directed both towards the self and towards others) that may be detrimental to its successful execution. The writing climate at SLCC appears to be similar to that found at many other institutions of higher education: for all stakeholder groups, writing is very important, yet is also arduous, arbitrary, adversarial, and potentially traumatic" (23).

These results weren't surprising; this statement could possibly describe the writing culture of any institution of higher education. But, now we had data to back up what was common knowledge and could develop programs based on it.

Additionally, this study shifted the emerging WAC program away from one of the primary aims of many Writing Across the Curriculum initiatives: "to increase the amount and frequency of student writing" (INWAC 2014, 2). It turned out that students at SLCC already wrote a lot, and frequently. Nearly 90 percent of courses at SLCC included writing assignments, and the students wrote more than their peers in comparable institutions. An analysis of 2010 Community College Survey of Student Engagement data revealed that SLCC students had a statistically significant higher mean response to "Prepared two or more drafts of a paper or assignment before turning it in" and "Number of written papers and reports of any length" (Rousculp 2015). These data did not include anything about the quality of these writing assignments or experiences, but increasing the amount and frequency of student writing was not going to be an immediate priority.

Further, the research showed that SLCC students have many and varied institutional resources to support their writing, including the Student Writing and Reading Center, faculty consulting, peer-mentoring programs, career advising, and disciplinary writing support and events. On the other hand, faculty, staff, and administrators—whose work lives are replete with writing—were offered little to no support. While faculty had access to some development opportunities for writing instruction, they had no support for their own writing needs, and neither did staff or administrators. A WAC program focused only student writing would miss two-thirds of the culture of writing at the college.

Given these circumstances, the WAC program would start with the immediate writing needs of faculty, staff, and administrators while quietly developing support for student writing that did not impact faculty workloads. For students, the WAC program's website provided a centralized resource of the many student writing support services at the college. The program also "translated" English Department student learning outcomes for faculty across the college and helped clarify the distinction between face-to-face, hybrid, and online composition course environments for a student audience. Along with the Student Writing and Reading Center, the WAC program collected an accessible and friendly set of grammar and style websites for faculty and students. That was it; we did not engage with "pedagogy," or "faculty development," or "improving student writing" at all.

To my supervisors, I reasoned that a faculty-, staff-, administrator-focused approach was essential to the long-term success of the student portion of the WAC program at SLCC. In this way, we could establish the program's relevance for all and reduce the risk of alienating faculty (Walvoord 1996). In addition, I recruited members of the first WAC Advisory Committee specifically to establish a matrix of representation of departments/areas and institutional roles across the college: associate deans from Accounting, Finance, and Economics and Communication and Performing Arts; directors of the Library, First Year Experience, and Faculty Services, and Student Life and Leadership; staff from Staff Development and Aviation and Related Technologies, faculty from English and Health Professions; a tutor from the Student Writing and Reading Center, and a student from Student Leadership. Everyone had to belong to Writing Across the College in order for it to succeed.

The research WAC undertook revealed many, many writing needs. In the following sections, I present three of the first initiatives that the Writing Across the College program undertook—seeing faculty as writers, making staff writing visible, and creating transparency with students—as it entered its second year of operation.

SEEING FACULTY AS WRITERS

Since faculty were the most resistant to the idea of a WAC program, regardless of its name change, it was essential that we focus first on their own writing needs (e.g., syllabi, letters of recommendation, assignments) in order to highlight their identities as writers themselves.

A new faculty evaluation process that required all faculty to submit a digital professional portfolio as the primary artifact for their performance became a key opportunity for the WAC program to demonstrate its support for faculty writing. Although the portfolio requirement was approved by all stakeholders at the college, there was no shared understanding of what the portfolio should contain, nor its discursive expectations, other that it had to address teaching, professional activity, and service, accompanied by a "self-assessment statement."

At commencement that year, panic wafted through the faculty ranks. The professional portfolio was a new writing assignment without clear expectations of how to do it, or how it would be evaluated. Faculty found themselves in their students' shoes and were as unsure, nervous, and insecure as might be expected. Unlike their students, however, faculty did not have institutional support, nor did their institutional roles as "experts" in their fields permit them to ask for guidance, even though earning an advanced degree does not automatically confer confidence in writing to its bearer. Further, SLCC, like many community colleges, has a large contingent of faculty in industry and technical fields (e.g., culinary arts, dental hygiene, diesel systems technology, HVAC, radiologic technology, welding). Many faculty in these areas did not have positive experiences with writing in their own education. For various reasons, it can be daunting for a faculty member to ask for help.

Within this vacuum of support, the WAC program proposed to associate deans that we create a set of resources to aid faculty in the development of their professional portfolios. Working with two associate deans, I synthesized recommendations from Peter Seldin's 2009 and 2010 academic and teaching portfolio publications (Seldin and Miller 2009; Seldin et al. 2010) with SLCC's tenure and rank evaluation standards to create a set of guidelines for portfolio structure, writing strategies, and expectations. After receiving approval from the associate deans, the WAC program worked during the summer to create a package of videos, handouts, workshops, and individual consultations for faculty, which was presented to all faculty at the start of the next academic year.

In the three years since, the WAC program has worked closely with associate deans, deans, the provost, and the Faculty Senate to bring clarity to the faculty evaluation process, its required professional portfolios, and their expectations.

MAKING STAFF WRITING VISIBLE

One of the most poignant findings in the "State of Writing Report" was that SLCC staff had no support for their professional writing requirements at all. Repeatedly, staff members whom I interviewed spoke of increased writing demands (e.g., web content, reports, proposals, plans) for which they had received no training. They also had to anticipate and quickly adapt to the changing styles and expectations of incoming supervisors. Staff writing was often lambasted with moralizing critiques of "correctness and style" even when those critiquing made similar and frequent errors as well. Many staff were insecure about their writing, while others were downright afraid of it. They dreaded sharing their writing with their supervisors, even though they had to continually produce more and more of it.

The staff culture at SLCC, however, provided an opening for the WAC program to directly address their writing needs. The college has long provided professional development opportunities for staff, but, until the WAC program emerged, none of them addressed writing needs. Even so, staff enjoyed attending workshops and the Staff Association and Staff Development administrators welcomed the WAC program's offer of creating workshop opportunities for them. These bodies initially requested workshops on "correct grammar and style."

Instead of resisting the literacy ideologies that underpin focus on correctness, the WAC program took them up directly and imported a workshop that had been developed for the Community Writing Center, called "GrammarPhobia," which explored linguistic, social, and political issues of correctness. This was accompanied by the development of a hard-copy and digital college-wide style guide in collaboration with the Institutional Marketing office and a "Get the 'Write' Style" workshop. This workshop also delved into ideologies behind style determinations and demonstrated how to use the style guide to assert agency in the face of admonition from superiors.

The staff response was immediate, with multiple workshops completely filling to the brim for the entire year. In the three years since, the WAC program offerings have expanded to other staff writing needs, including email, desk manuals, meeting minutes, and individual consulting on specific writing needs.

CREATING TRANSPARENCY WITH STUDENTS

While the WAC program did not initially focus on writing instruction for students, the State of Writing report revealed some serious concerns regarding expectations of writing assignments on the part of faculty and students. Like most of the findings of the report in regards to student writing, this was not a surprise. Dan Melzer's 2014 *Assignments Across the Curriculum* demonstrates the complexities of writing assignments and their interpretation by students, and many Writing Across the Curriculum programs focus on improving assignment clarity through faculty workshops.

Engaging with faculty directly about their writing assignments was not an option, however. Faculty did not trust what "a WAC program" might require them to do, and the risk of antagonizing them was too great. Instead, Writing Across the College wanted to start from a place of agreement between faculty and students, to locate those expectations for writing assignments that both groups already agreed upon, and to make these expectations public.

In our second year, the WAC program launched a study to determine what these shared expectations were. A survey of thirty-five statements about writing assignments was distributed to students and faculty. The results were striking in their disunity. Only two statements out of the thirty-five received unanimous agreement: "Students have a right to ask questions about a writing assignment," and "Faculty have a responsibility to respond to student questions about writing assignments." Several other statements elicited high agreement among both groups, including "Students have a responsibility to take writing assignments seriously and put significant effort into them" and "Students have a right to know how their writing will be evaluated." Others, though, showed serious disagreement: "Faculty have a right to have different expectations for student writing than other faculty do" (students: 73 percent, faculty: 96 percent) and "Students have a right to see what their professors think is good writing" (students: 100 percent, faculty: 57 percent).

While the statements with the highest degree of difference would shape future priorities for the WAC program, those with high agreement served as a draft for the "Student and Faculty Bill of 'Writes' and Responsibilities." I then met with the Faculty Senate and the Student Senate and Executive Council for their endorsement of the statements. There was a slight hiccup in the Faculty Senate because it was perceived by some members that this document would be another metric by which they would be evaluated (demonstrating how quickly Walvoord's 1996 "they-side" identity could emerge). After some slight revision, and removal of the term "rights," all bodies approved the document, which was then added to the SLCC First Year Handbook for Students (2017) and SLCC faculty orientations.

A CHANGE AGENT / AGENT OF CHANGE

When does a program become an "agent of change"? William Condon and Carol Rutz (2012) claim that WAC reaches this level of an Institutional Change Agent when it is fully integrated into the institution, and "viewed as part of the team" (378, 374). Cox et al. (2018) denote the fourth stage of sustainable WAC development as "Leading for Sustainability" (169). Yet, WAC programs have been named as agents of change for more than three decades (McLeod 1988), and many WAC programs have come and gone in that time; some have reinvented themselves, others have disappeared, still others have emerged from where nothing was before.

The Writing Across the College program at SLCC has broadened the definition of WAC to suit its own locality and to make possible educational reform that might last longer than the enthusiasm of its participants or the tenure of its founding director. We did this so that the WAC program might belong to the entire culture of writing at the college and possibly become a meaningful member of that entire culture. By doing so, the SLCC program does not fit neatly into the WAC taxonomies and stages presented in this chapter. Some of our work falls into the Institutional Change Agent category or Leadership stages, while others are still Foundational, or are still Planning or Developing.

For example, the WAC program's role in the faculty evaluation process has certainly evolved into a Leadership and Change Agent status, an unusual placement for a "writing across" program. It also currently leads and determines the process for evaluating the college's General Education "Written Communication" outcome as a part of the larger student learning outcomes assessment program, and WAC has become the most-contacted authority for staff on writing-related matters. On the other hand, there has been little success in terms of engaging faculty directly with writing pedagogical matters, through workshops or self-paced online courses. And, the statement about writing assignment expectations described earlier has shown little impact on the quality of writing assignments. An assessment conducted the following year showed no significant impact on students who had been presented with the document in a classroom setting (Smits-Seeman 2016). On yet another hand, however, a single meeting between myself and the associate dean of a department resulted in a complete writing assignment sequence change for all sections of one of their introductory courses.

As Paula Mathieu (2005) argues in *Tactics of Hope*, change may be consequential in ways that we cannot predict when we set out to make it, nor are our institutional definitions of change necessarily the most meaningful in the lives of those we seek to affect. Opening up the purpose of a WAC program to the entire college has created more opportunities for it to become fully integrated within the college and to become meaningful and important to the professional lives of the people who work here. By doing so, we have increased the chances that the Writing Across the College program will be able to positively impact the entire culture of writing at the college and, by extension, will allow the WAC program to slowly build positive changes in the ways students experience writing instruction across the entire college.

Going about making change is wholly contingent on the institution's local contexts, histories, agents and bodies, and intentions. At SLCC, the same (or overlapping) actors tried three times over two decades to develop a WAC program that could hold on longer than an initial burst of enthusiasm. The affordances granted by my senior faculty status, along with the trust the institution placed in me, were key to getting the SLCC WAC program started. Even so, more important than my individual affordances was to envision "writing across" as more than student writing, which inevitably puts a burden on faculty before trusting reciprocity is established between them and WAC. It is too easy for WAC to be shuttered onto the "they-side" (Walvoord 1996) when it attempts to move beyond enthusiasm towards sustainable change. I believe it is important to recognize opportunities that may not look like "Writing Across" as we know it. Recognizing that everyone writes in a college institution and providing tactical support and making change for all writers (wherever possible) opens doors to an institutional identity from which sustainability may strategically emerge.

POSTSCRIPT

In the year and a half since I drafted this chapter, the SLCC WAC program has proposed and gained approval of a writing intensive (WI) agreement that will provide institutional support for faculty across the college who wish to implement WI pedagogies. This agreement limits class size and adds an additional contact hour for WI courses for faculty load. Faculty who apply for and are granted WI designation for their course sections will spend that additional hour serving in the Student Writing and Reading Center tutoring students from across the college. With this load agreement, faculty who teach multiple WI sections should be able to decrease their teaching load by one section per semester.

Creating and implementing a WI faculty development program were together one of the first priorities I was handed when I was appointed to my position. Had I taken it on at that time, I have no doubt that it would have failed, because its success would have rested solely on individual faculty: WAC had no status from which to request institutional support beyond small stipends for training. Now, five years later, we have a viable structure from which to develop a sustainable writing intensive program. I do not yet know the shape of that program, nor how long it will take us to get there, but, at least I know it will be possible to do so.

NOTE

1. This difference might be explained by Thaiss and Porter's inclusion of descriptive prompts such as "Components of a WAC Program" (e.g., faculty seminars/workshops, all-college/university writing committee, writing lab/tutorials, writing

fellows, on-campus consultant) and "Curricular Elements" (e.g., WAC first year writing course, lower-division writing intensive [WI] courses, upper-level WI courses, adjunct writing courses attached to courses in other disciplines) while Roberts asked the open question, "Does your college have an institutionally-designated Writing Across the Curriculum or Writing in the Disciplines program?"

REFERENCES

Condon, William, and Carol Rutz. 2012. "A Taxonomy of Writing Across the Curriculum Program: Evolving to Serve Broader Agendas." *CCC* 64.2: 357–82.

Cox, Michelle, Jeffrey Galin, and Dan Melzer. 2018. *Sustainable WAC: A Whole Systems Approach to Launching and Developing Writing Across the Curriculum Programs.* Champaign, IL: National Council of Teachers of English.

Gardner, Clinton. 2010. "Introduction." Writing Across the Curriculum at the Community Colleges: *Beating the Odds, special issue of Across the Disciplines* 8.3. https://wac.colostate.edu/atd/special/cc/.

International Network of WAC Programs (INWAC). 2014. "Statement of WAC Principles and Practices." https://wac.colostate.edu/principles/.

Linkon, Sherry Lee, and Matthew Pavesich. 2015. "An Affordance Approach to WAC Development and Sustainability." *WAC Journal* 26 (Fall): 22–35.

Mathieu, Paula. 2005. *Tactics of Hope: The Public Turn in English Composition.* Portsmouth, NH: Heinemann.

McLeod, Susan. 1988. "Translating Enthusiasm into Curricular Change." Strengthening Programs for Writing Across the Curriculum, special issue of *New Directions for Teaching and Learning*, 36, edited by Susan H. McLeod: 5–12. San Francisco: Jossey-Bass.

McLeod, Susan, and Susan Shirley. 1988. "National Survey of Writing Across the Curriculum Programs." Strengthening Programs for Writing Across the Curriculum, special issue of *New Directions for Teaching and Learning*, edited by by Susan H. McLeod, 103–30. Hoboken, NJ: Wiley and Sons.

McMullen-Light, Mary. 2010. "Great Expectations: The Culture of WAC and the Community College Context." Writing Across the Curriculum at the Community College: Beating the Odds, special issue of *Across the Disciplines* 8.3. ed. Clinton Gardner. https://wac.colostate.edu/atd/special/cc/.

Melzer, Dan. 2014. *Assignments Across the Curriculum: A National Study of College Writing.* Boulder, CO: Utah State University Press.

Roberts, Leslie. 2008. "An Analysis of the National TYCA Research Initiative Survey Section IV: Writing Across the Curriculum and Writing Centers in Two-Year English Programs." *Teaching English in the Two-Year College* 36.22: 138–52.

Rousculp, Tiffany. 2014. *Rhetoric of Respect: Recognizing Change at a Community Writing Center.* Champaign, IL: National Council of Teachers of English.

Rousculp, Tiffany. 2015. "The State of Writing at Salt Lake Community College: Writing Inventory and Climate Assessment." Report. Salt Lake Community College Writing Across the College, Salt Lake City.

Russell, David. 1990. "Writing Across the Curriculum in Historical Perspective: Toward a Social Interpretation." *College English* 52.1: 52–73.

Seldin, Peter, and J. Elizabeth Miller. 2009. *The Academic Portfolio: A Practical Guide to Documenting Teaching, Research, and Service.* San Francisco, CA: Jossey-Bass/Wiley.

Seldin, Peter, J. Elizabeth Miller, and Clement A. Seldin. 2010. *The Teaching Portfolio: A Practical Guide to Improved Performance / Tenure Decisions,* 4th ed. San Francisco, CA: Jossey-Bass/Wiley.

SLCC First Year Handbook for Students. 2017. "First-Year Experience. Salt Lake Community College." https://www.slcc.edu/oss/first-year-handbook.aspx.

Smits-Seeman, Rochelle. 2016. "Writing Across the College—Writing Expectations Assessment." Report. Salt Lake Community College Institutional Research and Reporting, Salt Lake City.

Thaiss, Chris, and Tara Porter. 2010. "The State of WAC/WID in 2010: Methods and Results of the US Survey of the International WAC/WID Mapping Project." *CCC* 61.3: 534–70.

Townsend, Martha. 2008. "WAC Program Vulnerability and What to Do About It: An Update and Brief Bibliographic Essay." *WAC Journal* 19 (August): 45–61.

Walvoord, Barbara E. 1996. "The Future of WAC." *College English* 58.1: 58–79.

Writing Across the College (WAC). 2016. "WAC Mission Statement." Salt Lake Community College, Salt Lake City. http://www.slcc.edu/wac/mission-statement.aspx#:~:text =WAC%40SLCC%20collaboratively%20develops%20initiatives,%2C%20faculty%2C %20and%20administrators.

7

MAPPING TRAJECTORIES OF ALP WITHIN DEVELOPMENTAL WRITING EDUCATION

Leah Anderst, Jennifer Maloy, and Neil Meyer

One of the current trends across developmental education, and within the field of basic writing more specifically, is the Accelerated Learning Program model, commonly referred to as ALP, in which students take their developmental writing class in the same semester as their first-year writing (FYW) course. While ALP can be considered one iteration of a long movement to mainstream students identified as basic writers, it was conceived in its current form in 2007 by Peter Dow Adams at the Community College of Baltimore County (CCBC). Within this model, a group of about ten to fifteen students who have been deemed through placement procedures as in need of writing remediation enroll in a developmental writing course as a corequisite to a FYW course taught by the same instructor and also consisting of a group of about ten to fifteen "mainstream" students. The goal of ALP is to allow students to complete their developmental writing course in the same semester as their FYW course. Because the class size of the ALP developmental writing course is small, and because it is taught by the same instructor as the first-year writing course, students develop a sense of comfort and strong community in their developmental writing course, encouraging students to share their writing and their questions with one another as they complete their first-year writing assignments.[1]

In the ten-plus years since its inception at CCBC, ALP has been adopted and adapted by hundreds of schools—both two-year and four-year—across the United States. While these programs are resource intensive, depending upon small class sizes and extensive instruction, the positive effects of such programs have been documented through institutional research and scholarship. Community College of Baltimore County's ALP website showcases higher retention and pass rates of ALP students in their developmental writing, FYW, and second-semester

https://doi.org/10.7330/9781646421428.c007

required writing courses as compared to students enrolled in traditional developmental writing courses. This research on pass rates is confirmed by a 2010 study conducted by the Community College Research Center (Jenkins et al. 2010).[2] Likewise, Katie Hern and her colleagues involved in the California Acceleration Project have confirmed lower attrition rates among ALP students as compared to students in traditional basic writing courses (Hern and Brezina 2016). Individual instructors and writing program administrators of ALP also describe the program's ability to increase confidence among ALP students (Anderst et al. 2016a) and cultivate community among students.

A growing body of recent academic and nonprofit research has demonstrated that stand-alone remediation, where developmental coursework precedes college level work, may not serve students effectively as it is currently designed. In this research, students assigned to developmental, or remedial, writing, reading, and math courses often face one or more semesters taking stand-alone courses that may or may not provide credit toward graduation but that often drain students' financial aid, extend their time to graduation, and ultimately cause some students to drop out. For example, Juan Carlos Calcagno and Bridget Terry Long (2008), studying under the auspices of the CCRC the outcomes of some 100,000 community college students in the state of Florida, claim that "remediation might promote early persistence in college, but it does not necessarily help community college students on the margin of passing the cutoff make long-term progress toward a degree" (3). In another study, Thomas Bailey et al. (2010) found that "between 33 and 46 percent of students, depending on the subject area, referred to developmental education actually complete their entire developmental sequence," and they also found that "developmental education completion rates are negatively related to the number of levels to which a student is referred" (256, 259). In her recent article, "Beyond Tradition: Writing Placement, Fairness, and Success at a Two-Year College," Jessica Nastal (2019) discusses the ways in which prevailing placement and course structures in traditional remediation affect students based on racial and ethnic as well as gender lines, with Black and male students disproportionately disadvantaged. Researchers within City University of New York (CUNY) have noted some of these negative impacts of developmental coursework as well.

The "Report of CUNY Task Force on Developmental Education,"[3] published in 2016, began by lamenting that in fall 2015, 74 percent of CUNY students were deemed to need a developmental math course, 23 percent needed developmental reading, and 33 percent needed writing remediation. In light of this reality as well as their review of research on developmental education, the task force recommended a reexamination of placement procedures in an attempt to reduce the number of students assigned to developmental courses, expand corequisite or accelerated models, offer intensive and immersive programs that do not require students to use their financial aid, and eliminate high-stakes testing (like the CUNY-wide writing exam) as the sole measure for exiting remediation. A recent report by the non-profit Center for an Urban Future, making the rounds via local New York media outlets, affirms the task force's findings by claiming that one of the top reasons students at CUNY are graduating in such low numbers is "too many students are pushed into developmental education, a track that greatly increases the chances of dropping out" (Hilliard 2017, 9). Likewise, one of the CUNY Task Force report's recommendations for increasing graduation rates is to "expand the use of alternatives to remediation" (43), which includes "designing corequisite instruction models that bypass developmental education" (38). These corequisite reforms, as well the boosting of the Accelerated Study of Associate Programs (ASAP)— which provides wraparound services such as free Metro cards, free books, and additional advising to eligible students—have been lauded as national models in a variety of publications such as the *Wall Street Journal, the PBS NewsHour,* and the *New York Times.*

Research appears to show, then, that traditional, stand-alone remediation, and especially multisemester developmental sequences, may not be providing most students the access to a college education that these courses would seem to offer. Perhaps in response to some of this research, as well as to local budgetary pressure, legislative bodies have begun efforts to reduce or eliminate traditional remediation, threatening the existence of some developmental courses.

Accelerated Learning Programs, however, serves as a beacon of hope for those who are invested in providing additional support to underprepared students, as currently corequisite models are acknowledged by many researchers and the upper echelon of college administration as one of the few acceptable alternatives to traditional remediation. One of the most important features of ALP for its many stakeholders may be its name: Accelerated Learning. The term *accelerate* has universal appeal for all invested groups, as it connotes speed, increased velocity, and quick success. Within this program, students are more quickly immersed in credit-bearing FYW, with extra support, ensuring their hastened success in required writing as well as increasing the probability that they will successfully complete other credit-bearing courses. Students appreciate

ALP because their time in required writing courses is *accelerated* from two semesters to one, and they also, as Rebecca Mlynarczyk (2016) discusses, see themselves as *accelerated learners* rather than remedial, basic, or developmental writers. Faculty support ALP because the *learning* that takes place in required writing courses is *accelerated* not just in the sense of time but also by pedagogical best practices such as small class size, intensive interactions with faculty, and carefully scaffolded curriculum across basic and FYW. Finally, college administrators have an investment in ALP because it lessens the financial drain to students often associated with traditional remediation while increasing their retention rates and, potentially, speeding up students' time to degree completion. While national graduation rates and time to degree completion can be difficult to measure for two-year schools, according to most reports, six-year graduation rates for students who enter community college following high school hover at 39 percent nationally (Fink et al. 2017, 2), and the US Department of Education states the official graduation rate of community college students is 25 percent (Juszkiewicz 2017).

The early research on ALP is promising, and it dovetails with the growing body of scholarship that shows the longer students remain in remediation, the less likely they are to move on to credit-bearing courses as well as to graduate. As we will demonstrate, our experiences with ALP at our university—CUNY—confirm the many successes and benefits of this model. However, we want to argue here that the sea change of acceleration in developmental education, and in higher education more generally, must be examined carefully within historical trends in basic writing as well as within a neoliberal "austerity" model of education. As a historical examination of basic writing and developmental education demonstrates, reform in this field often occurs in cycles and in bouts of change that are adopted quickly and sometimes without input from and adequate preparation by all of the stakeholders involved in such changes. And when these changes are mandated by state and local governments or by university structures that oversee large systems of institutions, applying a blanket reform may negatively impact local program models that do support communities of students.

As Janet Quint et al., authors of a 2013 study on the Developmental Education Initiative state,[4] "scaling up is hard to do," when it comes to implementing changes on a large scale, particularly in times of economy austerity. Despite the preliminary evidence of the success of models such as ALP, we must think critically about the potential downsides to acceleration. In their analysis of the expansion of developmental education initiatives in fifteen community colleges, Quint et al. argue for "caution" regarding "the speed with which community colleges can meet highly ambitious goals, when less ambitious objectives require time, resources, communication, engagement, and commitment" (2013, 75). Our experiences on our own campus and within our larger university system convince us that localized reform efforts driven by true collaboration between faculty and administrators can have important positive impacts on students. When, however, remediation reform responds primarily to institutional crises from a top-down approach, history has shown that they won't always be effective and that another crisis will inevitably arise. In addition to this, when reform efforts are primarily funded by external, nongovernmental education initiatives, their approach, their design, and their methods tend to reflect the market logic of neoliberalism, which characterizes these funders rather than reforms born out of the needs of local student populations and local faculty expertise.

CONTEXTUALIZING ALP WITHIN HISTORIES OF BASIC WRITING

Histories of basic writing often are written as a series of crisis events in higher education. As both Mary Soliday (2002) and Jane Stanley (2010) argue, changes in remediation policies often take place as responses to the entry of new student populations into higher education as well as to enrollment and curricular issues. Concerns over standards—by faculty, administrators, and even the public at large—often result in reforms to determine college readiness and ultimately lead each time to a new batch of students assigned to remediation. Through her historical examination of remediation in the California system, Stanley argues that changes in remediation policy ultimately become quick fixes to a concern over changing demographics rather than meaningful research-based curricular reforms. Stanley argues that writing plays a special role in these crisis events, as it was—and is—used as a tool for academic elites to exemplify the inadequacies of new student populations. Stanley states, "Complaints about students' writing have served Californians just as well as they have served other Americans as a way to register publicly, if indirectly, dismay over the disruption of the social equilibrium caused by these new additions to the student body" (2). As Stanley articulates here, writing is a tangible student production, and thus it is available for "reformers" to examine for evidence of inadequacy and the need for remediation.

Mary Soliday's *The Politics of Remediation: Institutional and Student Needs in Higher Education* demonstrates that shifts in remediation policies from the nineteenth century onward were often responses by the institution to shifts in the economy rather than primarily a response to students' educational needs. Looking at CUNY and City College alongside national trends around remediation, she describes how university policies often were mediated by the influence—be it financial or political—of foundations, nonprofit organizations, educational companies, and government officials. Thus, larger politics of the institution often dictated the conditions of student access and also student need at any given period in CUNY's history. Another essential fact of CUNY's basic writing history, and remediation histories in general, is the ahistorical context of crisis events at any given point in the historical trajectory. Soliday writes of the "considerable gap between memory and practice" that "dramatizes the peculiar historical amnesia surrounding postsecondary remediation in American culture" (2002, 20–21). Remediation—especially in reading, writing, and mathematics—has existed in American institutions of higher education since its beginnings. As Jamie Merisotis and Ronald Phipps (2000) state, "those halcyon days when all students who enrolled in college were adequately prepared, all courses offered at higher education institutions were 'college level,' and students smoothly made the transition from high school and college simply never existed. And they do not exist now" (69). However, we fail to remember the cyclical nature of remediation histories in moments of institutional crisis. The current moment in developmental education reflects this: even though recent research demonstrates important problems with stand-alone "traditional" models of remediation, and some of the same research also shows comparative improvements for students enrolled in corequisite models, the rhetoric surrounding this research often mischaracterizes the problem as a crisis, a situation that is new, growing, or sudden. In fact, American colleges and universities have always worked to support students they deem underprepared.

INCORPORATING MEMORY INTO PRACTICE AT CUNY

In our attempts to contextualize ALP within a larger history of remediation, we offer our own historical narrative of remedial writing at CUNY, both in its evolution at specific moments in its history as well as its move toward acceleration locally and universitywide. As CUNY is the largest urban university system in the United States, we see it as a microcosm of shifts and trends in public higher education across the country. Within the confines of one city, CUNY encompasses many varieties of postsecondary education. The system comprises seven two-year community colleges, eleven four-year senior colleges, and six graduate schools. This large system educates college and university students at all levels and across all five of the city's boroughs. As CUNY has expanded in terms of students, offerings, and costs, it has also been a key site in the ideological battles around who is able to access an affordable college education.

Since its inception as the Free Academy, New York City's first public college that admitted its inaugural class of young men in 1849, CUNY has aimed for an expansive and liberal mission: to offer educational opportunities to a wide variety of the city's young people. The Free Academy, which became CUNY's flagship campus, the City College of New York (CCNY); the many municipal colleges that came under CUNY's umbrella when the system officially organized itself in the early 1960s; the specialized and graduate schools that have since been established; and the most recent addition, Guttman Community College, founded in 2011, all work toward this mission of making higher education accessible and open to as many of the city's students as possible. Two major barriers to any college education have also impacted CUNY and its students in shifting ways throughout its history, ways that bear on our current conversations surrounding remediation: cost, whether in tuition, materials, or time taken away from a job, and academic preparation. Two particular moments in CUNY's past carry important resonances for our current moment and the widespread drive to accelerate developmental coursework: 1970s open admissions policy and 1999s removal of remediation from the senior colleges.

Quite famously, in the fall of 1970, CUNY admitted its first class of "open admissions" freshmen across the system of colleges. This revolutionary gesture, which was precipitated by widespread student and faculty demonstrations and demands for greater admission of students of color in particular, opened CUNY's doors wider than they had been previously. Prior to 1970, the four-year colleges maintained competitive admissions requirements (an average high school grade of 83 percent), while the two-year colleges admitted students whose academic preparation was deemed less sufficient, but they too limited admissions (to students whose high school GPA averaged 75 percent) (Hechinger 1971). The new policy guaranteed admission to one of the CUNY colleges to any graduate of a New York City high school, without regard to whether their diploma was academic or professional. While the senior colleges remained competitive but with lower benchmarks during this period, the two-year colleges removed all admission requirements. In its first year of open admissions, CUNY admitted 9,000 students across the campuses who would have been excluded under the old criteria and 12,000 in its second year (Hechinger 1971). Open admissions had profound effects across CUNY, in particular increasing the numbers of students served by the university. And while open admissions did mark an increase in less-prepared students admitted and, therefore, in remedial courses offered at the senior colleges, these colleges had long been offering and filling precollege courses.

Prior to open admissions, in fact, CUNY had a strong model for how best to serve its newest students, especially its lower-income students whose prior study may not have prepared them for college coursework. This program was SEEK. Search for Education, Elevation and Knowledge was created in 1966 to serve the very small number of Black students attending CUNY, and its inaugural group centered at City College but soon spread to the other CUNY four-year campuses (Resnik and Kaplan 1971). Through SEEK students benefited from waived admissions requirements, free tuition, a weekly stipend, free textbooks, and individual tutoring on top of any remedial coursework they might require. Created collaboratively by CUNY faculty and administrators as well as by members of the New York State government, who ensured the program would remain in place and part of the university's budgetary structure, SEEK's roots within CUNY have grown, and the program remains a presence on eleven of CUNY's four-year campuses. At the two-year colleges, College Discovery (CD) served and continues to serve a similar student body over the same period (The Percy Ellis Sutton SEEK and College Discovery Program 2016). Both SEEK and CD, though, have remained comparatively small. From 1990 to 2017, SEEK and CD combined have consistently served between 10,000 and 15,000 undergraduate students each year across all of the undergraduate-serving campuses.[5] Further expansion of SEEK and CD seems a financial impossibility for CUNY, and, as Soliday points out, funding was the biggest concern in CUNY's open admissions policies and programs of the 1970s: "What eroded support for open admissions and fueled much of the anger was the unwillingness of the city and state to fund it properly" (99). In SEEK, in CD, and in open admissions, we see an important precursor to CUNY's current push to transform developmental coursework into corequisite models alone. Initially created locally and on smaller scales, ALP courses support students' needs well, but scaling up across a university system whose open-access policy remains a key part of its mission will require a consistent and a significant stream of support from the university, something the university was not able to do in the wake of open admissions. Because open admissions, a major policy change, was not accompanied by a commensurate increase in funding and resources, CUNY came under fire in the decades following 1970 for what was seen as the program's increased costs and lowered standards.

So, in 1999, when CUNY's board of directors voted to remove all remediation from the senior colleges, they in effect created a two-tier system, segregating to the community colleges—which remained open access—underprepared, "at-risk" students from their better-prepared counterparts who would attend the competitive senior colleges. The board's vote was controversial and resisted by many student and faculty groups within the university, but, marshalling a rhetoric of concern for lowered standards across the colleges, for the high costs of remedial courses, and for the idea that the once proud university needed rescuing, the vote passed with a wide margin.

This move to eliminate remediation from senior colleges was part of a larger effort to reform CUNY with a new focus on what was posited as diminishing standards. A report called *The City University of New York: An Institution Adrift* (Mayor's Advisory Task Force 1999), composed by a task force commissioned by then mayor Rudolph Giuliani, based its findings on studies conducted by consultants at PricewaterhouseCoopers, RAND Education, and a faculty member at Fordham University Graduate School of Education.[6] The report was publicized in a series of articles in the *New York Times*, as Linda Adler-Kassner and Susanmarie Harrington (2002) document in *Basic Writing as a Political Act: Public Conversations about Writing and Literacies*. They argue that the representation of CUNY's remediation policies in this report drew upon what they call a "meritocratic narrative" in which higher education is an entry into the middle class and "a requirement of getting this education is amassing and reproducing objective literacy skills" (Adler-Kassner and Harrington 2002, 62). Adler-Kassner and Harrington demonstrate that the *New York Times* coverage as well as the report itself claim that CUNY's remediation structure did not ensure that students were able to master the skills they needed to succeed in college. The *New York Times*, they state, portrayed students as disempowered within that structure and therefore established the need for restructuring (64). Soliday claims that critics at the time blamed remediation for lowering standards as well as causing financial strain on universities (106), and the report supported this as it posited increased access as "synonymous with remediation" (118). By associating remediation and access, CUNY was able to restructure the university and "downsize" remediation by establishing that "remedial programs were the source of CUNY's woes, not economic or cultural shifts" such as the privatization and defunding that accompanied these changes (Soliday 2002, 116).

As Brian Cafarella (2014) notes in his historical overview of developmental education in the United States, "There is a sharp contrast in how college leaders and state legislators measure success in developmental education in the present day from that of their counterparts forty to fifty years ago" (n.p.). Whereas success following the open-enrollment trends of the 1960s was measured primarily by the important increases in students served by colleges—by *access* to college, in other words—today colleges and legislatures measure success by rates of retention and by how quickly students can be accelerated through developmental coursework. Cafarella explains that this "paradigm shift" is paralleled in another shift: decisions regarding developmental coursework are often now made by bodies external to colleges, such as by state and local legislatures, rather than by college administrators or faculty. So far, CUNY has resisted impositions on its developmental curriculum from outside the university;[7]; however as evidenced in recent reports, CUNY has acted on a university level to require all campuses to develop corequisite models and to move toward the elimination of a majority of stand-alone developmental courses. In the midst of another "literacy crisis," negotiating designs of corequisite instruction on individual campuses alongside CUNY-wide mandates reveals the tensions inherent in scaling up ALP.

THE EMERGENCE OF ALP AT CUNY

Currently each of CUNY's community colleges has its own developmental curriculum within a variety of academic departments. Yet up until very recently, exit from reading and writing remediation was standardized across the university according to particular scores on high-stakes exit exams.[8] Amidst universitywide policies and placement requirements that have altered how students are placed into and exit from remediation, all of CUNY's community colleges have created their own forms of ALP, based on faculty and administrative collaborations that examined the specific needs of students and the available resources and structures of each college. The creation of ALP at one of the two-year schools that is part of CUNY, Queensborough Community College (QCC),[9] demonstrates the appeal of ALP for all invested parties at the college as it offers increased student access while addressing current institutional crises.

Before the inception of ALP, QCC's developmental writing and reading and English as a Second Language (ESL) courses were housed in the Academic Literacy Department, an entity entirely separate from the English Department, where introductory composition and literature courses were taught. None of the courses in the Academic Literacy Department awarded students credits toward graduation, and all required eligible students to use their financial aid. For faculty members in both departments, the best option seemed to be to work within the existing course structures in our two departments and create a corequisite upper-level developmental writing course (with 14 students) and a FYW course (with 14 ALP students and 10 mainstream students). Even though the administration was quite encouraging of these efforts, the disciplinary stratifications necessitated careful collaboration across departments to create an aligned curriculum for both classes that clearly showed how students could use their Academic Literacy writing course to both prepare for the exit exam and to be supported in their FYW course. Queensborough Community College piloted two sections of ALP courses in spring 2014, and each subsequent semester ALP course offerings grew as participating faculty members documented pass rates on the exit exam as well as students' passing grades in FYW. The academic departments and administration saw that ALP was working for both "native" English-speaking and ESL students (Anderst et al. 2016a). In our pilot semester, spring 2014, 70 percent of students enrolled in our ALP sections passed while just 44 percent of students passed who were enrolled in our stand-alone upper-level developmental courses. In fall 2014, when we increased our numbers of sections and students, our pass rate comparison continued to outpace the stand-alone courses: 56 percent of ALP students passed while 46 percent of non-ALP students passed (Anderst et al. 2016a, 18).

As more sections were added each subsequent semester, students continued to benefit from this form of accelerated learning by reducing the amount of time they spent in the remedial track as well as by enrolling in a developmental course with a small cap size. Faculty benefited from ongoing professional development and possibilities for collaboration. The administration continued to support ALP and encouraged faculty to continually expand the eligibility requirements for students to bolster enrollment. All of these benefits paved the way for the Academic Literacy and English Departments to merge into a single department and for new, meaningful discussions about writing to take place amongst diverse faculty members. Eventually, we created an integrated reading and writing ALP, through which students with developmental needs in both areas may participate in ALP and reduce their developmental course requirements. The collective efforts of faculty and administrators working together to build a program based on best practices in developmental education resulted in a successful ALP model that addressed many of the specific needs of QCC's student population using existing structures on our campus. This production at a local level has largely yielded positive results for students.

LaGuardia Community College, where Meyer teaches, has a similar story of local development and positive results for students. Their ALP course was inspired directly by the CCBC model and designed for the campus by a LaGuardia faculty member, Dr. Heidi Johnsen, among others. Over several years, the English department went from twelve ALP sections in the first year of the course to fifty-seven during the 2018–2019 school year. Each year faculty reviewed the pass rates and student success in subsequent writing courses, changing the placement profile to make the course available to more students flagged as in need of remediation. Along with this, the department held regular professional development on the best practices in ALP pedagogy, continued by Dr. J. Elizabeth Clark after Dr. Johnsen.

Both QCC and LaGuardia offer examples of local faculty investing in accelerated composition through research, faculty buy-in, and careful planning. However, we find ourselves in a moment at which we are questioning our ability to push forward with more ALP sections for more students alongside the sharp reduction in stand-alone developmental course offerings in our department. By way of illustration, we present two student scenarios, with the students' names changed, to exemplify the benefits as well as some of the limitations of the ALP model for our students.

Jie is a young woman who came to the United States from China a few years prior to enrolling at QCC. She lived with her parents in a neighborhood of Queens, where she is mainly surrounded by other Chinese speakers and businesses, and she has a part-time retail job in her neighborhood, where she interacts primarily with Chinese customers and colleagues. Before enrolling in classes at QCC, she took classes through CUNY's Language Immersion Program (CLIP), a low-cost, intensive English language program that hosts classes in spaces on each of the CUNY two-year colleges. Jie speaks, writes, and hears English almost exclusively at school, and while her work in CLIP helped her pass CUNY's reading entrance exam (ACCUPLACER), she did not pass the writing entrance exam (CATW) and had to take developmental writing. Historically, QCC has tracked English Language Learners (ELLs) into a separate stream of developmental reading and writing courses from that of native English speakers (NES), so under our old model, Jie may have been placed into a stand-alone ESL-designated developmental writing class one or even two levels below English 101, our credit-bearing college writing course. Because our ALP model mixes students from these two streams into one, Jie enrolled, with other ELL students as well as NES students, in the highest-level developmental writing linked to a section of English 101, and, for her, this corequisite option offered some continuity from her intensive and immersive CLIP classes. With ALP, she completes more writing, reading, and speaking in English than she would have in one ESL developmental class alone, and her focus on the course materials meant that she made important progress in both her fluency in English and in her facility with college-level writing and reading over the semester. She passed both classes in the ALP pair, and she moved on to English 102 and to courses in her major, including writing intensive courses.

While the intensity of ALP may have been just what worked well for Jie, for some students, it can become burdensome alongside a full course load. Another QCC student whose placement test results placed her into developmental writing, fared less well in the courses. Abigail was a returning, Black student. Following high school, she got married and divorced and had a child in between who was a toddler when she enrolled in ALP classes. Even facing all of her life demands, Abigail decided to jump right into college when she enrolled at QCC. Over the last few semesters, CUNY has become focused on improving time to degree specifically by encouraging more students to enroll in a course load of fifteen credits.[10] While grounded in the goal of improving students' chances to earn a degree, the "15 to Finish" campaign overlooks the fact that for some students, dedicating more time to their initial classes is what allows them to learn. For advisors at QCC, however, ALP, specifically its *accelerated* model, pairs well with this momentum campaign.

Entering QCC at this moment, Abigail was encouraged by an advisor to enroll in eighteen credits spread over six courses. She reported that the advisor had characterized the two classes that make up ALP (seven credit equivalents) as more or less the same amount of work and difficulty as one ENGL101 class (three credits). So this misunderstanding of the ALP course's structure and intensity combined with a mandate to increase students' per-semester credit hours, pushed Abigail over an already high fifteen credit goal into a number of credits that contributed to her inability to pass her courses.

Early in the semester, Abigail was eager, focused, and hardworking. In only a few weeks, though, she was spread thin between her many classes, her part-time job, and her family commitments. Eventually, she withdrew from one of her other courses, and this freed her up to catch up on some of her missed coursework so that she passed the developmental portion of the ALP class pair but not ENGL101. Abigail's overburdened semester caused her a good deal of stress in her first year back to school, and it was simply too challenging for her to catch up once she got behind. Looking at her record alone, Abigail certainly was a good fit for ALP courses. She benefited from the small class size and the attention her instructor was able to provide, but she floundered in the face of a university policy that aims to increase overall graduation statistics at the expense of students who simply need more time and more breathing room.

By and large, we have seen a good deal of student success with ALP on our two campuses (QCC and LaGuardia Community College), and this reflects both the research and anecdotes of ALP faculty as well as current research in developmental education across CUNY as well as the country; however, the student scenarios above also reveal the possible thresholds for ALP, helping us to understand whom the program works for and who might be disadvantaged by default ALP placement without alternatives offered within English departments. For example, the two stories highlight only the experiences of students who can enroll in courses full time. Part-time or evening and weekend students, on the other hand, may be excluded from ALP altogether because the times we tend to offer these classes combined with their longer meeting times favor students whose schedules are flexible. Our analysis of student success and struggle in ALP comes at the same time that CUNY administration is establishing ALP as the default placement for a majority of CUNY students deemed in need of remediation. Although there is significant overlap between our experiences and the ambitions of these CUNY reforms, our institutional and student examples also reveal the nuance of developing ALP courses along with the complicated needs of a diverse student body, whose developmental writing needs cannot always be met with a single, one-size-fits-all, intervention. As we will see, massive changes to writing remediation at CUNY and across the nation can eliminate barriers to student access to credit-bearing courses but might also leave fewer options for students with complex lives and nontraditional student profiles.

CONTEXTUALIZING ALP IN HIGHER EDUCATION'S CURRENT AUSTERITY CRISIS

The benefits of these reforms cannot—and most definitely should not—be ignored or even underestimated. Important changes such as the increase of corequisite instruction to the structure of developmental education have indeed accelerated students' progress as they support best practices in writing instruction such as process-based writing assignments, small class size, and faculty support rather than depending upon high-stakes testing. Across CUNY, a total of 1,045 sections of corequisite courses were offered to 16,786 students for the years 2013–19. Students in corequisite composition courses were 16 percent more likely to complete six composition credits in two years than those students who began in traditional, noncredit remediation (Watanabe-Rose 2019). The benefits of such a course are obvious, and much of these data come prior to CUNY's massive scaling up of corequisites like ALP.

But our above narrative detailing QCC's move to ALP courses reveals the difficulty of doing such change the right way: researching best practices, involving multiple college stakeholders, measuring student outcomes, and considering local structures and concerns. Such effective change at QCC required significant investments from the college, and those courses—with their smaller class sizes and additional course time—require continuing resource commitments. This commitment to resource-intensive coursework stands a bit at odds with current state support for higher education. To take CUNY as an example: "Over the past forty years at CUNY, the ratio of tuition paid by full-time students to public funding has shifted from zero to about 50 percent for students, many of whose annual family incomes are below $30,000. Within that same time frame the proportion of classes taught by full-time faculty has diminished from almost 100 percent to less than 50 percent" (Fabricant and Brier 2016, 3). Ultimately, CUNY is working to reform developmental education—by changing placement and exit procedures for developmental education and increasing accelerated learning and corequisition instruction—at the same time as it faces the reality of austerity. The concern becomes underfunded reforms, reforms paid for by increased student tuition, or reforms guided fundamentally by the goal of cost saving rather than student learning.

The trends at CUNY are representative of a national disinvestment in public higher education. John Quinterno (2012) writes that "real funding" for full-time students dropped 26.1 percent from 1990 to 2010 (2). Almost as important, he notes that the recessionary cycles that define the modern economy are having a disproportionate, negative impact on college funding; since 1979, with each new recession, the "length of time for higher education funding to fully recover . . . has lengthened" (2). As the nation emerged from the Great Recession of 2008, funding levels for public higher education did not return in kind. Michael Mitchell and Michael Leachman report that even as state revenues have returned to pre-2008 levels, state funding for public higher education has not (1–2). This process—of higher tuition, fewer full-time faculty, and prolonged periods of austerity—is worth keeping in mind as we contextualize the current enthusiasm for expanding ALP and corequisite courses within the austerity framework of higher education funding.

Although often not supported with additional state funding, recent years have seen significant state interventions in colleges that bear both directly and indirectly on remedial education, including Tennessee (2010), Connecticut (2012), Florida (2013), and Colorado (2014). Perhaps most ambitiously, in April 2017, the California State Assembly passed a bill that requires California community colleges to use student GPAs as a measure to place students, in hopes that this move—much like the August 2017 executive order by the California system's chancellor to eliminate all remedial courses and replace them with corequisite models—will help more students enter directly into credit-bearing courses.

These major reforms have encouraged composition scholars to proactively respond and situate them in the large body of composition scholarship and best practices, for example, the Two Year College Association's "White Paper on Developmental Education Reforms" ("TYCA White Paper" 2015). The authors warn that "the very existence of the open-admissions two-year college is thrown into question by state mandated developmental education reform initiatives" (233). The authors also note that these massive interventions are usually made with little direct input from faculty and scholars and with little attention to the discipline's body of research (237). Among their recommendations, the white paper authors call on funding for "strong academic support systems for students" and support for "ongoing professional development for all developmental educators" (228). These recommendations prioritize expertise of local faculty, an attention to specific student populations, and buy-in from the larger college community. These recommendations then align with previous versions of remediation support, such as CUNY's SEEK program described earlier, or the development of ALP at the Community College of Baltimore County. But these recommendations also get to the central tension between developmental educators and legislators at this moment: a heightened intervention in the structures of college education (often with limited faculty input) alongside continued austerity-level funding.

At CUNY, this gap between reduced state support and increased classroom needs is being bridged through outside private funding and support, most notably, through a recent grant from Strong Start to Finish (SSTF). Funding of SSTF comes from the Bill and Melinda Gates Foundation, the Great Lakes Higher Education Corporation and

Affiliates, and the Kresge Foundation. It describes itself as a "network" that brings together current research on best practices in college education with philanthropic funding that allows institutions to scale up these practices ("About" 2017). Strong Start to Finish describes this work as helping colleges improve retention and completion rates for the most marginalized student populations. In 2018 CUNY was awarded a $2.1 million grant from SSTF, described in a press release "to support faculty-led work replacing traditional, stand-alone remedial courses with high-impact corequisite courses and workshops" ("CUNY Awarded"). What might also be most notable here is the scale: "CUNY aims to double the number of new students completing math and English gateway courses each year to 16,000 and reduce achievement gaps between black or Hispanic students and Asian or white students." The Gates Foundation's interest in remediation predates its involvement with SSTF, and the foundation and its affiliates have worked for years to encourage states to slash developmental college education and to tie college budgets to graduation rates (Mangan 2013). However, while SSTF sees itself as bringing evidence-based reforms to institutional-wide policy, the TYCA white paper specifically cautions against such massive standardization of locally created policy.

One reason for the caution is that organizations like the Gates Foundation largely leave educators and scholars out of private institutions' research and decision-making processes. This was certainly true of developmental writing faculty at CUNY. Until 2018, CUNY relied on a "do-or-die" exit exam from its highest-level, non-ALP-designated developmental writing courses, the CUNY Assessment Test in Writing (CATW). But faculty had advocated for years to end this punitive testing model, and the CUNY Writing Discipline Council (WDC) made ending high-stakes testing one of its chief priorities. The WDC represents writing program administrators (WPAs) from every CUNY undergraduate-serving campus and this body (of which all of the authors of this chapter have served as members at some point) began advocating for changes to remedial testing in 2015. Despite bringing evidence of the disparate impacts of high-stakes testing and the successful alternatives implemented at other schools, CUNY did not move to change their writing remediation policy until prompted by SSTF and its grant money. Local expertise was ignored until validated by an outside funding source, to the detriment of students needlessly held back by a punitive testing regime.

The massive changes proposed by groups like SSTF may build their work from the best practices in developmental reform, but they often lack attention to local stakeholders or individualized campus needs and histories. So, whereas our successes with ALP at LaGuardia and a QCC have been born from our locally created models, with massive interventions from nonprofits and state governments, the nuance that created ALP at CCBC gets lost.

Soliday and others have pointed out that the various "literacy crises" are the product of particular cultural and political shifts. This new literacy crisis is not driven by shifts in student populations (such as the open-admissions era) but by shifts in funding for college education and, therefore, who gets heard in curricular discussions. The austerity budgets of the past decades have chiseled away at state support for colleges and have forced students to share in a larger part of the burden as colleges increase tuition. Nonprofits step in, and directly fund reforms that aim to reduce the class- and race-based differences in college graduation rates. But these interventions frequently sideline on-the-ground stakeholders, ignore institutional histories, and apply reforms without local input or context. We can see possible tensions between LaGuardia and QCC's local implementation of ALP against the recent CUNY-wide investment in corequisites. As schools move toward ALP and similar corequisites through NGO and/or legislative fiat, standing firm on the principles outlined by the TYCA White Paper on Developmental Reforms and their students' and institutions' needs will be more important than ever.

CONCLUSIONS AND FURTHER CONSIDERATIONS

As we try to contextualize ALP within larger histories of basic writing and literacy crises, we must also consider how ALP is being implemented within current constructions of crisis in higher education. In many ways, the growth of ALP marks an exciting period in the history of basic writing and developmental education more generally. Up until quite recently, the growth of ALP has been one that follows a grassroots model for development: a group of dedicated faculty and college administrators at CCBC built a developmental education model based on best practices within the fields of developmental education and composition studies. This group from CCBC, led by Peter Dow Adams, shared resources—in the forms of course materials, research, formal and informal advice, and ultimately a national conference—with other community colleges across the country in order to support community college English and developmental education departments. These efforts were largely faculty informed, if not faculty driven, and took local circumstances—student population, student need, campus priorities and resources, and administrative perspectives—into consideration. Our examples of QCC's and LaGuardia's development of ALP demonstrate how our locally rooted designs were informed by the resources that CCBC has made available for other schools to use and adapt based on specific needs.

However, we are wary of current top-down approaches by legislatures and educational organizations to mandate and standardize corequisite education and to tie it to funding for such programs. Positing corequisite programs such as ALP as a possible solution to the current higher education crisis of low graduation rates may be sound given the positive, albeit somewhat limited, data that link ALP to higher pass rates and graduation rates. However, if the implementation of such programs is mandated through a top-down process that is tied to funding, local campuses may lose their autonomy in designing programs based on the needs of specific student populations. What is more, if ALP does not adequately solve the crisis of low graduation rates as it has been positioned to do within such mandates, it may be stripped of the substantial resources it requires to be sustained, especially if ALP is increasingly funded by third parties providing temporary financial support for specific academic initiatives. Tying funding to—and even measuring success by—college graduation rates is understandable from the outside looking in, but it is problematic for faculty working intensively with students who are underprepared for college. Many of the barriers to graduation are factors beyond curricular control, factors such as family obligations, transportation issues, work pressures, and financial limitations. In their histories of basic writing, Soliday and Adler-Kassner and Harrington identify these same life factors. Not only, then, are the institutional challenges to basic writing the same as in the 1990s' crisis, so are the student realities that often are lost in the crisis rhetoric.

ALP is an incredibly effective model, as CCBC demonstrates with its documentation of the national growth of ALPs in a variety of colleges, and as we describe in reflecting on our local implementations of the model. However, it is important for us to understand that like any programmatic innovation, ALP is not a one-size-fits-all solution for all college students who have been identified as in need of additional academic support. If ALP is presented as such within our current higher education crisis, particularly when this crisis is occurring in a moment of austerity, we need to think carefully about what this means in terms of access and allocations of resources. Open access may be threatened when the dwindling resources available to developmental education are allocated to ALP courses that work for many but not all, the not all being some ELLs (who could be excluded from these programs or go through these programs without getting the types of support they would need prior to entering ALP), as well as adult and nontraditional students who attend part time and may again need more support. As Christie Toth et al. (2019) note in a recent issue of the *Journal of Writing Assessment*, the Council of Learning Assistance and Developmental Education Associations (Toth 2019) and a recent US Department of Education report (2017) argue for a careful consideration of a swift mass elimination of remediation. The council warns that the end of traditional remediation might limit access and therefore heighten disparities; the Department of Education states that "appropriate placement and completion of developmental courses could relate to persistence and degree completion" (8). English departments may be mandated to eliminate developmental education courses and implement ALP for as many students as possible under the auspices of helping students enter credit-bearing courses immediately and promising to keep them out of the remedial quagmire and on the road to efficient college success. However, if students who need more support have no alternative but to drop out if they are overwhelmed with corequisite models, we ultimately deny them access.

While acceleration is an appealing concept to legislators, educational organizations, administrators, faculty, and students, we must be aware of the potential risks in excessive speed. The alternative licensure program has generated exciting changes throughout the field of developmental education and has served many thousands of students well. However, it is essential for stakeholders in accelerated learning to consider what alternatives will be available for students who may need different types of immersion at different paces.

NOTES

1. More information and details about the ALP model and its various iterations can be found in the introduction of *Basic Writing e-Journal*, issue 14.1, a special issue focused on ALP and guest-edited by Anderst, Maloy, and Jed Shahar (Anderst et al. 2016b).
2. This study was funded by Lumina Foundation's "Achieving the Dream."
3. The report describes the members of the task force as the chairs or co-chairs of the CUNY Reading, Math, and English Discipline Councils, members of the CUNY Central Office, and administrators from individual campuses (1–2).
4. The Developmental Education Initiative was funded by the Bill and Melinda Gates Foundation and the Lumina Foundation.
5. As a comparison, CUNY's total undergraduate enrollment in fall 2017 was 244,420, so SEEK and CD combined accounted for 4.5percent (SEEK/CD total: 10,881); see CUNY Office of Institutional Research (n.d.).
6. http://home.nyc.gov/html/records/rwg/cuny/pdf/adrift.pdf.

7. In his budget proposal for fiscal year 1999, then mayor Rudolph Giuliani proposed outsourcing all precollege courses to for-profit outfits, potentially reducing the students at CUNY's community colleges by 75 percent. His proposal failed (Selingo 1998, A4).

8. City University of New York mandated multiple-measures assessment for students to "exit" from developmental reading courses in fall 2016 and from developmental writing courses in fall 2017.

9. For another description of QCC's ALP creation, please see Anderst et al. 2016b.

10. This push to enroll students in fifteen credits each semester may be linked to the 2017 introduction of New York State's Excelsior Scholarship, which provides free tuition to students who enroll in thirty credits or credit equivalents per year. "Tuition-Free Program" (n.d.).

REFERENCES

"About." 2017. Strong Start to Finish. strongstart.org/about.

Accelerated Learning Program. n.d. Community College of Baltimore County. Accessed June 24, 2021. http://alp-deved.org/.

Adler-Kassner, Linda, and Susanmarie Harrington. 2002. *Basic Writing as a Political Act: Public Conversations about Writing and Literacies.* New York: Hampton Press.

Anderst, Leah, Jennifer Maloy, and Jed Shahar. 2016a. "Assessing the Accelerated Learning Program Model for Linguistically Diverse Developmental Writing Students." *Teaching English in the Two-Year College* 44.1: 11–31.

Anderst, Leah, Jennifer Maloy, and Jed Shahar. 2016b. "An Introduction to Acceleration: Some History, Some Questions, Our Stories." *Basic Writing e-journal* 14.1 https://bwe.ccny.cuny.edu/ALPEdsIntro.html.

Bailey, Thomas, Dong Wook Jeong, Sung-Woo Cho. 2010. "Referral, Enrollment, and Completion in Developmental Education Sequences in Community College." *Economics of Education Review* 29 (April): 255–70.

Cafarella, Brian V. 2014 "Developmental Education: Then and Now." *Research in Developmental Education* 25.4.

Calcagno, Juan Carlos, and Bridget Terry Long. 2008. "The Impact of Postsecondary Remediation Using a Regression Discontinuity Approach: Addressing Endogenous Sorting and Noncompliance." NBER Working Paper No. 14194. July.

"CUNY Awarded $2.1 Million Grant to Scale Equity-Focused Student Success Strategies." 2018. City University of New York, February 6. http://www1.cuny.edu/mu/forum/2018/02/06/cuny-awarded-2-1-million-grant-to-scale-equity-focused-student-success-strategies/.

CUNY Office of Institutional Research. n.d. *Current Student Data Book by Subject.* http://www2.cuny.edu/about/administration/offices/oira/institutional/data/current-student-data-book-by-subject/.

Fabricant, Michael, and Stephen Brier. 2016. *Austerity Blues: Fighting for the Soul of Public Higher Education.* Baltimore, MD: Johns Hopkins University Press.

Fink, John, Davis Jenkins, and Takeshi Yanagiura. 2017. "What Happens to Students Who Take Community College 'Dual Enrollment' Courses in High School." *National Student Clearinghouse Research Center.* https://ccrc.tc.columbia.edu/media/k2/attachments/what-happens-community-college-dual-enrollment-students.pdf.

Hechinger, Fred M. 1971. "Open Admissions: Prophets of Doom Seem to have Been Wrong." *New York Times,* March 28.

Hern, Katie, and Jennifer Brezina. 2016. "Transforming Remediation: An Essential Part of Campus Equity Efforts." *Diversity and Democracy* 19.1. *Association of American Colleges and Universities.* https://www.aacu.org/diversitydemocracy/2016/winter/hern.

Hilliard, Tom. 2017. "Degrees of Difficulty: Boosting College Success in New York City." Center for an Urban Future. https://nycfuture.org/pdf/CUF-DegreesofDifficulty_Dec.pdf.

Jenkins, David, Cecilia Speroni, Clive Belfield, Shanna Smith Jaggars, and Nikki Edgecombe. 2010. "A Model for Accelerating Academic Success of Community College Remedial English Students: Is the Accelerated Learning Program (ALP) Effective and Affordable?" *CCRC Working Paper*, 21. *Community College Research Center*. https://ccrc.tc.columbia.edu/media/k2/attachments/remedial-english-alp-effective-affordable.pdf.

Juszkiewicz, J. 2017. *Trends in Community College Enrollment and Completion Data*. Washington, DC: American Association of Community Colleges.

Mangan, Katherine. 2013. "How Gates Shapes State Higher-Education Policy." *Chronicle of Higher Education*, July 14. https://www.chronicle.com/article/How-Gates-Shapes-State/140303?cid=cp14.

Mayor's Advisory Task Force. 1999. "The City University of New York: An Institution Adrift." June 7.

Merisotis, Jamie P., and Ronald A. Phipps. 2000. "Remedial Education in Colleges and Universities: What's Really Going On?" *Review of Higher Education* 24.1: 67–85.

Mitchell, Michael, and Michael Leachman. 2015. "Years of Cuts Threaten to Put College Out of Reach for More Students." *Center on Budget and Policy Priorities*, May 13.

Mlynarczyk, Rebecca W. 2016. "Acceleration vs. Remediation: What's in a Name for Composition Studies?" *Basic Writing eJournal* 14.1. https://bwe.ccny.cuny.edu/Mlynarczyk.htm.

Nastal, Jessica. 2019. "Beyond Tradition: Writing Placement, Fairness, and Success at a Two-Year College." *Journal of Writing Assessment* 12.1. https://journalofwritingassessment.org/article.php?article=136.

The Percy Ellis Sutton SEEK and College Discovery Program. 2016. 2015–2016 Annual Report. http://www2.cuny.edu/wp-content/uploads/sites/4/page-assets/academics/academic-programs/seek-college-discovery/SEEK-CD-2015-16-annual-report_WEB.pdf.

Quint, Janet, Shanna Smith Jaggars, D. Crystal Byndloss, and Asya Magazinnik. 2013. "Bringing Developmental Education to Scale: Lessons From the Developmental Education Initiative." *MDRC*. https://www.mdrc.org/sites/default/files/Bringing%20Developmental%20Education%20to%20Scale%20FR.pdf.

Quinterno, Jose. 2012. *The Great Cost Shift: How Higher Education Cuts Undermine the Future Middle Class*. New York: Demos.

"Report of CUNY Task Force on Developmental Education." 2016. City University of New York, June 1. http://www2.cuny.edu/wp-content/uploads/sites/4/page-assets/about/administration/offices/undergraduate-studies/developmental-education/Proposed-Recommendations-of-RTF-06.17.16.final_.pdf.

Resnik, Solomon, and Barbara Kaplan. 1971. "Report Card on Open Admissions: Remedial Work Recommended." *New York Times*, May 9.

Selingo, Jeffrey. *Chronicle of Higher Education*, February 13, 1998, A4.

Soliday, Mary. 2002. *The Politics of Remediation: Institutional and Student Needs in Higher Education*. Pittsburgh, PA: University of Pittsburgh Press.

Stanley, Jane. 2010. *The Rhetoric of Remediation: Negotiating Entitlement and Access to Higher Education*. Pittsburgh, PA: University of Pittsburgh Press.

Toth, Christie. 2019. "Directed Self-Placement at Two-Year Colleges: A Kairotic Moment" *Journal of Writing Assessment* 12.1. https://journalofwritingassessment.org/article.php?article=134.

Toth, Christie, Jessica Nastal, Holly Hassel, and Joanne Baird Giordano. 2019. "Introduction: Writing Assessment, Placement, and the Two-Year College." *Journal of Writing Assessment* 12.1. https://journalofwritingassessment.org/article.php?article=133.

"Tuition-Free Degree Program: The Excelsior Scholarship." n.d. Accessed June 24, 2021. https://www.ny.gov/programs/tuition-free-degree-program-excelsior-scholarship.

"TYCA White Paper on Developmental Education Reforms." 2015. *National Council of Teachers of English.*

US Department of Education. 2017. "Developmental Education: Challenges and Strategies for Reform." January. https://www2.ed.gov/about/offices/list/opepd/education-strategies.pdf.

Watanabe-Rose, Mari. 2019. "Corequisite Remediation: Some National and CUNY Perspectives." Restructuring First-Year Writing at CUNY: Access and Equity in the Twenty-First Century conference. April 5.

8

ACTORS AND ALLIES
Faculty, IT Work, and Writing Program Support

Rochelle Rodrigo and Julia Romberger

As institutions that include digital mediated courses in their curriculum at a variety of levels increasingly move to include more digital technology infrastructural support for their classes, faculty and graduate students who have scholarly expertise in various technologies because of their research foci and pedagogical practices are often being called upon to do service work that goes beyond committee work. This undertaking might be due to department and college needs for professional development or advising for and maintaining infrastructure development or through necessity to complete their own agendas—often both. For example, Rochelle (Shelley) was hired in her first full-time position because she could teach online writing courses. At the conclusion of her fifth year, the campus instructional technologist was offered a better position elsewhere, leaving the institution only the summer months to fill the position before the next academic year started. Shelley wanted a sound hiring search cycle for this, what she believed was an important position; therefore, she offered to be acting instructional technologist for the year. She was assigned the acting position and did not teach courses all year long (except the required "how to teach online" course).

This example of a writing program technologist (WPT) is a relatively positive story; Shelley was committed to robust technological support and engaged in labor that was outside of her regular purview to make sure the technologies were supported. In this instance, the labor was both compensated, she was fully reassigned for the year, she was visible, and the position came with a title and an office. Oftentimes, however, many examples of the type of work completed by WPTs are invisible. The 1998 Conference on College Composition and Communication's "CCCC Promotion and Tenure Guidelines for Work with Technology" explicitly discusses the value of technological work done by faculty who have expertise in that area that extends beyond the scholarly into

https://doi.org/10.7330/9781646421428.c008

the practical. Specifically, the guidelines discuss the committee work that writing studies scholars with this expertise might be asked to do. However, the question of other forms of service—such as running department instructional computer spaces or maintaining web servers and presences—is not addressed, nor are suggestions made for application of such guidelines to contingent faculty and graduate students. This lack of discussion is particularly concerning, for these last two populations may be more vulnerable to the expectations of being "good departmental citizens" by fulfilling the needs of requesters that aren't completely cognizant of the amount of work being asked for and yet less well positioned to argue for the value of their work.[1] This usually invisible work is also not visible in this document. This absence may in part be related to the fact that much of this work—especially the pedagogical support and the career advancement support provided through maintaining and advocating for IT infrastructure and professional development workshops—qualifies as care work, as Robinson defines it in chapter 5 in this collection. At times it is affective, but more often is supportive and nurturing of pedagogical change and risk taking along with providing fundamentals necessary for research and teaching. Although the 2015 update to the 1998 "CCCC Promotion and Tenure Guidelines for Work with Technology" provides a few more examples of the type of service work that might be done by listing "department and organizational websites, as well as developing and maintaining listservs, databases, archives, surveys, and online forums," the document then suggests referencing tenure and promotion case studies that are over eight years old. Writing studies is lacking scholarship about this, many times invisible, specialized labor. Whether or not this technologically themed labor is visible or not, it is being done, in many cases to the benefit of writing programs and the units in which they are housed. There are likely many reasons that this labor is not particularly visible, but some of it is clearly connected to wider sociocultural understandings of technology. It might be suggested that part of the reason that the WPT has not been clearly identified as a separate, professional position as the WPA has is because of the nature of the work itself. Early discussions and journals saw the technology as integral to the writing process. The work to bring technology into play within these spaces was not a task clearly separate from supporting best teaching practices unlike the work of a WPA (e.g., the managing of staffing, resources, and professional development), the WPT's work is often taken on because it is seen as a critical part of teaching. And yet WPTs often end up doing administrative work similar to WPAs—indeed, the data indicate that WPAs and

WPTs can at times be the same person. In addition, Andrew Feenberg (2017), among others, has written about how technology that supports labor becomes an integral part of that labor and thus essentialized into it. This absorption leads to a sense that the work with the underlying technology itself is invisible as the technology itself is. It is likely that nearly any writing program of reasonable size has a WPT or two, but it is unlikely that those people hold a named role or position. In the survey we conducted in 2016–17, only 50 percent of the forty respondents had a job description. The lack of job descriptions and the tendency to see it as essentialized into other work, in other words, are two parts of the same coin that can lead to a significant downplaying of the amount of time and the expertise WPTs may be employing, which opens up the possibility of advantage being taken.

In this chapter, we will contextualize the impact of Information Technology (IT) in the academy and in writing programs. We will then share our study results that introduce and define WPTs and discuss how and why they might be helpful to both WPAs and their institutions at large along with some of the challenges they face in getting their work understood as well as some of the larger challenges of encouraging those doing WPT work to see themselves as a coherent, and significantly sized, group of individuals.

IT AND THE ACADEMY

In the 1990s, there was a noticeable burst of technologically mediated classes, especially distance-learning courses, in higher education (Allen and Seaman 2004; Carnevale 2005; Dutton and Loader 2002) and writing courses (Harrington et al. 2000; Hewett and Ehmann 2004; Palmquist et al. 1998). The statement "there is no evidence that enrollments [in distance-learning courses] have reached a plateau" (1) that Elaine Allen and Jeff Seaman made in 2004 is just as relevant to writing programs in 2019, when institutions like the University of Arizona (2014), Arizona State University (2015), and University of Nevada, Las Vegas (2018) posted job advertisements for online writing program administrator positions. Information Technology/ies (IT), however, have/has been changing higher education for a lot longer.

In *The World Is Flat: A Brief History of the Twenty-First Century*, Thomas Friedman (2016) discussed the rapid rate of technological change and our need to stay caught up: "The great challenge for our time will be to absorb these changes in ways that do not overwhelm people or leave them behind. None of this will be easy. But this is our task. It is inevitable and unavoidable" (49). As various technologies have prompted change in higher education, IT departments have grown and changed as well. In 2002, Dennis Jones and Dewayne Matthews reminded readers that IT has become ubiquitous in higher education, supporting all aspects of the institution, including instruction, and academic and student support services, as well as administrative logistics and facilities (3). This growing need for IT support has shown itself in the growth of size of central IT units and the number of president/provost cabinet-level chief information officer (CIO) positions that emerged in the 1990s and 2000s. Many articles—published by EDUCOM, CAUSE, and EDUCAUSE[2]—continue to discuss ways to manage the transformation and change of higher education by IT (Brunt 1994; EDUCAUSE n.d.; Grama 2013). Thomas Warger (2006) specifically discussed the difficulty that many campus media and IT support teams are having in trying to keep up with the ever-increasing number of newer technologies.

Just as IT departments, and their corresponding administrative needs, grew with the increasing impact of IT on institutions, many institutions similarly either started, or increased the size of, their pedagogical units (centers for teaching excellence, quality, or teaching and learning—units tasked with the continuing professional development of the faculty and sometimes staff), starting in the 1970s (Tiberius 2002) through the early 2000s with the "explosion of technology use in college teaching" (Sorcinelli et al. 2006, 4). Reporting out on three large empirical studies about professional development practices in higher education, C. McKee and colleagues conclude that "the obvious inference to be drawn is that from Centra in 1976 to POD Network in 2001 to the work of McKee and colleagues in 2010, professional educators have always been eager to advantage their students by attempting to add the latest advancement to their instructional practices" (20). These pedagogy units have not only always been invested in helping faculty better facilitate learning using various technologies; this emphasis has obviously grown with the increase in online and computer-mediated teaching practices.

IT AND ENGLISH STUDIES

Writing studies as a field felt the impact of rapidly changing computer technologies very early on, which perhaps accounts for the significant influence it has had upon rhetoric and composition and technical communication as disciplines and the longtime connection of faculty within this field with the technology. The major standardization of word processing (primarily with Microsoft Word even though there are alternatives like WordPerfect and Open Office) along with the continued development of either campus- or text-company-developed software that address various writing stages and processes (like McGraw Hill's *Connect*, Pearson's *MyWritingLab*, and Cengage's *MindTap*) demonstrate a need for instructors and, therefore, WPAs in particular, to stay abreast of communicative technological change. New writing technologies aside, even major changes in Microsoft Word—the track-changes feature for example—have had the ability to greatly impact how writing instructors teach writing with technology.

Writing faculty understand the close connection between writing and technology as evidenced by the Council of Writing Program Administrators (Council of Writing Program Administrators 2008), adding a "Composing in Electronic Environments" section to the "WPA Outcomes Statement for First-Year Composition" and then in 2014 completely integrating digital composing throughout the outcomes in the third edition of the Outcomes Statement (Council of Writing Program Administrators 2015). After the National Council of Teachers of English (NCTE) joined the Partnership for Twenty-First-Century Skills, it published a research brief on Twenty-First-Century Literacies and a position statement defining Twenty-First-Century Literacies. To help their students succeed in the twenty-first century, an increasing number of writing instructors are making a commitment to teaching with technology.

If only because of basic logistical concerns, human resources, student enrollment, and so on, WPAs have, at minimum, a tangential relationship with IT support of institutional infrastructure. With the growth of online learning and institutional administrators demanding that entire curriculums be accessible online, as well as with the growing popularity of computer-mediated composition and multimodal composition, WPAs are becoming more closely connected to both IT as well as pedagogy units. The changing infrastructure of university IT systems continues to grow in importance when an administrator starts, or is directed by, upper level administration, to implement programmatic review and/or assessment. Increasingly the offices responsible for institutional assessment desire assessment strategies that can be easily quantified so that data might be technologically integrated with assessment data from other units for "data driven decision making" (Hrabowski et al. 2011). Much writing assessment scholarship promotes various digitized assessment options like RaiderWriter from Texas Tech (Department of English, Texas Tech University n.d.) and the various ePortfolio initiatives across the nation. Even if digitizing the assessment process is not required, no WPA has the physical space to continue archiving copies of assessment materials (i.e., stacks and stacks of student papers) and will probably need to digitize copies of assessed documents.

The writing about *paying attention to technological change* has been on the WPA's office wall for quite a while. And if said administrator wants to be "critical" (Selfe 1999) of the technologies they're implementing, or not get trapped in another uncritical adoption of a technological solution or railroaded off to "Cooltown" (Rice 2007), they will probably want to identify and work closely with their local WPTs. Writing program technologists are also often well positioned to advocate for critical technology implementation based upon an understanding of student technology access in turn based upon various institutional variables as well as larger discussions about tech company data collection policies and terms of service. Writing program technologists are usually in a position to evaluate proposed technologies with an experience and knowledge base, particularly in terms of writing program's curricular goals, which may be quite different from those of other course types, something that WPAs simply do not have time to do. We are not claiming that WPAs do not have the intellectual know-how to do the work of sustaining technology-rich programs; a growing number of WPAs are also WPTs. Instead, we want to acknowledge, along with Rice and Richard and Selfe, as well as all the authors in Dánielle Nicole DeVoss and colleagues' *Technological Ecologies and Sustainability* (2009), that this work is both intellectually rigorous and time consuming. In "Remediating Writing Program Administration," Carrie Leverenz lists a paragraph of multimodal composing applications she needs to learn "if I want to be able to remediate the writing program I direct" (2008, 47). Richard Selfe's book *Sustainable Computer Environments* (2004) is entirely dedicated to help writing faculty, and therefore administrators, to develop "technology rich" environments; it emphasizes the need to plan, pay for, and assess digital environments in writing programs. We are not adding to the list of things that an WPA needs to do to design, develop, and sustain a technology-rich program; instead, like Selfe (2004), we are suggesting that WPAs who are not also already technology savvy should not, and hopefully need not, tackle the technology alone. Tracing the current discussions about surveillance and privacy and how these concerns impact technology adoption in universities where Family Educational Rights and Privacy Act (FERPA) laws require us to rigorously protect student grade information, for example, is just one more conversation that WPAs perhaps should track, but may not have the time or background to. WPTs often do.

THE STUDY

During the summer of 2012, we conducted a series of twenty-three interviews that collected data about the job descriptions, types of work, and compensation of those who might describe themselves as the "techie" in their English department. We were primarily interested in the following questions:

- What type of technology-related service are "technologically knowledgeable" faculty in English department doing?
- How is this service valued and/or compensated?
- How is this work articulated by faculty and administration?

Prior to the 2012 Computers and Writing conference, we obtained IRB approval to use a convenience and opportunity sampling to select our interviewees. We wanted participants who had completed some type of technologically related service to the department, college, or institution that does not fall under their general teaching and/or research requirements. After the conference we only had about ten interviews, so we personally followed up with individuals we had seen and/or chatted with at the conference.

During the twenty-three interviews we conducted we asked the following questions:

1. What is your technology service title, and what is the description of your assigned duties (e.g., manage a computer lab, manage a web server, provide professional development)?

2. Please describe any unassigned duties.

3. Approximately how many hours during a semester these duties take to discharge? Are there hours over summer?

4. What type of compensation do you receive (e.g., course releases, stipend, etc.)?

5. What are your impressions of how the labor is perceived (invisible, essential, "easy," etc.)?

6. Do you keep records of the time and resources you expend?

7. Can you share with us a representative anecdote or two about this labor and how it is valued (or not)?

It is important to note that within this set of questions, we deliberately chose not to include institutional size or type because individual WPT contexts can vary so greatly it seemed likely that they could be identified by information within their answers. We did not wish to put anyone's career in harm's way because of their answers. Based upon the idiosyncrasies of some of the institutional contexts we heard about, this seemed to be a well-founded concern.

Although our data produced interesting information about the type, value, and (in)visibility of "English Techie" work (data already presented as a traditional report of empirical research by Rodrigo and Romberger 2017), it also helped us to develop, define, and provide examples of the following WPT archetypes. The WPT archetypes can help WPAs identify, ally with, and support WPTs while developing and supporting robust, digitally mediated research and teaching programs. Each archetype was founded upon looking at similarities of description across categories of responsibility—service work performed, articulated connections to pedagogy, and articulated connections to research agenda. This isn't to claim that any one of these categories is all encompassing and that the definition could not be expanded upon or other archetypes discovered. We realize that given the number of WPTs out there, this is a quite small sample size.

WRITING PROGRAM TECHNOLOGIST ARCHETYPES

We see the writing program technologist as defined by several fundamental characteristics we list below. The following is our overarching articulation of a WPT's identity followed by the archetypal subsets that we encountered.

Who Is a Writing Program Technologist?

Usually the fundamental raison d'être for a writing studies faculty member's or graduate student's decision to take up a WPT position in their institution is their research interests and/or research agenda. In institutions where a faculty member's job security is dependent upon obtaining tenure, research is one of their higher, if not the highest, priority(ies). And in institutions where job security is not associated with research, a faculty member's research agenda is also highly personal because they are completing it above and beyond articulated job responsibilities. Writing program technologist scholars are highly motivated to help maintain the technologies and the technologically mediated spaces needed to conduct their research. Therefore, the traditional responsibility of conducting and writing up research is complicated by the need to access and maintain technologies that are the objects of research studies and/or facilitate the processes of conducting research.

Almost all writing faculty are invested in technological access for students, in the least instance so that students can type and print (or digitally submit) major writing projects. However, the growing number of distance or hybrid writing courses (Harrington et al. 2000; Hewett and Ehmann 2004; Palmquist et al. 1998), as well as the growing number of writing studies faculty teaching either multimodal projects in first-year composition courses and/or separate digital writing courses (McKee and DeVoss 2013), implies a growing number of writing faculty highly invested in technologies that support their teaching as well as student learning/ composing. Beyond preparing for and conducting their courses, Faculty members who are WPTs are what Richard Selfe calls the "teacher/ leaders" (2004, 28), interested in acquiring and maintaining both the hardware and software used in their instruction and assessment practices and the spaces (physical and virtual) in which these are situated.

The third articulated space of responsibility is that of departmental service and/or departmental administration. Generally, a WPT who is actively supporting technological access and maintenance issues as a part of their departmental service and/or administrative responsibilities do so because they are motivated by their technologically mediated research and teaching responsibilities. However, even if some technological issue is not the direct topic of a given service or administrative responsibility, committee chairs and department administrators are invested in digital communication and collaboration technologies to better facilitate traditional service and administrative work. Service and administrative work now gets done in shared documents and drives as well as in meeting spaces set up for external members to come in via audio and/or video conference meeting applications. For example, even if the WPT researcher and/or instructor is not a member of the personnel or application committee, they may be asked to help construct and maintain digital working environments supporting these committees. Many WPTs find that their articulated spaces of responsibilities begin to overlap because of the close relationship between their teaching, research, and service activities.

Tech Service Archetype

After transcribing and coding these interviews, patterns of identities began to form. Historically, the identity from which other identities seem to have emerged is the tech service actor. This identity was performed mostly through the work of purchasing, maintaining, and troubleshooting the technological infrastructure of a department. Tech service actor 1.0 work has been categorized as "plug[ging] in machines," "crawling under the desk and hooking together computer labs," "butt-in-the-air" work.

These types of techies often know what technologies are out there to help support particular initiatives and teaching practices or know how to find out what is available. They are also capable of acting as "translators" between IT staff and WPAs and other faculty who are not as conversant with technological jargon. However, more than one interviewee mentioned that they don't, or rarely, do that type of work anymore, and there wasn't much interview data to suggest that this type of work was still common. Instead, their archetypal profile fits what we have termed tech service 2.0.

As IT departments grew and took over the work of installing and maintaining hardware, a second generation of tech service actors emerged. The tech service 2.0 actor still might help troubleshoot hardware and software as well as manage the department website; however, the change in the role and its responsibilities comes from the change in institution-wide IT support. As IT departments expanded, techies from specific departments were not required to help build labs and image computers. Instead, tech service 2.0 actors are more likely to focus on supporting technological activities associated with the specific discipline and department. This support can be offered in an official capacity, as with department-offered workshops and include unit level titles like "Technology Applications Mentor," "department technology coordinator," or "e-course coordinator for the English department." Tech service 2.0 work can also stay unofficial, with titles such as "the tech guru," the person to whom everyone goes when they have a technology related question. Interviewees described some of their tech service 2.0 work as revolving around several frequently identified terms such as training and professional development. This role can be seen in the following quotes, "I did Bb training, Wimba training, and helped faculty with technology needs as they arose" and "I've led workshops on using LiveText, which is our ePortfolio and assessment software package that the university subscribes to. . . . I have led workshops on basically supplemental materials for texts that we've been teaching that are online so using YouTube videos in the classroom to support a novel that we're teaching in first-year writing or uploading and using resources on Blackboard." Another part of the tech service 2.0 WPT's work is connected to supporting and guiding infrastructure decisions and maintenance. For example, one interviewee said, "If the chair wants to know what to buy, what we need, I'm one of the two or three people that they email to say, 'How much does this cost?,' 'Where can we get it for?,' etc. So, I have no title; it's not a formal thing—it's just I'm one of the people who knows what to do, so we get tasked with that." Similarly, another interviewee discussed how they handled things like "dealing with the support staff, making plans for budgets; there was a student worker who I supervised directly; people would come to my office to ask for help all the time. The person who worked in the job before me basically did anything he was asked to do." Our tech service 2.0 WPTs did a lot of the same pedagogical and administrative support that Selfe (2004) associated with his "teacher/leader" group.

By definition, both tech service archetypes are hopefully willing and able to help administrators with technology implementation on a department, unit, and/or program level. Historically, tech service 1.0 archetypes probably helped many departments get computer-mediated classrooms for their course offerings. Many of our interviewees who fit into the tech service 2.0 archetype explicitly mentioned helping with official technology mediated pedagogical support like workshops and open office hours/support. Tech service 2.0 archetypes who specialize in technologically mediated pedagogies might also help administrators make explicit connections with campus pedagogy units.

Technology Liaisons / Policy Makers

The longer a tech service actor maintains the role of supporting the implementation and maintenance of technology mediated actions at the unit level, the more likely they are to make connections external to the unit. Over time, tech service actors often find themselves performing more intellectual work as decision makers and policy generators departmentally and, at times, extradepartmentally. In this capacity, they become technology liaisons / policy makers. In this capacity, they can advocate for the general digital infrastructure needs of the writing program as well as the research and pedagogical agendas of various faculty. Interviewees described technology liaison / policy maker work at the college and university as well as at the unit level that comprised guiding and setting policy and facilitating networking between invested stakeholders across administrative structures. These WPTs are often overtly tapped for their knowledge and expertise by others, such as with this interviewee who told us, "[the associate dean in charge of facilities] asked me to be on at least two different committees talking about computer and software needs for the college. Talking about life cycles for new computers for faculty—how long we could go for that. We made up a recommendation; I worked with four other faculty." In fact, this type of request was a reasonably frequent theme that showed up again: "Last semester I was on a pilot study because the college is really asking for an innovative teaching methodology" and again,

I'm the chair of the instructional technology committee, which is a university-wide committee made of faculty members, IT staff, some representatives of units on campus like the library and media services that are involved in either purchasing or deploying instructional technologies. My chairship of that committee is a totally voluntary thing, but service on university-wide committees is strongly encouraged and even largely expected of faculty at the university, so I self-selected onto ITC (Instructional Technology Committee) as opposed to being on an honors committee or a curriculum committee or some other such thing. . . . [T]he committee actually provides input on purchase decisions made by IT; we meet once or twice a month as a full group that includes the director of IT to provide feedback and often input and sometimes guidance on decisions that IT makes about timing for outages, for example for maintenance for the email server or for whether a certain software package needs to be renewed when the contract comes up or what the specs on faculty hardware might be for faculty computers.

Along with addressing requests that they lend their expertise to various committees and decision processes across campus, these WPTs often also took the lead in creating connections between stakeholders on campus as seen in the following interview where the WPT said, "[we] decided that we needed to meet with the vice president of technology and set up a committee, faculty advisors, and find out how everything worked. And, we set one up at the college level as well." This other interviewee was dealing with monetary issues: "With budget cuts we had less available and so in order to make things run a little more smoothly his thought was like, let's see if we can get people who actually know what they're doing to talk to other people."

Some technology liaison / policy maker archetypes in our data end up leaving the writing-focused units for positions like "Interim Director of Instructional Technology" or "Coordinator of Innovative Teaching Initiatives." Technology liaison / policy maker archetypes are great individuals to help an administrator start connecting more deeply with IT and/or campus pedagogical units. Technology liaison / policy maker archetypes will also be very likely to work with mentoring faculty on various technologies and developing teaching with technology workshops within a department harkening back to the tech service 2.0 archetype. The difference is that the liaison / policy maker has the opportunity to work across the institutional administrative system rather than remaining strictly within the unit. Usually they are motivated to do such work because they want to keep their unit running smoothly, which can require working at a variety of levels where decisions happen. They also can be an additional voice of support in advocating for resources, space, time, and faculty development.

Master Architect

Our last archetype, the master architect, is a very particularized WPT. This person often has a research and/or teaching agenda that requires the building of an infrastructure that does not conform with general IT needs for security and uniformity that allow for ease of management across a multidisciplinary institution. Such an architect often supplements their technology domain with outside resources and seeks institutional autonomy. One interviewee discussed his role as master architect thusly: "My research, you know, goes back and forth between the theoretical kind of stuff, which is mostly what I've published, and the more pedagogical concerns." Becoming a master architect takes a level of commitment and sacrifice that not everyone is either willing or capable of undertaking, as this interviewee makes clear:

> I had to work really hard to get that to happen and initially to get that to happen it had to come out of my own hide. I just had to bleed service to get it started and so I started with one classroom, thirteen sections. When I started, I was doing a ton of digital technology work. Revising curriculum, developing material spaces, working with the new teachers, training the new teachers, and all of it was coming without any sort of course release, without any sort of title recognition, it just, if there was going to be digital composition and digital writing it just had to start somewhere; and if I had gone into it guns blazing and said, "You need to give me administrative position before I do this," it never would have happened. So, it started for the first two years, or actually year and a half, without any sort of administrative role.

And the master architect often has to be able to do liaison work in order to make it happen as this interviewee did:

> The agreement would be that I would be the one who maintains all of the technology in the lab because I wanted a very specific set up in there and I didn't trust anybody else to do it, and so far that's been a fantastic thing. . . . I image out the machines every semester; so there's a master machine that I create; usually three or four and then I sync up. There's nineteen computers in the lab so I have eighteen opportunities to screw up, then once I finally get it right then I do a metal to metal copy of that machine's hard drive and then push that out to the other eighteen machines in the lab.

Master architect archetypes usually have near IT-level expertise in hardware and software related issues; they have to in order to demonstrate their ability to maintain a secure digital environment outside of IT's purview. Whereas master architect archetypes are less likely to do general IT-related service—they already put in a lot of time with their own environments—they can be persuaded to work with administrators when goals are aligned. They also are often repositories of knowledge regarding acquisition of resources and pockets of money internal and external to the institution that administrators might not be aware of. Additionally, like the WPT tech service archetypes, they also are able to operate as a translator when discussing complex technical issues between IT staff and WPAs and other faculty.

As already demonstrated by how some individuals shifted from tech service to technology liaison / policy maker roles, individuals may shift in their roles, and/or might hold multiple roles simultaneously. Obviously, there are a variety of ways in which these writing program technologist archetypes might help various WPAs; however, we suggest that strategically leveraging the strengths and the motivations of the archetypes within the overlapping alliances will benefit both the WPT as well as the administrator. Writing program technologist as technology liaisons, program and student advocates, and mentored and networked partners within and outside the university system can assist WPAs on a number of levels, but the nature of and the effort required for this labor also need to be acknowledged by the institution.

WPTS AND OTHER ADMINISTRATORS WORKING TOGETHER

In short, these WPT archetypes are ideal individuals to help twenty-first-century WPAs grow and maintain their departments or units. Writing program technologists often have networks based on the type of work they do, as we chart below, that can be highly valuable to WPA work. We are not explicitly outlining ways WPTs might contribute to a program; there is much scholarship about how writing programs need support for teaching with various technologies. Instead, we emphasize and provide ideas on the labor and power support issues related to this type of work. When considering ways of fostering alliances with WPTs, administrators might wish to consider uncovering the following information about WPTs and how they are already enmeshed in the technology decision making of the university. We recommend administrators start with identifying the WPTs in the department (table 8.1); there might be more than one—many rhetoric, composition, and technical communication graduates leave graduate school prepared to meet the WPA Outcomes Statement with its integrated emphasis on composing in a variety of (digital) environments. Knowing which of the archetype(s) each WPT fits can help an administrator develop an understanding of what the WPT might bring to the alliance. Additionally, knowing what the individual's professional needs and personal motivations are—be they

Table 8.1. WPT archetypes and networks

	Tech Service	Tech Liaisons / Policy Makers	Master Architects
Types of Work/ Activities	Wants to get the work of digital composition done; may help with both logistics (hardware and software) as well as pedagogy and research/assessment methods	Helps research, make decisions, and institute policies about using specific technologies within the department/ program and/or across the campus	Sets up very specific technologically mediated environments to facilitate personal technologically mediated research and/or teaching agenda
Potential Networks	Usually works with faculty and staff internal to the department or writing program	May be networked with both official and unofficial technology leaders in the department and on the campus at large	Usually closely networked with IT staff and administrators; probably has good working knowledge of institutional processes and policies regarding IT

pedagogical or research driven or both—can be helpful in negotiating alliances as well (Rodrigo and Romberger 2017).

Administrators will probably benefit from identifying and working within a WPT's current connections and prior experiences. Obviously, WPTs are interested in the growth of IT; however, IT may also benefit from the expertise of WPTs in helping describe, theorize, and assess technological use across the campus. Writing program technologists can also be advocated for students through their understanding of how technology use is affected by issues of access and privacy when implementation decisions are being made. Often, WPTs were experimenting with technology for teaching or research long before adoption across campus. Similarly, some pedagogical units also recognized the expertise of WPTs in terms of digitally mediated teaching and learning. Investigating alliances the WPT already has in play with IT and pedagogical units across campus can assist an administrator in fostering a broader network of alliances across the campus with the growing number of units involved in utilizing and making decisions about technological infrastructure that supports the mission of the institution. Making visible the networks and experiences of various players, like WPTs, can help administrators manage and maintain, even grow, the technological infrastructure of their various programs, departments, and other units.

Both administrators and WPTs will benefit from making this working relationship more explicit. The original emphasis of our interviews was on the (in)visibility of tech service work. For example, one interviewee used the metaphor of sled dog work or racing to described visible and invisible tech service labor:

> There's the hard work to get things started, like you're a sled dog and you've got your runners on your sled are frozen in the ice and you've got to break it free and you just, and that's like really, really hard work. Then, you kind of trudge and you get it going, and then you've got it going, but then you've got to keep it going. And, the keeping it going is actually, in some ways, I think more invisible labor because if you're starting something and it catches and it goes, it's visible, it lurches forward. But, once it's rolling and people are just used to watching it go around the track or whatever they forget.

For example, setting up a new computer-mediated classroom is a very visible "lurch" of labor. McKee and DeVoss, plus Richard Selfe, along with one interviewee, agree that sustaining the lab space can take as much work as starting it. The interviewee describes how "there was no communication with the people [about] how do you refresh these computers when they get old and everything. And, finding out all of that took an inordinate amount of time. Well, it turns out that it's done through student technology fees. . . . [S]o I found out about that and started writing and they began part of my duty, to write the student technology fee proposals." Certain administrators, especially evident in scholarship about WPAs, are already sensitive to their identities constructed as invisible (Jewell 1980), negative "service" (Bullock 1987), and "marginal" (Gunner 1999); therefore, the identities need "pragmatic self-awareness" to help become more visible and valuable to others (Bushman 1999). Writing program technologists should understand both the desire to find allies in getting work done as well as the need to make those allies and their work both visible and positively valued. One interviewee discussed writing a "memo of understanding that switches my job duties." "Because," they explained "this position didn't exist before I came here."

Similarly, WPAs should work with WPTs in negotiating the work that the WPTs do for the unit. If the institution has a well-developed IT department for hardware and software support, the WPT should, as one of our interviewees said, "absolutely set boundaries." Another interviewee emphatically claimed, "I made it clear that I don't do hardware in this position. We have a fine technology services department." Therefore, if someone from IT can help set up email and printers, the WPT should not do that work. Similarly, if the campus's pedagogy unit has robust support for the learning management system (LMS), the WPT should not be showing someone how to use the Blackboard or

Moodle grade book. Instead, WPTs and WPAs should be negotiating work that is writing-centric technology support work, like designing and delivering "Teaching Writing Courses Online" and "Teaching Writing in a Computer Media Classroom" workshops or acting as a liaison in a decision-making capacity regarding what LMSs would work better for the teaching and learning of reading and writing or which tutor-tracking software would work best in the writing center environment.

In an environment where almost all administrators are asked to do more with less, identifying allies to help with various responsibilities, big and small, is worth the time and effort. Using the WPT archetypes can help identify actors and start productive conversations with potential allies, leading to a working relationship that benefits all including the faculty the WPA administers.

CODA

After thirteen years of agitating each time administrators changed to make the position of WPT more visible in the English Department and the resources needed to effectively manage the labor of this position (a once-per-year course release), Julia worked with the department to get the WPT position, its responsibilities, and its compensation codified into the constitution. This codification makes the labor clearly valued and more easily passed along to other vested faculty without fear of losing the resources necessary to do it.

NOTES

1. The data from a survey we conducted from 2016–17 showed that of 40 respondents completing, 23 were tenure-line, 9 were full-time non-tenure-line with renewing contracts, 2 were contingent with non-renewing contracts, 4 were graduate students, and 2 listed themselves as other (Institutional Review Board [IRB]: University of Arizona 1610903901).

2. One of the precursor "technology and higher education" organizations to EDUCAUSE, EDUCOM started in 1964 with a five-year, $750,000 grant from the Kellogg Foundation (Heterick 1998). The impact of IT in higher education is not just in relation to teaching and learning. The other precursor organization that started in 1962, CAUSE, emerged from the College and University Machine Records Conference (EDUCAUSE n.d.).

REFERENCES

Allen, I. Elaine, and Jeff Seaman. 2004. "Entering the Mainstream: The Quality and Extent of Online Education in the United States, 2003 and 2004." The Sloan Consortium. Online Learning Consortium. secure.onlinelearningconsortium.org/publications/survey/entering_the_mainstream2004.

Brunt, William R. 1994. "A Model for Change." EDUCAUSE. library.educause.edu/resources /1993/1/a-model-for-change.

Bullock, Richard H. 1987. "When Administration Becomes Scholarship: The Future of Writing Program Administration." *WPA: Writing Program Administration* 11.1–2: 13–18. http://associationdatabase.co/archives/11n1-2/11n1-2bullock.pdf.

Bushman, Donald. 1999. "The WPA as Pragmatist: Recasting 'Service' as 'Human Science.'" *WPA: Writing Program Administration* 23.1–2: 29–43. http://associationdatabase .co/archives/23n1-2/23n1-2bushman.pdf.

Carnevale, Dan. 2005. "Online Courses Continue to Grow Dramatically, Enrolling Nearly 1 Million, Report Says." *Chronicle of Higher Education* 51.44. www.chronicle.com/article /Online-Courses-Continue-to/121228.

Conference on College Composition and Communication. [1998] 2015. "CCCC Promotion and Tenure Guidelines for Work with Technology." National Council of Teachers of English. http://cccc.ncte.org/cccc/resources/positions/promotionandtenure.

Council of Writing Program Administrators. 2008. "WPA Outcomes Statement for First-Year Composition." http://wpacouncil.org/aws/CWPA/pt/sd/news_article/243055 /_PARENT/layout_details/false.

Council of Writing Program Administrators. 2015. "WPA Outcomes Statement for First-Year Composition (3.0)." http://www.wpacouncil.org/positions/outcomes.html.

Department of English, Texas Tech University. n.d. "First-Year Composition." Texas Tech Department of English. Accessed April 22, 2014. www.depts.ttu.edu/english/fyc/.

Devoss, Dánielle Nicole, Heidi A. McKee, and Richard Selfe. 2009. *Technological Ecologies and Sustainability*. Computers and Composition Digital Press. Computers and Composition Digital Press. ccdigitalpress.org/book/tes/index2.html.

Dutton, William. H., and Brian D. Loader, eds. 2002. *Digital Academe: The New Media and Institutions of Higher Education and Learning*. New York: Routledge.

EDUCAUSE. n.d. "CAUSE History." https://www.educause.edu/about/mission-and -organization/our-history#.

Feenberg, Andrew. 2017. *Technosystem: the Social Life of Reason*. Cambridge, MA: Harvard University Press.

Friedman, Thomas. L. 2006. *The World Is Flat: A Brief History of the Twenty-First Century* (Updated and Expanded). New York: Farrar, Straus and Giroux.

Grama, Joanna Lyn. 2013. "A Transformative Period: Is Higher Education IT Having an Identity Crisis?" *EDUCAUSE Review Online*, June 3. er.educause.edu/articles/2013/6/a -transformative-period-is-higher-education-it-having-an-identity-crisis.

Gunner, Jeanne. 1999. "Identity and Location: A Study of WPA Models, Memberships, and Agendas." *WPA: Writing Program Administration* 22.3: 31–54. http://associationdatabase .co/archives/22n3/22n3gunner.pdf.

Harrington, Susanmarie, Rebecca Rickly, and Michael Day, eds. 2000. *The Online Writing Classroom*. New York: Hampton Press.

Heterick, Robert C. 1998. "Educom: A Retrospective," *Educom Review* 33.5 www.educause .edu/ir/library/html/erm/erm98/erm9853.html.

Hewett, Beth L., and Christa Ehmann. 2004. *Preparing Educators for Online Writing Instruction: Principles and Processes*. Urbana, IL: National Council of Teachers of English.

Hrabowski, Freeman A., John J. Suess, and John Fritz. 2011. "Assessment and Analytics in Institutional Transformation." *EDUCAUSE Review* 46.5: 15–27. er.educause.edu/arti cles/2011/9/assessment-and-analytics-in-institutional-transformation.

Jewell, Walter. 1980. "The Contribution of Academic Leadership to Academic Excellence." *WPA: Writing Program Administration* 3.3: 9–14. http://associationdatabase.co/archives /03n3/wpa03n3All.pdf.

Jones, Dennis, and Dewayne Matthews. 2002. "The Transformation of Instruction by Information Technology: Implications for State Higher Education Policy." Western

Cooperative for Educational Telecommunications. wcet.wiche.edu/sites/default/files/Transformation-of-Instruction-by-IT-White-Paper.pdf.

Leverenz, Carrie. 2008. "Remediating Writing Program Administration." *WPA: Writing Program Administration* 32.1: 37–56. http://associationdatabase.co/archives/32n1/32n1leverenz.pdf.

McKee, C. William, Mitzy Johnson, William F. Ritchie, and W. Mark Tew. 2013. "Professional Development of the Faculty: Past and Present." *New Directions for Teaching and Learning*, no. 133: 15–20. http://doi.org/10.1002/tl.20042.

McKee, Heidi A., and Dànielle Nicole DeVoss, eds. 2013. *Digital Writing: Assessment and Evaluation.* Computers and Composition Digital Press / Utah State University Press. Computers and Composition Digital Press. ccdigitalpress.org/book/dwae/.

Palmquist, Mike, Kate Kiefer, James Hartvigsen, and Barbara Goodlew. 1998. *Transitions: Teaching Writing in Computer-Supported and Traditional Classrooms.* Greenwich, CT: Ablex Publishing Corporation.

Rice, Jeff. 2007. "Cooltown—The Place of Intellectual Work." *WPA: Writing Program Administration* 30.3: 93–109. http://associationdatabase.co/archives/30n3/30n3rice.pdf.

Rodrigo, Rochelle, and Julia Romberger. 2017. "Managing Digital Technologies in Writing Programs: Writing Program Technologists and Invisible Service." *Computers and Composition* 44: 67–82. https://doi.org/10.1016/j.compcom.2017.03.003.

Selfe, Cynthia. L. 1999. Technology and Literacy: A Story About the Perils of Not Paying Attention. *College Composition and Communication* 50.3: 411–36. Accessed August 8, 2021.

Selfe, Richard. 2004. *Sustainable Computer Environments: Cultures of Support in English Studies and Language Arts.* New York: Hampton Press.

Sorcinelli, Mary Deane, Ann E. Austin, Pamela L. Eddy, and Andrea L. Beach. 2006. *Creating the Future of Faculty Development: Learning from the Past, Understanding the Present.* San Francisco: Jossey-Bass.

Tiberius, Richard G. 2002. "A Brief History of Educational Development: Implications for Teachers and Developers." *To Improve the Academy* 20.1: 20–37 https://doi.org/10.1002/j.2334-4822.2002.tb00571.x.

Warger, Thomas. A. 2006. "Supporting the Newest New Technologies on Campus." PowerPoint presented at the North East Regional Computing Program Conf., Worcester, MA. EDUCAUSE. events.educause.edu/special-topic-events/nercomp-annual-conference/2006/proceedings/supporting-the-newest-new-technologies-on-campus.

PART 3

Transforming Curriculum

In this section, authors highlight curricular initiatives and innovations that have gained traction in writing studies in the last few decades. Debates about basic writing and developmental education, linguistic diversity, multilingual writing and writers, and online writing programs that are highlighted in part 2 are explored here in detailed case studies. Chapters focus on transformative course design by highlighting our methods in practice: classrooms that use the archives, that center on linguistic diversity and World Englishes, and that use the pedagogies of online writing instruction and course design. The first three chapters in part 3 emphasize, broadly, our increasingly diverse student populations. How do we meet the needs of generation 1.5 students? What do cultural and linguistic diversity look like in our writing programs? How can World Englishes help us build a stronger curriculum for our multilingual—and monolingual—student populations, whether well-prepared international students, those who identify as refugees or immigrants, or US-educated multilingual students with a range of literacy skills across multiple languages?

We encourage readers to think about these chapters not only in terms of the students at their center but also as models for best practices: we contend that the insights offered here can improve student learning across *all* of our student populations. The student demographic is changing across institutional type; more students speak more than one language, are returning after a gap in their formal education, have dependents, work full time, have a disability, are experiencing the consequences of structural racism and poverty, and now, have been deeply impacted by the lived realities of COVID-19 in America and abroad. It's more important than ever that we build curricular approaches that are inclusive and responsive; it is equally important that our pedagogical practices meet the needs of all students and particularly those who may be marginalized in multiple ways. How might we do this? These chapters showcase how: a drill down into course design, the ways in which

https://doi.org/10.7330/9781646421428.p003

we can employ our most cutting-edge theories and methods in practice to engage diverse students. The chapters collectively leave us with some answers to a key question posed by the volume: How can in writing studies educators across institutional contexts create and sustain curriculum that serves students, navigates institutional constraints, and employs our best practices in the field?

9

PERSONAL CHOICE
Connecting Lived Experience to Academic Experience as Essential Empowerment in Basic Writing

Ruth Benander, Brenda Refaei, and Mwangi Alex Chege

Transformation of our lowest-level basic writing course arose out of a need to address the demand for developmental education reform. Researchers such as Thomas Bailey et al. (2010) and Doug Shapiro et al. (2014) reported the state of developmental education as broadly lacking in positive results. At the same time, developmental educators such as Peter Adams et al. (2009) were experimenting with accelerating developmental writing. The "TYCA White Paper on Developmental Education Reforms" was written in response to legislative initiatives to reform developmental education, and the TYCA Executive Committee was concerned that developmental education experts were not consulted about the best practices in reforming developmental reading and writing courses. They noted that not enough time and money were devoted to such large-scale programmatic changes to ensure student success. Also at issue was the definition of "success" in two-year colleges (TYCA Research Committee 2015). Graduation and retention data should not be the only data points used to assess the quality of basic writing courses.

The revision of our lowest-level reading and writing course occurred in the midst of these national trends. We developed modules to scaffold each writing assignment. Because students work through the modules at their own pace, the instructors are able to circulate around the room as students work on their literacy activities. Students documented and reflected on this work in their ePortfolios. Our college is an open-access branch campus of a research university. According to our college's Institutional Research Office, about half of our students transfer to the four-year, selective admissions colleges after obtaining their associate's degree at our campus. Other students complete technical degrees offered at our campus, such as nursing, dental hygiene, radiologic

https://doi.org/10.7330/9781646421428.c009

technology, and veterinary nursing. More than half of our students are first-generation students, nearly a quarter are African American, and nearly half of our student population is nontraditional-aged students. As a regional campus of a research university, we do not have many English language learners, and the majority of the English language learners at our college are "generation 1.5" (Harklau et al. 1999). Many students report feeling insecure about their finances, and nearly all hold jobs in addition to taking college classes.

We received both time and money to develop a pilot for our revised course design. The design was assessed through a research study of student portfolios from the redesigned course that focused on how the redesign affected the complexity of student writing. We also compared student choices of topics to the approaches of reading and topic choice in four major textbooks.

Basic writing courses at our institution have a long history. In the 1990s and early 2000s, there were three basic writing courses: Preparatory Reading and Writing I, Preparatory Reading and Writing II, and Preparatory Composition. The paired reading and writing courses were six credit hours on the quarter system to allow enough instructional time for the linked reading and writing instruction. Students were, and still are, placed into our writing courses through an in-house placement test, which consists of reading an article, summarizing the article, producing a reaction to the article, and creating a reflection on how the piece of writing turned out. These placement tests are read by faculty of the English Department, and, using a common rubric, students are placed in a writing course. Around 2011, we noticed that fewer students were placing into the Preparatory Reading and Writing I course. This was also the time at which institutions in Ohio were moving from quarters to semesters. In this move, the Preparatory Reading and Writing I course was dropped, and the Preparatory Reading and Writing II course was reduced to three credit hours and renamed Introduction to Academic Literacies. In the conversion, an attempt was made to keep reading as an essential component of the course, but some elements of reading instruction had to be removed to fit the shorter class-time. This revised course was guided by a carefully chosen textbook that asked students to read and write in response to the readings. However, all of the readings and all of the writing assignments were determined by the instructor.

Integral to our transformation of this basic writing course was incorporating student choice and promoting flexibility to accommodate a diverse student population through a culturally responsive pedagogy.

When students choose their own topics and their own readings, and use their own voices, they have greater investment in their writing. For students who are beginning to develop an academic identity, it is important to learn to analyze, synthesize, and create new knowledge in the context of topics in which they have some background and experiential knowledge. In particular, students from backgrounds radically different from their instructors are restricted when these instructors assign topics and readings, which may be foreign to the experiences and interests of students. Therefore students in basic writing courses should read and write about topics they feel connected to, which will allow them to explore and extend their developing critical reading and writing abilities. In our innovative basic writing course, we have found that students choose more complex topics and write more nuanced essays when they are in control of these choices.

EXISTING LITERATURE

Basic writing curriculum takes a variety of forms, from traditional modes-based to innovative Accelerated Learning Programs (ALPs). In identifying important threshold concepts that composition instructors need to keep in mind, Kathleen Blake Yancey (2016) writes that the variety in writers' histories, processes, and identities "is troublesome because it speaks to the complexity of composing itself and to the complexity of the task of helping students learn to compose" (53). She asserts that differentiation in writing instruction is needed. One way to achieve that differentiation is through students' choices of writing topics. Supporting student autonomy as a way to increase their engagement involves allowing students to choose their own readings and writing topics.

Students in basic writing courses often have histories that vary greatly from their instructors' experiences. Cia Verschelden (2017) examines how adverse life experiences, such as poverty and discrimination, reduce the amount of "brain bandwidth" available for students to tap into while learning. "Brain bandwidth" refers to the cognitive resources for learning. Verschelden notes that students who experience racism, sexism, or other issues need pedagogical approaches that scaffold learning to help them engage meaningfully with the learning experience. Geneva Gay (2013) advocates culturally responsive teaching involving students' own cultural understandings of how they learn as a way of making learning relevant. According to Gay, this kind of connection facilitates "students' agency, efficacy, and empowerment" (49). Students are more likely to take ownership of their writing on a topic they can relate to and have experience with compared to one that is given to them by the instructor.

In response to calls for basic writing reform (e.g., P. Adams et al. 2009), we redesigned the new semester-long course to promote greater student autonomy using an emporium model as a guide, as suggested by Twigg (2003, 2011) and elaborated in Refaei and Benander (2016). The emporium model is distinct from ALP, in that it is not paired with another college-level writing course, and from the studio model, in that it does not have additional hours attached to it.

The emporium model has been relatively well documented for developmental math studies. Twigg founded the National Center for Academic Transformation (NCAT), which identified the Emporium Model as an effective strategy for teaching college and developmental-level mathematics because it requires active student engagement. The center ("How to Redesign" 2013) identified eight elements needed to redesign math courses for them to meet their definition of Emporium Model, including course design, active learning, computer mediation, prompt assessment, personal attention, focused time on task, supervision of progress, and assessment. Research into success rates of developmental math students learning through the Emporium Model have been mixed. Susan English (2016) found that students in an Emporium Model developmental math course experienced better course success, course completion, and success in college-level courses than students in a traditionally facilitated course. In terms of student experience, Angela Boatman and Jenna Kramer (2019) report that students enjoyed the flexibility and accessibility of the Emporium Model math instruction, and students felt like they experienced fewer barriers to learning math. However, Whitney Kozakowski (2019) found that students were less likely to complete an Emporium Model math course or take following courses than students in traditional instruction courses.

In all of these realizations of the Emporium Model for math, students engage in online work with instructors to assist when they have questions. Writing courses realize the Emporium Model in a slightly different manner, since writing does not immediately lend itself to online practice in the same way that mathematics might. Barbara Roseborough (2016) reports a comparison of an Emporium Model developmental writing course and a traditional instruction course in which students performed at a similar success rate in the two courses, but those in the Emporium Model course experienced a higher level of success in the following college-level English course. However, it is not clear how much writing the students in this study did. Brenda Refaei and Ruth Benander (2016) specify that their adaptation of the Emporium Model from developmental math to developmental writing involved students researching and writing essays based on their own topic choice, with the instructor available for questions during the class session. The computer instruction, in this case, involved writing modules that prompted students through the steps of the writing process. Refaei and Benander report, while retention in the Emporium Style courses was similar to traditional instruction courses, student success in Emporium Style college-level English courses was greater.

The key element of the Emporium Model is giving students control of their learning process. Adams and McKusick (2014) discuss the importance of contextualizing a developmental writing curriculum to make it relevant and meaningful so as to motivate students, guided by the consideration: "What are the best ideas we can come up with for helping students become more successful writers and readers?" Among the topics they cover, they "emphasize how much effective writing is the result of serious thinking" (21). Allowing students to choose their own topics invites students to think critically about an issue they can relate to, or care about. Jessica Nastal (2019) writes, "Writing should mirror the curriculum it serves, and the curriculum should offer students the opportunity to develop their ideas and communicate their thinking in their own patterns and varieties of language . . . we must revise methods and develop opportunity structures 'to advance access, power, agency, affiliation, and impact for all learners'" (para. 14). Sarah Stanley (2017) discusses how giving students agency allowed Tejada, one of her students, to find her voice. She recommends teachers, "Affirm identities by opening 'tiny doors' . . . Resist predetermining the micro activity by using your privilege to decide on which sentence [in our case topic] of your students' writing are up for discussion. Instead, invite your students to be front and center directing and participating in sociocultural response" (22). We argue that students' interest in their writing and their agency of choice are important contributions to the classroom.

In addition, students with disabilities often begin their college career in basic writing courses. Michael Wehmeyer and Karrie Shogren (2016) write specifically about students with disabilities, but their observations can be insightful for all students. They observe, "Fundamentally, however, a focus on promoting self-determination has increased in importance in synchronicity with the emergence of greater civil rights protections and enhanced community and school inclusion for people with disabilities" (561). In the principles of Universal Design for Learning, if we make writing accessible for everyone by helping students make connections between their lived experience and their academic experience, regardless of specific ability, everyone benefits. Allowing students to choose topics related to their experiences gives them the opportunity to bring into their writing "prior experiences" and "frames of reference." Allison Harper Hitt (2015) writes about how writing instructors need to move from thinking about helping students overcome deficits to thinking about how to work with students to create learning experiences accessible to their personal circumstances. Wood (2017) contributes to the discussion of accessibility by pointing out that concepts of time, or how long different parts of the writing process take, also need to be examined so that all students can find appropriate approaches for their writing needs.

Some scholars in the field of composition have also addressed the connection between choice, and students' self-efficacy, motivation, and success (Blake et al. 2016; MacArthur et al. 2016; Sullivan 2011). In examining the specific role of interest on reading, writing, and learning, Suzanne Hidi (2001) notes that learners "who have individual interests in activities or topics focus their attention, persist for longer periods of time and enjoy their engagements more, are more likely to use strategic processing and tend to learn and write better than those without such interests" (202–3). Hidi suggests that when students are engaged in their topics, they do write better.

In basic writing, there may be a reluctance to allow students much autonomy by instructors who may not have confidence that students will make good choices. Tracie Barber and Victoria Timchenko (2011) commented that instructors were highly concerned about increased workload in allowing students to choose their own topics, but they report that offering the choice enhanced not only student engagement, but also faculty engagement in the assessment process. Generally, these studies suggest that the "supported autonomy" approach may be the most effective strategy for students to feel motivated to learn.

WRITING TOPICS IN BASIC WRITING TEXTBOOKS

Textbooks often guide curriculum in basic writing. We examined four textbooks by major textbook publishers for basic writing to explore the complexity and diversity of writing topics students could encounter. Three books take a modes-based approach, while the fourth uses a thematic approach. Two of the modes-based books focus exclusively on paragraph writing and grammar exercises. The two other books ask students to write slightly longer essays on assigned topics such as to tell a

Table 9.1. Analysis of approach, focus, and purpose of readings in basic writing textbooks

Textbook Title	Approach	Focus	Purpose of Provided Readings	Final Assignment
Laurie Kirszner and Steven Mandell, *Focus on Writing: Paragraphs and Essays*	Modes	Paragraphs and grammar	Readings model the mode, not connected to writing prompts	Personal reflection; assigned topic
K. Flachmann, *Mosaics: Reading and Writing Essays*	Modes	Short essays	Readings model the mode, not connected to writing prompts	Source based paper; choice of topic
W. Royce Adams, *Viewpoints: Readings Worth Thinking and Writing About*, 7th ed.	Themes	Paragraphs and grammar	Readings are analyzed for structure; last assignment connected to writing prompt	Source based paper; assigned topic
Bob Brannan, *A Writer's Workshop: Crafting Paragraphs, Building Essays*, 3rd ed.	Modes	Short essays	Modeling the mode, not connected to writing prompts	Source based paper; choice of topic

story about their lives that has changed how they view themselves. These four books end with chapters on research writing in which students choose a research topic and are advised to use three to five sources. Our analysis is presented in table 9.1.

The four textbooks vary in the amount and type of texts students are exposed to. In the most basic paragraph modes texts, students are given models of student-generated texts. For instance, one textbook uses a conservation theme for the writing assignments. In one chapter the assignments include topics such as "Stores should only sell energy-efficient light bulbs," or "A large local company (or your college) should encourage carpooling to help reduce emissions." The writing assignments do not require students to interact with texts in their writing. The other two modes-based books introduce persuasive/argument writing that ask students to identify a debatable topic and to identify any texts that may have contributed to students' thinking about the topic. The fourth book provides a thematic approach that asks students to read texts about topics like cross-cultural communication. Students then choose a text and topic from the book to use as the basis for the essay.

Placement of the research assignments as the last chapter means that if faculty follow the order of the books, students may never engage in the research writing chapters, depending on how long it takes any given course to work through the chapters. Although students in basic writing courses do have problems with editing and paragraphing, they also need to learn how to write from texts in order to succeed in the writing activities commonly found in first-year composition. To acquire this skill, students need the opportunity to practice the reading activities writers use when writing from sources. In the basic writing classroom, instructors should be able to help students with the reading practices they will need to write from sources.

TRANSFORMATION OF A BASIC WRITING COURSE FOR STUDENT CHOICE

Implementing choice of topics and readings in our redesigned developmental writing course facilitated the flexibility that allowed students to choose the next course they would attend and how they would create a portfolio to demonstrate their competencies. In this way, choice is incorporated into the course in two ways. First, students choose whether they want to go directly to first-year composition or to the next level of developmental writing. Students develop a portfolio of their work to demonstrate their readiness for the next course they are aiming for. This flexibility in preparing their portfolios is so important in terms of breaking through the limitations of standard academic English and recognizing the various competencies and literacies of all of our students. Members of the department who teach developmental courses and first-year composition assess the portfolios.

The portfolio assessment is based on rubrics derived from the learning outcomes of each course. For example, one of the learning outcomes students must master in order to progress to the next course is incorporating ideas from readings to support a thesis. In the portfolio assessment, the assessor looks at the body of work represented in the portfolio to see the progression of the students' mastery of making connections between the texts they read and their essay theses. Another course learning outcome is reflection. The portfolio is an excellent way for students to document their development as reflective writers from their initial reflections at the beginning of the course to their final course reflections.

This transformation of the course also changed the way we taught the course. We developed a series of modules in our learning management system (LMS). In each module, students read the writing assignment prompt and find an article or articles they want to write about. They complete a reading log in which they summarize the article, analyze the article, and reflect on their reading strategies. Students then use the reading log to complete an outline to help them organize their ideas. They paste the outline onto an ePortfolio page to develop their draft. This draft is peer reviewed and teacher reviewed before students complete the final draft. The process below illustrates how reading logs, outlines, and drafts progress in an essay's development.

1. Annotate an article.
2. Write a Reading Log (summary, insights, citation).
3. Paste the annotations into an outline.
4. Paste the outline into a draft.
5. Edit the draft.

This process of having students choose their writing topics and readings allows instructors to work individually with students on their unique needs. Each class session begins with a check-in with students. As students work, the instructor circulates the room engaging in miniconferences to address questions, issues, and concerns. Instructors are able to provide this individualized instruction due to the low course capacity of fifteen students. Unlike a traditional classroom, students drive the direction of their learning during each class.

To guide students' academic reading and writing development, the essay prompts encourage students to respond with increasing complexity over the course of the semester. Essay 1 asks students to respond to a reading, linking their personal experience to that of the author's experience. Essay 2 asks students to choose two articles on the same topic, explain how each article offers a different perspective on the topic, and conclude with a synthesis of the two perspectives. Essay 3 asks students to identify a problem, find two to three sources that deal with the problem, and offer a solution to that problem taking multiple perspectives into account. Essay 4 asks students to make an assertion about a topic that is controversial, find sources offering the points of view of different stakeholders involved in the controversy, and make a recommendation of what should be done to address the needs of all stakeholders. Each writing assignment has an associated rubric that outlines what a student needs to do to develop an assignment appropriate for acceptance into first-year composition or to the next level of basic writing.

STUDENT PERFORMANCE

In spring 2015, we redesigned our lowest level basic writing course to allow students to choose the topics and readings used in their essays. These essays are curated in ePortfolios, which include students' reflective writing and process writing. To investigate how the element of choice has increased the complexity of student writing in this Institutional Review Board–approved study, we analyzed the topics and textual references in students' work. We compared the complexity and diversity of student-nominated topics with those recommended for basic writers in four basic writing textbooks offered by four different publishing companies.

We looked at the portfolios of thirty students. Each student portfolio contained four essays, completed over one semester. For this study, we did not analyze the first essay because it is teacher directed. We assign the reading and writing topic, so we can work with students on the reading, writing, and technology processes they will use in the course. There are four readings in this unit, and students can choose any of the four so we are able to begin the course with some choice for students. In this analysis, we looked at essays 2, 3, and 4, for a total of ninety essays. We recorded the topics of each essay and the works cited for each essay. We then completed a descriptive analysis of the student topics. For the sources students cited, we analyzed them according to three types of genre: websites, popular news magazines, and scholarly journals.

Student Choice of Writing Topics

In an analysis of the second, third, and fourth essays students wrote, the most common topics covered social issues, such as the role of father figures in child development, the legal challenges of obtaining child support, and the racist history of blackface. The secondmost popular topic covered scientific issues, such as overfishing, the health implications of breastfeeding, and the controversy over mandatory HIV testing. Other topics included climate, predominantly hurricanes, immigration, current politicians, and exploration of specific careers (see figure 9.1).

Figure 9.1 shows the variety of topics that students chose over the semester. Students were able to choose the topics and articles they were interested in exploring. This choice led to a wider variety of topics than can be covered in a textbook. In our analysis of basic writing textbooks (see table 9.2), the writing assignments provided such prompts as "describe your favorite meal, choose a controversial issue, discuss your encounters with nature, or read *The US Expatriate Handbook Guide to Living and Working Abroad.* Write an essay summarizing what you read and what you learned about cross-cultural differences." The topics suggested by the textbooks do not engage students in the type of reading and writing activities they will need for their first-year composition course at our college. Samples of writing prompts from these textbooks are presented in table 9.2.

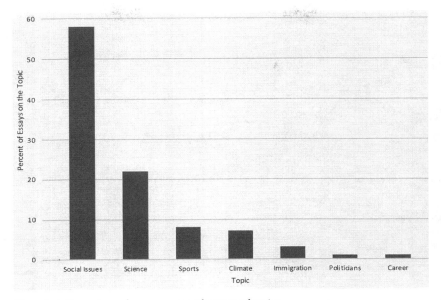

Figure 9.1. Percentage of essays on specific types of topics.

In self-determination theory, the three principle elements of competence, autonomy, and relatedness are all addressed in the students' choices of their writing topics. Students have the autonomy of choosing their topics, supported by their previous knowledge so that they feel a certain competence to become involved in the topic, and the topics are of current importance to them so that they feel the relevance of learning more about these issues. In this basic writing course, students chose a variety of topics related to their interests that allowed them to freely demonstrate their personal abilities to analyze and develop writing topics.

Student Choice of Sources to Support Their Writing Topics

Analysis of the sources that students used to support their second, third, and fourth essays shows they chose a diverse range of sources. As reflected in figure 9.2 below, the most referenced type of source is topic-oriented websites, such as *Science News for Students*, *Web MD*, the *Conversation*, and *Justice.com*. The second most commonly cited type of source is news sites that cover current events in real time, such as *CNN*, the *Guardian*, the *Washington Post*, and the *New York Times*. Third is magazine sites with extended text that provides a deeper dive into

Table 9.2. Sample writing prompts from the beginning, middle, and end of selected basic writing textbooks

Textbook Title	Sample First Assignment	Sample Midpoint Assignment	Sample Final Assignment
Kirszner and Mandell, *Focus on Writing: Paragraphs and Essays*	p. 33 "Should community service—unpaid work in the community—be a required part of the college curriculum?"	p. 253 "An unusual recipe How to find an apartment Applying for a job A religious ritual or cultural ceremony A complicated task you do at work A do-it-yourself project that didn't get done"	Units 4, 5, 6, and 7 focus on sentences and grammar. p. 459 "Working in a group of four students, list ten nouns (five singular and five plural)—people, places, or things—along the left-hand side of the paper."
Flachmann, *Mosaics: Reading and Writing Essays*	p. 131 "What direct encounters have you had with nature? What are some of the details of these encounters? Was your general impression of these encounters positive or negative?"	p. 381 "Choose a controversial issue on your campus or in the news that interests you. Write an essay that presents your opinion on this issue."	pp. 419–88 "The assignment is spread out over several pages in chapter 21, pp. 453–65 and is implied in the process directions: Choose a subject, write a thesis statement, find sources to support your thesis."
Adams, *Viewpoints: Readings Worth Thinking and Writing About*, 8th ed.	p. 33 "In your journal, re-read your objective summary of Pete Hamill's essay, 'The Wet Drug.' Now write your subjective reaction to his essay."	p.190 Pursuing Possible Essay Topics: "Go online and read more from another chapter in The US Expatriate Handbook Guide to living and working Abroad. Write an essay summarizing what you read and what you learned about cross-cultural differences."	p. 429 Pursuing Possible Essay Topics: "Pick one of the essays on nuclear power and write an argument against the author's viewpoint. Show the fallacies . . . in the argument. Or, agree with one of the authors, but provide your own arguments."
Brannan, *A Writer's Workshop: Crafting Paragraphs, Building Essays*, 3rd ed.	p. 22: "Tell a story about some event in your life that you remember well and that has affected your view of yourself, another person, or the larger world."	p. 386: "In this assignment, you will tackle an issue (a debatable topic), taking a clear position and defending it in an essay of 500 to 600 words."	p. 443: "This assignment asks you to choose a topic and develop an essay of about three pages that uses information you find in books, magazines, and newspapers and on the Internet to support your thesis."
Sample Student Self-Selected Topics	Contrasting their experience with an article: chronic traumatic encephalopathy, does capitalism cause poverty?, and English as an official language in the United States.	Synthesizing three perspectives: ethics in accounting; race, biology, and culture; and how technology changes sports.	Argument: emotional contagion, the importance of father figures for young men, and nihilism versus Christianity.

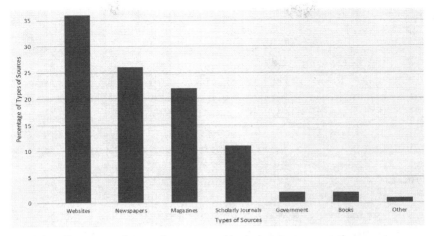

Figure 9.2. Percentage of types of sources used in students' essays over the semester.

current topics, such as *Time, Huffington Post,* the *Atlantic,* and *Scientific American.* For the purposes of this study, sources were classified into the three categories using the following criteria: websites are topic oriented, newspapers cover current events in real time, and magazines cover current topics in more depth. Students also cited scholarly sources even though it was not a requirement, such as *Philosophy of Science, Family Law Quarterly, Journal of the American Medical Association,* and *Journal of Ethnic and Migration Studies.* Some students also used government sources, mostly the Center for Disease Control (CDC) and the World Health Organization.

In addition to using a diverse range of sources, the analysis shows, the number of sources increased as students progressed from essay to essay. For instance, a total of 71 sources were used in the second essay, 73 in the third essay, and 98 in the fourth essay. The complexity of sources also increased as students progressed, as demonstrated in the students' use of scholarly sources and books. Three scholarly sources were used in the second essay, 11 in the third essay, and 13 in the fourth essay. Similarly, two books were used in the second essay and three in the fourth essay.

CONCLUSION

Based on research findings in multiple disciplines, we believe that offering choice is culturally responsive teaching for all students that addresses their need for competence, autonomy, and relatedness. Currently, basic writing textbooks do not seem to support student choice of topics and may actually offer topics that do not allow students to demonstrate their real abilities. In addition, some basic writing textbooks may not connect readings to writing prompts such that the skill of reading for writing is not clearly connected.

Given the diverse populations that are represented in basic writing courses, Jaqueline Rodriguez and Stacey Hardin (2017) suggest that culturally responsive teaching can guide our choices to "teach our students how to capitalize on their experiences, their backgrounds, their cultural knowledge, their will and their grit to be purposeful in making decisions about their future" (101). We find that when given choice, students will select complex topics and readings appropriate for their personal level and directly applicable to their writing. As students gain fluency in reading and writing, the readings and essays become more complex over time.

Admittedly, this approach to basic writing can be challenging to apply. For example, the teacher must be able to scan readings quickly in order to be able to guide a student in appropriately identifying the main idea. Also, the teacher must be able to think quickly and explain key concepts on the spot, tailored to a given student's understanding. Another challenge involves giving up teacherly control and trusting the students to embrace the power of their choice. It is true that this type of teaching is energy intensive, and students may actually be resistant to making choices. However, we find that these two hurdles are not so high. The students' increased engagement makes it easier for the instructor to talk about topics of interest. We find that it is easy to trust the students to choose readings appropriate for their own level, since their interest in a topic seems to draw them to readings that are appropriate and often challenging. The final portfolios these novice academic writers create are interesting, often insightful, and appropriately challenging for their level. Our advice is to trust yourself as a teacher, and trust your students as readers and writers to choose well.

REFERENCES

Adams, Peter, Sarah Gearhart, Robert Miller, and Anne Roberts. 2009. "The Accelerated Learning Program: Throwing Open the Gates." *Journal of Basic Writing* 28.2: 50–69. https://files.eric.ed.gov/fulltext/EJ877255.pdf.

Adams, Peter, and Donna McKusick. 2014. "Steps and Missteps: Redesigning, Piloting, and Scaling a Developmental Writing Program." *New Directions for Community Colleges* 167: 15–25. https://doi-org.uc.idm.oclc.org/10.1002/cc.20107.

Adams, W. Royce. 2013. *Viewpoints: Readings Worth Thinking and Writing About.* 8th ed. Boston: Cengage Learning.

Bailey, Thomas, Dong Wook Jeong, and Sung-Woo Cho. 2010. "Referral, Enrollment, and Completion in Developmental Education Sequences in Community Colleges." *Economics of Education Review* 29.2: 255–70. https://ccrc.tc.columbia.edu/publications /referral-enrollment-completion-developmental-education.html.

Barber, Tracie, and Victoria Timchenko. 2011. "Student-Specific Projects for Greater Engagement in a Computational Fluid Dynamics Course." *Australasian Journal of Engineering Education* 17.2: 129–37. https://doi.org/10.1080/22054952.2011.11464055.

Blake, Michelle F., Charles A. MacArthur, Shannon Mrkich, Zoi A. Philippakos, and Ilknur Sancak-Marusa. 2016. "Self-Regulated Strategy Instruction in Developmental Writing Courses: How to Help Basic Writers Become Independent Writers." *Teaching English in the Two Year College* 44.2: 58–175.

Boatman, Angela, and Jenna Kramer. 2019. "Content and Connections: Students' Responses to a Hybrid Emporium Instructional Model in Developmental Mathematics." Center for the Analysis of Post-secondary Readiness. CAPR working paper.

Brannan, Bob. 2010. *A Writer's Workshop: Crafting Paragraphs, Building Essays.* 8th ed. New York: McGraw Hill Education.

English, Susan. 2016. "A Comparison of Students' Success in Emporium Model Developmental Mathematics Courses versus Traditional Developmental Mathematics Courses." PhD diss., Morgan State University. ProQuest (10188539). https://mdsoar.org/han dle/11603/9928.

Flachmann, K. 2018. *Mosaics: Reading and Writing Essays.* Boston: Pearson.

Gay, Geneva. 2013. "Teaching to and through Cultural Diversity." *Curriculum Inquiry* 43.1: 48–70. https://doi.org/10.1111/curi.12002.

Harklau, Linda, Kay M. Losey, and Meryl Siegal. 1999. *Generation 1.5 Meets College Composition: Issues in the Teaching of Writing to U.S. Educated Learners of ESL.* Mahweh, NJ: Lawrence Erlbaum Associates.

Hidi, Suzanne. 2001. "Interest, Reading, and Learning: Theoretical and Practical Considerations." *Educational Psychology Review,* 13.3: 191–209. https://doi.org/10.1023/A: 1016667621114.

Hitt, Allison Harper. 2015. "From Accommodations to Accessibility: How Rhetorics of Overcoming Manifest in Writing Pedagogies." PhD diss., Syracuse University.

"How to Redesign a College-Level or Developmental Math Course Using the Emporium Model." 2013. The National Center for Academic Transformation. (2013). https:// www.thencat.org/Guides/Math/TOC.html.

Kirszner, Laurie G., and Steven Mandell. 2010. *Focus on Writing: Paragraphs and Essays.* New York: Bedford / St. Martin, 2010.

Kozakowski, Whitney. 2019. "Moving the Classroom to the Computer Lab: Can Online Learning with In-Person Support Improve Outcomes in Community Colleges?" *Economics of Education Review* 70 (June): 159–72.

MacArthur, Charles A., Zoi A. Philippakos, and Steve Graham. 2016. "A Multicomponent Measure of Writing Motivation with Basic College Writers." *Learning Disability Quarterly* 39.1: 31–43. https://doi.org/10.1177/0731948715583115.

Nastal, Jessica. 2019. "Beyond Tradition: Writing Placement, Fairness, and Success at a Two-Year College." *The Journal of Writing Assessment* 12.1. https://journalofwritingassessment .org/article.php?article=136.

Refaei, Brenda, and Ruth Benander. 2016. "Using an Emporium Model in an Introduction to Academic Literacies Course." *Basic Writing eJournal* 14.1. https://bwe.ccny.cuny .edu/Refaei%20&%20Benander%20.pdf.

Rodriguez, Jaqueline, and Stacey Hardin. 2017. "Culturally Responsive Teaching to Support All Learners." *What Really Works with Exceptional Learners,* edited by Wendy Murawski and Kathy Lynn Scott, 100–116. Thousand Oaks, CA: Corwin.

Roseborough, Barbara. 2016. "A Comparative Study of Two Instructional Models in Developmental Education Writing Programs." PhD diss., Walden University, Minneapolis, MN.

Shapiro, Doug, Afet Dundar, Xin Yuan, Autumn T. Harrell, and Phoebe Khasiala Wakhungu. 2014. *Completing College: A National View of Student Attainment Rates—Fall 2008 Cohort* (Signature Report No. 8). Herndon, VA: National Student Clearinghouse Research Center. Accessed August 10, 2021. https://files.eric.ed.gov/fulltext/ED556471.pdf.

Stanley, Sarah. 2017. "From a Whisper to a Voice: Sociocultural Style and Anti-racist Pedagogy." *Journal of Basic Writing* 36.2: 5–25.

Sullivan, Patrick. 2011. "'A Lifelong Aversion to Writing': What If Writing Courses Emphasized Motivation?" *Teaching English in the Two Year College* 39.2: 118–40.

Twigg, Carol A. 2003. "Improving Learning and Reducing Costs: New Models for Online Learning." *EDUCAUSE Review* 38.5: 28–38.

Twigg, Carol A. 2011. "The Math Emporium: Higher Education's Silver Bullet." *Change: The Magazine of Higher Learning* 43.3: 25–34.

TYCA Research Committee. 2015. "TYCA White Paper on Developmental Education Reforms." *Teaching English in the Two-Year College* 42.3: 227–43.

Verschelden, Cia. 2017. *Bandwidth Recovery: Helping Students Reclaim Cognitive Resources Lost to Poverty, Racism, and Social Marginalization.* Sterling, VA: Stylus.

Wehmeyer, Michael, and Karrie Shogren. 2016. "Self-Determination and Choice." *Handbook of Evidence-Based Practices in Intellectual and Developmental Disabilities,* edited by Nirbhay Singh, 561–84. Augusta, GA: Springer. https://link.springer.com/content/pdf/10.1007%2F978-3-319-26583-4.pdf.

Wood, Tara. 2017. "Cripping Time in the College Composition Classroom." *College Composition and Communication* 69.2: 260–86. https://prod-ncte-cdn.azureedge.net/nctefiles/resources/journals/ccc/0692-dec2017/ccc0692cripping.pdf.

Yancey, Kathleen Blake. 2016. "Writers' Histories, Processes, and Identities Vary." In *Naming What We Know: Threshold Concepts of Writing Studies Classroom Edition,* edited by Linda Adler-Kassner and Elizabeth Wardle, 52–53. Logan: Utah University Press.

10

LEVERAGING THE TRANSLANGUAGING LABOR OF A MULTILINGUAL UNIVERSITY
SJSU's Transformation to a Postremedial Writing Community

Cynthia M. Baer

Under the utopian aegis of consensus, students can learn to agree to disagree, not because "everyone has their own opinion," but because justice demands that we recognize the inexhaustibility of difference and that we organize the conditions in which we live and work accordingly.

—*John Trimbur (1989)*

This chapter takes shape somewhere between case study and prospectus. It does not, in other words, narrate a program transformed, but one transforming. Its transformation is systematic, transactional: as a leader and participant, I both change it and am changed by it. And it is historical: the program drives and is driven by deeper cycles of institutional learning locally and nationally in higher education. The current "crisis in higher education," whether real or, as Linda Adler-Kassner (2017) suggests, rhetorical, is a response to changing demographics that we have too long resisted (319–23). Our demographics, not just administrative reports on higher education, both demand and afford the change, the learning, to which we are called.

As part of the California state system of comprehensive, public universities, my campus's mission is to leverage our state's diversity as we build new norms and values for inclusive twenty-first-century multilingual learning. Critical to success is our dismantling the remediation programs and policies that have enforced the traditionally closed language borders of higher education. In 2014, we implemented a Stretch English program, which extends the traditional one-semester college writing course into a two-semester course. This "stretched curriculum"

https://doi.org/10.7330/9781646421428.c010

offers added time and support that some students need as they transfer high school experiences into the university classroom (Glau 2007). The cohorted and mainstreamed Stretch classrooms move us beyond the logic of remediation to redistribute the labor of the translanguaging required for an inclusive, equitable, and sustainable multilingual learning community.

Everyday languaging calls us to speak and listen, to write and read, across language difference, or the differences we embody in language. We adjust to anomalies in the moment: we translate, transform, negotiate. That is, as communicative agents, we actively process perceived "error" and confusion in the shared target language to stabilize communication. As Min Zhan Lu and Bruce Horner (2011) explain, "meaning is necessarily always the product of translation across difference" (4). This languaging activity is no different in higher education; we do it all the time, as do our students. At stake in our current transformation is the way higher education has distributed this labor, absorbed it into its system of mastery, of exclusivity. We have traditionally tested novices on entry to identify deviations from a stipulated norm, and we have remediated difference to reduce inefficiencies, whether these be measured as student learning and success, as professor workload, or as instructional resources.

Only now, forty years into an age of increased migrations, is my campus rethinking this labor. San José State University (SJSU) is one of the most ethnically diverse campuses nationwide; our student population is 41 percent Asian, 27 percent Hispanic, 17 percent white; 3 percent Black, >1 percent Pacific Islander or Native American; and almost 10 percent identify as Other (SJSU 2017). Represented in these data is a globe of languages. Appendix 10.A details the geography of our learning system. Given our demographics, translanguaging is inevitably a mechanism of our learning. It has become a conscious practice for those of us working the Stretch. As Stretch mainstreams our classrooms, it disrupts the institutionalized remediations that have kept us from the work of translanguaging, exposing a historical resistance to the learning our multilingualism calls and commits us to.

Five years into our transition out of remediation, I appreciate how, on a globalizing planet, these same demographic shifts have been and are reshaping academic campuses and lives beyond my own. They drive the sense of "crisis" that Adler-Kassner (2017) asks us to seize as a disciplinary opportunity—the practice that Horner, Lu, and other second language theorists and practitioners call us to engage equitably, defining "translanguaging" as a disposition to difference (Horner et al. 2011).

The case I describe is thus relevant within higher education across the United States, not just in California, because the lessons of those who teach and learn on our campus in San José, California, are the lessons of our collective future together in higher education. Especially in a political climate of intensified and intensely contested migrations, the case now unfolding at SJSU feels timely beyond my own thirty-seven-year history and experience at one campus. Indeed, as I speak to colleagues and students about our future at SJSU, it is our capacity to become a beacon for dialogue across cultures and languages that stands out: If SJSU can leverage our internal dissensus to transform diversity into learning, what work might we do to develop public consensus for a working, thriving democracy?

THE HISTORY OF OUR DISSENSUS AND THE LABOR OF READABILITY

In 2011, the same year that second language (L2) compositionists called us all to the values and practice of translanguaging (Horner et al. 2011), external reviewers called SJSU faculty to a renewed practice and study of writing, one informed by the last fifty years of "research into writing practices and writing development generated in the field of composition and rhetoric" (Adler-Kassner and Anson 2011, 8). Perhaps because they converged in my own history, I see these two calls as inherently related, but, in fact, SJSU's experience is reflective of—and illuminating for—national considerations of the same set of issues around multilingualism, writing pedagogy, "treating" error, and teaching labor. Our local response to difference came out of the same forum of university languaging that had directed writing studies nationally, distributing writing studies across several increasingly siloed university disciplines and departments: linguistics, rhetoric, and literature. Wherever first-year composition retained its original Harvardian belles lettres response to language difference, writing instruction was, in those same fifty years, remediated in successive attempts to accommodate in the learning system remedial writers, developmental writers, basic writers.

On our campus, by 1987, the disciplinary split into linguistics and literature had literally fractured entry-level writing: When linguistics split off into its own department, Linguistics and Language Development (LLD), it took the remedial composition courses (LLD 1 and LLD2) with it. The Department of English continued to host unchallenged a traditional belles lettres freshman writing program (English 1A). This fragmentation institutionalized opposing disciplinary responses to difference, leaving in place as the dominant value the emphasis on student "error" rather than the negotiations of uptake between writer and reader. Institutionalized into departmental structures and balkanized as competitors in a college budget, by 2011, "discussions about the possible consolidation of programs . . . introduced a certain degree of territorializing and wagon-circling that also threaten[ed] to block a much-needed openness to change" (Adler-Kassner and Anson 2011, 5).

Our siloed writing programs left unchallenged "the concerns expressed by faculty at all levels about the 'underdeveloped' nature of students' writing abilities as they move through the curriculum" (Adler-Kassner and Anson 2011, 9). This campus-wide concern, read in the context of current L2 composition theory and practice, is an instance of collective, institutionalized uptake—or failure of uptake. Four years into our Stretch, I read this failure, not as the neglect of a fifty-year history of writing studies, but as the product of a fifty-year history of basic writing and remediation that runs alongside the history of scholarship that has urged us away from it, to a new disposition to reading, receiving difference. Sheltering students from the demands of normativity also shelters faculty from the need to redefine norms.

As Paul Kei Matsuda (2006) explains, containment programs stifle faculty learning by sheltering them from the dissensus otherwise natural to a multilingual learning system (638). In Horner and Lu's terms, such programs "take as the norm a linguistically homogeneous situation: one where writers, speakers, and readers are expected to use Standard English or Edited American English—imagined ideally as uniform—to the exclusion of other languages and language variations" (Horner et al. 2011, 303). I would go further: such programs police the norm of homogeneity through the practice of containment; containment both enforces the norm among new members and reinforces the norm among already established members. Systematically, it diminishes both writing and reading-writing agency for both students and faculty. In spring of 2014, as we geared up to pilot Stretch on my campus, I began to work across the aisle with the Academic English (AE) coordinator and the coordinator of the Language Development Center (LDC), which provided the two-unit support course for AE students in the lowest bands of tested English proficiency. My insight into just how deeply and rigidly "contained" we all were began here. Invited to sit in on a tutor meeting at the LDC, I witnessed firsthand the odd twist of remediation's logic: I found linguistics graduate students training to position themselves as sympathetic readers, nonetheless enforcing norms to police the line between standard and nonstandard English. They did this, they explained, so that students might "pass" in the normalized community once advanced. Left unchallenged was normativity itself. This is not homogeneity imagined; it is homogeneity policed through a collective agreement to "treat error."

Student and faculty labor in freshman composition have long been organized and trained to "treat" error "as an isolated item on a page" rather than a "flawed verbal transaction between a writer and a reader" (Williams 1981, 153). Even if we recognize the need to change this labor, we will no doubt still hear the perennial cry against students' failure to learn—"Why can't my students write?"—from colleagues as we walk across our campuses (Adler-Kassner 2017, 317). Adler-Kassner spends several pages outlining the story of an Educational Intelligence Complex and its diminished "just writing," whose narratives of the crisis of education organize around just such laments (319–26). Kassner's "Why can't my students write?" is an anecdotal version of studies Dana Ferris (2011) cites to offer the rationale for the treatment of error: Ferris notes, "accuracy matters outside of writing class" where "in some settings university professors and employers find language errors in writing distracting and stigmatizing" (14).

At the heart of this translation of reader distraction into writer stigma is a battle about workload. In professional development workshops across our campus, faculty lament the time it takes to read students' "unedited" work. But the remediation approach to readability workload not only "assume[s] that heterogeneity in language impedes communication and meaning," but also ensures that it does so, precisely because faculty trained to normative standards are never challenged to read beyond those norms and thus continue to stigmatize based on their own distraction (Horner et al. 2011, 303). Perpetuating "the myth of linguistic homogeneity" shifts the burden of translanguaging onto the "second-language writers who do not fit the dominant image of college students" and the instructors and tutors tasked to normalize them (Matsuda 2006, 638). Stretch English "problematize[s the] long-term implication" of this distribution of the languaging workload, and reorganizes that labor.

The lesson of the mainstreamed Stretch classrooms is clear: if translanguaging is a natural linguistic activity that allows for fluent transaction in everyday speech and text, remediation has been an academic intervention to contain the difference (at its perceived source) and thereby increase communication efficiency (readability) for listeners and readers already expert in the target language of the community. It is a labor policy—and one that has been anything but efficient.

On our campus the labor of translanguaging is measured in units spent to earn credit for the first of three general education requirements

in writing. Two tables in appendix 10.B demonstrate the unit savings that
Stretch English provides. Table 10.3 outlines how, on the remedial pathway, students could spend anywhere from 6 to 11 units to meet one 3-unit
requirement. The extra 3 to 8 units signify labor that students designated
"remedial" were enjoined to perform to ease the burden of readability for
a faculty hired but not trained to teach them. Those who did not meet the
locally established cut scores for college writing "eligibility" were required
to complete prebaccalaureate remedial courses. Predictably, the timed,
high-stakes tests directed L2 learners into high-unit pathways more often
than L1 learners; thus reinforced, test-based containment ensured continued need for remediation. These tests, which purport to measure student
ability, do not account for reader uptake; the expertise of the Educational
Testing Service (ETS) readers trained to the holistic reading was never
in question at SJSU. One of the strongest arguments for Stretch, among
both faculty and administrators in either of the writing programs, was not
only the pedagogical innovation it promised, but the relief of students
burdened in unit hours with the labor of translanguaging.

Interestingly, statewide demands for a more inclusive labor force are in
fact creating the economic demand for the pedagogical inclusiveness we
now pursue. It took a statewide call for increased production of college-
trained workforce to pressure the Chancellor's Office to address graduation rates and streamline general education—a "crisis" whether real or
rhetorical, nonetheless functional in this case—and to create a demand
for change from above the two departments with their siloed remedial
and first-year writing programs. Our new dean was eager to reorganize
the labor of remediation that was taking its toll on the college's budget.
In other words, Stretch gained administrative traction by making good
economic sense; it streamlined labor and reduced time to degree. Rather
than undermining writing pedagogy on our campus, as we so often fear
administrative reorganizations will do, the Stretch English reorganization
has (as its first proponents argued it would) helped us to recover a uni-
fied writing program from its historical division between two departments
and to put in place a curriculum that is innovating writing pedagogy on
our campus by teaching us all to stretch our translanguaging potential,
and to reap the administrative efficiencies in the process.

Using a "reflective rhetorical" model of self-placement, a student
now opts in to spend an extra three units on their learning (Leaker and
Ostman 2016). (See table 10.4 in appendix 10.B.) Acknowledging the
need for added support to meet the requirement, the state funds the
choice. As a result, our classrooms are now broadly heterogenous—a
mix of language histories and experiences, a range of tested expertise.

Five years later, with the new learning system in place, these same students are succeeding at rates commensurate with their peers. Students are learning to speak through difference; their instructors are learning to listen across language difference and to host difference in their multilingual classrooms.

One instance common to first-year writing may suffice: teaching the practices of annotation as a critical reading engagement for research. A common practice for such lesson would be to have students read something like Mortimer J. Adler's classic article "How to Mark a Book" (1940) and then individually practice what they have read. In a classroom designed to stretch the translanguaging capacity among all learners, this same assignment becomes a shared investigation into how we make—and mark—meaning as we read. For such an exercise, an instructor directs students to read individually Adler's essay, using whatever reading process and practice they normally use to keep track of what he is telling us about how we can use texts to make meaning. They are prompted to read the text purposefully, keeping an eye out for ideas that confirm, extend, or challenge their current reading practice. When students then convene to share what each has gleaned from the text, the instructor prompts them to share two things: the ideas they got from their reading, and the marks they made (or not) as they read. Exploring together how we read, students will necessarily share and discover varied practices. This peer-to-peer learning is critical to the purpose of probing current norms and practices while continuing to extend them by leveraging the differences among the group. A classroom thus designed to emphasize reciprocal learning engages and makes explicit the translanguaging students engage together. A follow-up discussion facilitated by the instructor can surface for the whole class a rich sharing of what they learned from the text and from each other—not only about annotation but also about the way we learn for ourselves and from each other.

In a multilingual classroom designed as a space where learning is transacted across difference, language difference itself becomes a critical component of natural transactional processes. Through each learning transaction, an instructor and their students are afforded equally the opportunity to practice listening across differences, cultural and linguistic (Jordan 2012, 122–23). Reflection (by individual learners and among the class) can surface the struggle, negotiation, improvisation, adaptation that define any one classroom languaging and learning event. The classroom is a functional space for multilingualism to flourish—and for students to flourish in it.

Thus situating students and faculty as collaborative researchers in a common inquiry is more than a curriculum; it is a curricular *stance* that enacts a specific disposition to difference. This stance acknowledges classrooms as functional university learning spaces, but activates reciprocal, reflective learning by leveraging all learners and modes of learning among the cohort. With the added time of Stretch English and a receptive, scaffolded support for their learning among their learning cohort, all students are able to enter college writing classrooms and thrive: 92 percent of all our students complete their first writing requirement in their first year. (Appendix 10.B includes success data for the last seven years in figure 10.1.)

STRUCTURING THE LABOR OF TRANSLANGUAGING THROUGH A PROGRAMMATIC CURRICULUM

The streamlined progress to degree that Stretch English affords our students is not just an economic expediency. If the history of our dissensus had produced an ever-proliferating increase of labor to satisfy faculty and professional demands for normativity, the history of our Stretch out of remediated writing has redistributed that labor by positioning us all, students and faculty, as co-learners within a multilingual learning system to disrupt the myth of homogeneity. The curriculum structures this redistribution of labor. Faculty and students engage in cross-disciplinary, cross-functional, evidence-based inquiry that moves all students onto a path toward the language leveraging futures we want for *and with* them. The shared inquiry creates space for all learners by displacing the treatment of error to emphasize instead the rhetorical learning and the negotiations of uptake that give students and faculty full reading and writing agency. This curriculum has thus drawn us all collaboratively into the "double loop" of deep organizational learning.

The work of implementing Stretch and its corresponding assessments has exposed the mechanisms of our writing labor across the campus learning system: (1) the co-labor of faculty and students to learn, (2) the co-labor of faculty to develop curriculum, and (3) the co-labor students and faculty to assess learning.

The Co-labor of Faculty and Students to Learn

If translingualism is a new disposition to difference, the Stretch writing curriculum structures the classroom to exercise this new disposition. The curriculum organizes the classroom as a multilingual contact zone, geared for deep transformation of knowing, and knowledge. Faculty and students work together for a full year to study a question relevant to students' current lives and studies. They may read *New York Times* together to explore the relationship between twenty-first-century literacies and our public lives as global citizens. They may investigate the cultural myths that structure private identity, or they may research college life and adult learning to explore their current transition into college learning. Whatever the specific theme, the inquiry is stretched across three modules of integrated reading and writing activities completed over two semesters; these modules engage student literacy within the learning community to expand the individual learner's knowledge and the group's.

The Stretch writing curriculum puts to work the scholarly work of writing studies over the last twenty-five years to define four best practices for an inclusive writing pedagogy.

1. The curriculum scaffolds inquiry to train the translanguaging disposition as the hallmark of the twenty-first-century rhetor (Jordan 2012; Canagarajah 2014).

2. The scaffolded inquiry integrates reading and writing to make and transmit new knowledge. Tapping the generative power of genre, students surface the often silent decision-making that characterizes writing as a social activity and an adaptive technology (Nowacek 2011; Bawarshi 2016).

3. Lower-stake, local writing tasks are emergent performances, rehearsals, for the more public, global writing projects. Students improvise to transform material for multiple audiences, purposes, and contexts, across several genres. This improvisation engages deep revision. With each iteration, each learner along the continuum of language development speaks the linguistic know-how that allows them, silently, to know with the genres we read and write (Canagarajah 2013, 2014, 2016; Reiff and Bawarshi 2011; Nowacek 2011; Schoenbach et al. 2012; Hyland 2014).

4. Reflection writing built into the sequence makes visible the cohort's learning, strategically targeting and surfacing metacognition at critical moments of transfer—lesson to lesson, unit to unit, semester to semester, course to course (Yancey 2016; Horner 2016; Inoue and Richmond 2016; Leaker and Ostman 2016).

Designed as a collaboration, our Stretch curriculum aligns writing practice with pedagogies for inclusivity and equity-minded instruction—as some faculty have put it, "bakes it right in." Apprenticed as readers and writers to authentic intellectual work within a community, students learn to adapt literacy practices to academic ends in the college classroom.

Pursuing a common inquiry engages all members of the learning community as accomplished novices led by an adaptive expert

(Committee on Developments in the Science of Learning 2000, 50). Their co-laboring draws on the prior knowledge each student brings to the classroom from their daily communities of practice; repurposing that prior knowledge and experience for academic study activates multilingual learning and exercises the dispositions of translanguaging. Situated in the immediate context of the classroom's shared inquiry, the artifacts of a writing task are valued according to their contribution to the shared work. The success of any one student or of the class depends on a communal disposition to reach across difference and to "understand the plurality of norms in a communicative situation and expand their repertoires"; they cannot "rely solely on the knowledge of skills they bring with them to achieve communicative success" (Canagarajah 2013, 43). Learning to co-construct meaning, we leverage the language of all learners to maximize learning for all, multilingual and monolingual, students and faculty.

This curriculum thus radically departs from the skills-first approach of remediation, which sets up edited academic English as the exclusive ticket to the higher-order inquiry of the college writing classroom. In the Stretch "contact zone," L2-L1 difference is not a problem to be solved, but a dialogue that catalyzes learning about how we learn across languages and the cultures they embody. "Meaning does not reside in the grammars [students and faculty] bring to the encounter, but in the negotiated practice of aligning with each other in the context of diverse affordances for communication" (Canagarajah 2013, 43). The innovations of this Stretch English curriculum in our multilingual learning community have asked us all to conceive language as a much more plastic medium for our mutual learning.

The curriculum affords all learners deepest contact with the translanguaging disposition—both the dynamics of its improvisations and the challenges of uptake. With the focus on the transactional relationship of genre—on the "brokering of uptakes" within the learning economy of the classroom—new lines of learning are exposed, for faculty and students alike. Interestingly, while it opens this rich field of rhetorical inquiry for students and faculty, this contact with genre studies has also exposed the mechanisms of our traditionally siloed university learning, mechanisms rigid enough to be nodes of resistance in the faculty learning system. Genre study is an area of rhetorical specialty that can be unfamiliar to a faculty who have studied in MA teaching English to speakers of other languages (TESOL), literature, and creative writing programs. The experiences of academic genres that our faculty have been trained to and that they carry forward as expectations into their own first-year composition classrooms are often grounded in what Anis Bawarshi has called a "fixated" understanding of and production of forms. Trained to the "dominant pedagogical approaches" themselves, faculty have had to work against their own tendency to seek the pseudo-mastery of genres "as relatively static objects to be taught and acquired as part of disciplinary and professional enculturation" (Bawarshi 2016, 244).

The shallow gains we see sometimes see in our students' portfolios can be traced back to our own prescribed and ritualized versions of a genre in lessons and assignment sheets; filling in the form, no matter how comforting that practice might be, is nothing compared to the deep gains we can afford students if we allow them the full field of genre play as their forum. And that means not trying to perfect products by preempting student rhetors' choices, but drawing attention to reader uptake as a phenomenon to be negotiated in any given performance. Thus, the challenge of this curriculum is that it apprentices faculty and students alike—not to the study of error and the prescription of form—but to the phenomenon of "uptake" (Bawarshi 2016, 248). The curriculum surfaces uptake, voicing it, making it visible both as we co-labor among ourselves to develop curriculum and as we co-labor to assess curriculum with students.

The Co-labor of Faculty to Develop Shared Curriculum

Within our learning system, embedding language learning within an inquiry-based writing curriculum has instigated fundamental change: restructuring labor to align with the now primary value of inclusiveness, old tension lines are blurring and new ones are exposed. Shifting our focus from the skills of the writer to writing as a rhetorical faculty that we cultivate has led to just that: cultivating a writing faculty.

While students have been cohorted, so have instructors. In our program, historically, instructors have been left to design their own curricula. So long as that curriculum aligns with general education writing outcomes, faculty are free to develop their own course. When we instituted our Stretch, we developed a template of core assignments—the inquiry-based exploration through genres—to achieve the pedagogical gains described above. We had the students' learning foremost in mind. We left open to the instructors the design of the inquiry itself—with the stipulation that they work in cohorts, not individually, to develop common themes. Here, we had faculty learning in mind. The co-labor of curriculum development makes explicit what would otherwise have been a silent, solitary labor to expand and adapt the traditional expertise each instructor brought to the cross-disciplinary curriculum. This collaborative work, however, surfaced the resistance to the interdisciplinary practice of multilingual writing instruction—namely, the limits to our institutional capacity to support faculty learning and the hidden labor of vulnerability when we task the faculty to change within an institution geared to "mastery."

Our current collaborations challenge the institutionalized mastery of disciplinary learning in a couple of important ways. Within this pos-tremedial learning system, the translanguaging our curriculum deploys unseats expertise as a fixed category. At the same time, to facilitate learning in this curriculum requires a broad base of knowledge, spanning the institutionally siloed disciplines of rhetoric and language development. This is a big ask from a faculty that has emerged from the discrete degree silos that advance us—or not—as academics. The fractured writing programs we had operated in before Stretch had not challenged our disciplinary engineering, which is much narrower than the curriculum we now operate. Faculty are called on to adapt; they are not simply experts in possession of knowledge that can be transmitted, but learners themselves whose expertise is constantly emergent within the inquiry as they seek together the activities and lessons that extend their own teaching repertoires. To accommodate the stretch toward inclusivity, we all stretch, students and faculty.

We saw as part of the early promise of our stretched multilingual writing program this redistribution of learning labor across the department rift between L2 writing studies and first-year writing studies. Our program hired from both departments, and we designed the curriculum to bring instructors together to cross-train as they developed shared curriculum "in light of competing knowledge and beliefs" (Canagarajah 2016, 266). We have not fully realized that promise, because of the barriers to faculty learning inherent in the systems of mastery that continue to institutionalize a remedial—and remediated—writing faculty. These barriers are both contractual and institutional. But the promise was and is there.

The Stretch writing curriculum calls faculty to work against the siloed experiences of their own graduate training. And they do, but not without burdens we did not originally foresee. In our first summer of preterm training, four of the seven faculty—all from the Academic English program—requested to form their own inquiry group, and thus a separate curriculum development team. This split us along traditional linguistic and English Department faculty lines. Initially, these instructors explained, their linguistic training warned them against asking

L2 students to read a newspaper—a highly culture-inflected genre of writing. But later, once it was clear that our students were reading the newspaper in the classrooms pursuing that inquiry, some voiced their discomfort to expose their limited rhetorical knowledge to English Department counterparts whom they imagined had more rhetorical training than they.

To this day, I do not fully understand the original split in writing culture on our campus; but this much is clear to me, its center of gravity has something to do with the idea of expertise that makes us, as faculty, so guarded about our own not-knowing that some fear to risk exposure among their colleagues across the departmental aisle and others choose inquiries aligned with their own literary backgrounds at the expense of exploring new intellectual ground with their students. Even though this program was requiring us all to apprentice ourselves to a new learning system, the group that split off from the line of inquiry originally proposed were much more comfortable to acknowledge and address their learning curve within their own smaller, more familiar intradepartmental cohorts. As a novice coordinator, I had not yet learned the need to establish among professionals a safe environment for professional risk-taking.

What finally united us as a faculty across disciplines was to find an authentic line of inquiry to solve a common teaching problem: how do we design for inclusivity? I aligned our faculty development work with the work of the California State University (CSU) Summer Institute in Teaching and Learning, to design a more inclusive instruction (Nilson 2016). Now part of a regional, not just local, effort to increase inclusive teaching practices, we started to work together to reform pedagogy. The critical gift of a Stretched writing program is time: a yearlong curriculum allows faculty to fundamentally redesign writing instruction. Faculty have worked together to study and to implement new pedagogies, design collaborative, active, research based lessons, and deliver them through an online learning management system. Most recently we are adapting Reading Apprenticeship practices to multilingual learning in a writing classroom; this framework for learning has given us a shared practice and language for describing our own and our student's learning along personal, social, cognitive, and knowledge-building dimensions (Schoenbach et al. 2012). Now structured as a community of practice, we occupy the same learning curve.

These new genres of writing instruction afford instructors new vantage points for their own learning within the interdisciplinary curriculum. In the collaborative active-learning classroom, student learning drives teacher learning. Instructors exercise their expertise to convene an exercise in the classroom, but as lessons are performed by the students, the lesson designer is free to observe closely the labor of the curriculum and to gauge directly the students' capacity for the work the curriculum exposes. Positioned as researchers in their own classrooms, they observe directly the results of the new pedagogies—and disciplines—they practice. The process once again makes writing instruction transactional, giving the expert room to adapt the lesson in light of the students' uptake of that lesson. Most faculty are energized by this process, though the vulnerability it exposes them to takes its toll as well. We have had faculty drop out or cycle out of this intense learning system.

The bottom line is—and faculty are aware of it—in Stretch English, your expertise will be tried. We have all had to learn to make room for this vulnerability, courting risk while mitigating failure. This is not a comfortable position for those who already belong so tenuously in a university culture of mastery. Nor does it make for a sustainable program; the program is continuously challenged to staff from a narrowly trained pool cut off from full university development. Non-tenure-line faculty are teaching faculty—their contract includes no assignment for research and scholarly or creative activity. This labor model works against developing a self-regulating writing faculty commensurate with their PhD counterparts teaching in the majors of the departments that hire them. Our current model and contract for the labor of these writing instructors do nothing to help us professionalize this faculty once they are with us, or retain them once we train them. The faculty labor contracts they work under are negotiated between administrators and unions to preserve a university that grants tenure as part of a rigid culture of professional expertise that insists on the exclusivity of some rather than the advancement of all. These are the faculty "facts on [our multilingual] ground."

The Co-labor of Faculty and Students to Assess Learning

Remedial instruction demands and produces a remediated faculty. Instructors are not remedial by nature but by (buy) design—the designed product of an instructional economy that displaces writing as a skill to be trained, not a knowledge base to be developed as a requisite university disposition to language and knowing. A skills-based, academic-writing course allows for "basic writing" as a low level of skilled know-how that grants universal authority across the disciplines; in such a writing program, we can all read for a "narrow band of competencies" and aim our teaching to that skills-based goal. San José State University is not out of these woods. Nor is the CSU. Written Communication I continues to be defined in our general education (GE) curriculum as a "skills based" course; the stipulated cutoff for the C– needed to earn credit for this requirement polices the language border to "college-level proficiency in English." Training this skilled know-how comes down largely to a demand for correctness at a formal level—sentence, paragraph, essay—"just writing" (Adler-Kassner 2017, 317). Neither students nor faculty, within such a writing universe, innovate and explore form as genre within the complex system of rhetorical composition; rather, they accept handbook and textbook definitions of genres and cut the cloth of any particular subject (topic) or subject (student or faculty member) to fit the pattern. Such "academic writing" is invented and policed by the writing academy to stabilize difference in language development learning for both students and faculty. It does not leverage the translanguaging potential of our globalizing multimodal network of writing and reading in the twenty-first century. To equip students and faculty as novice and expert rhetors within the complex system of texts we inhabit, academic writing is a pale substitution of basic skill for deep knowledge.

One of our first projects as a cohort was to redefine the course learning goals to articulate the stretched curriculum. As coordinator, I led the team to reform the assessment process. The updated *progymnasmata* of our Stretch English curriculum offers students, multilingual and monolingual, the opportunity to explore a "translingual literacy [that understands] the production, circulation, and reception of texts that are always mobile; that draw[s] from diverse languages, symbol systems, and modalities of communication; and that involve[s] inter-community negotiations" (Canagarajah 2013, 41). Our norming sessions are structured to verbalize this economy of uptakes and to engage faculty to observe patterns that may otherwise be "dismisse[d] or trivialize[d]'" (Lu qtd. in Bawarshi 2016, 248).

Once again, our process enjoins the co-labor of students and faculty. Responding to our self-assessment prompt—"help the Stretch faculty reading your essay to understand your progress in Stretch English"— students reflect on and document their progress toward the learning outcomes of the course. These are outcomes their audience, the Stretch faculty, have defined. Thus, as they write their reflective self-assessment, they translate the language of our program writing values to describe their progress. Their interpretation of our values reveals to us their own. "The student interpreted the learning outcomes" has become the most valued uptake among instructors: Reading these essays we gain insight not only into what they understand about the outcomes we have defined for them, but also, since these outcomes shape the instruction design to direct their learning, their essays provide feedback from learners on the learning we designed for them. It has taken time for us to learn to read these assessments receptively, not just as assessors, but as fellow learners. While early norming sessions showed faculty still rigidly clinging to formalist approaches to writing assessment, the scoring guide was designed to focus attention on uptake and guide faculty discussion to surface "what we really value" (Broad 2003).

Early on as we met in our cohort to develop the assessment exercise, I realized that my challenge as coordinator would be to break through the expectations of normativity that had been so deeply ingrained in our remediation culture. To break this pattern, I created a scoring guide that highlights writer performance and reader uptake, and I introduced Bob Broad's *What Do We Really Value: Beyond Rubrics in Teaching and Assessing Writing*. The scoring guide literally prompted faculty readers to map a student's writing performance, from strong to weak, across several dimensions of performance, the goal being to acknowledge the discrete writing values embedded in the task we had outlined in our prompt. It was interesting to watch how difficult it was for all of us to push error aside, to learn to read the argument that was in fact on the page—to give the student a mark in the "strong" column for defining a clear and useful argument, even though the same student received a "weak" mark in the column for "makes the text readable." By sharing our struggles to "map" values on this scoring guide, we have gained a technology in our own learning process. This technology prompts this faculty trained to ask, "Is this student a college-level writer?," to ask instead, "What work is this writing doing for me as the intended reader, and how might perceived difference be operating within the communication system that the text is organizing?" Uptake is a complex systematic question. Scoring even one essay surfaces a complex internal dialogue of the translanguaging adjustment.

Our practice of shared reading is useful precisely because it continues to surface the dialogue of values that our silent, private reading of student work never asks us to engage. We have to talk about the values and norms that operate our evaluations of student writing. And we are positioned to recognize the results of our own training to hear, or not, across difference. The second faculty reader's struggle illuminates the comparative ease with which I accommodate and graph the student's progress; reading my student's work together we notice both the first-time reader's struggle to read beyond the surface errors of the text and the trained reader's capacity to extend ourselves beyond that surface barrier. The value of the double reading is not just that the second reader is a check on instructor bias or a check on reliability or a statistical guarantor of validity; the value of the second reading is its measure of our own languaging practice and learning. Engaged as translanguaging agents in a multilingual community, we are not—as some may worry—biased in favor of our students. We have learned to read them. That is, we have in fact extended our translanguaging capacity. Our paired readings expose the mechanisms for learning that we can deliberately and programmatically leverage as our multilingual learning community learns to read across borders.

OUR STRETCH INTO THE DEEP ORGANIZATIONAL LEARNING OF "INEXHAUSTIBLE DIFFERENCE"

The history of remediation at SJSU is the history of a "traditional approach . . . at odds with" the "facts on [its own] ground[s]" (Horner et al. 2011, 303). In our journey out of remediation, we struggle to adapt within the forty-year history of global migration that shapes higher education globally for all of us in the twenty-first century. Our experiment has taught us much and challenges us to do more. For any campus similarly engaged in a transformation toward more inclusive, equitable—and sustainable—higher education, ours is a rich case study. Our stretch into a multilingual learning community has surfaced the labor of translanguaging that is our most promising lever of change for the deep organizational learning we seek.

A translanguaging learning system exposes the reciprocity of learning. If equity demands a new disposition to disciplinarity and difference, Stretch provides it: novice and expert co-labor as linguistic and rhetorical agents to negotiate new norms and values that drive learning, system wide. Apprenticeship activates their translingual learning so that faculty, students, and WPAs see the myth of homogeneity that has bifurcated our research and scholarship, divorced writing faculty from their students, splintered student cohorts into test-score placement categories and courses, and reduced advising to placement and policing. This Stretch has surfaced three kinds of labor we must now coordinate, facilitate, and sustain: (1) the reciprocal labor of classroom learning, (2) the labor of campus collaboration, and (3) the labor to reframe university infrastructure, aligning it with the emergent values of our multilingual community.

A translanguaging learning system also exposes the bias of traditional university organizations. Historically, our mechanisms to manage learning transfer have been unidirectional, running along the functional bias of a siloed and singular expertise that has characterized higher education. These traditional mechanisms must be restructured to make campus and system-wide learning reciprocal and collaborative if we hope to achieve the equity we seek. Specifically, in our case, there are lessons to be learned about the give and take of policy and practice in deep, and system-wide, organizational learning.

The program's greatest challenge has been to accommodate, reward, and grow the faculty learning needed to adapt to curricular innovations. Writing program administrators (WPAs) have been hired and engaged to manage this faculty learning. And much has been gained from this commitment. As we have argued for budgets to sustain the student-faculty learning cycle, WPAs have played a larger role in organizational learning—not only to build communities of practice among our faculty but also to distribute our learning up the chain to drive the campus-wide and the administrative learning cycles. Doing so, we have recovered the social system of our campus itself. Our locally designed self-placement practice is now embedded in freshman orientation; through this university process we now engage the larger campus community of faculty, advisors, instructional staff, and college and university administrators in our curricular innovation. We have found ready allies everywhere we go to realize a dynamic coalition of agents functioning together across institutional functions and across the borders of language difference, learning to hear each other.

Indeed, the great gains of the past five years would have been impossible at SJSU without new labor for specialists in rhetoric and composition: first-year writing is hosted at SJSU in a traditional English Department, but it is an English Department that has made a significant commitment to the labor of writing studies in the last five years. Since 2013, we have hired six tenure-line rhetoric and composition faculty to develop three levels of writing expertise: first-year writing, professional and technical writing, and writing across the curriculum. Two tenured full professors were hired to administer the Writing Across the Curriculum and the First Year Writing Programs. Two more assistant professors were hired to assist the administration of the program during this transition out of remediation. The three first-year-writing administrators share the program workload; among us we now have assigned time devoted to administration of writing equivalent to two full-time positions. This structural change in the labor of writing study represents a fundamental rethinking among campus leaders about the nature of writing itself and the role of writing as a university study on our campus.

Given the disciplinary expertise we lacked, we have been able to work the changes I have documented in this chapter.

Now that we have restored the systematicity of our learning community, it is glaringly apparent that a top-down faculty training model will not be self-sustaining. No effort to address student inequity will be sustainable if we do not also address the faculty inequity that requires three disciplinary experts to mentor learning for sixty adjunct faculty trained across four disciplines. Our classrooms themselves now afford us a platform for sustainable faculty development. Positioned alongside students as co-learners, teachers are researchers in their own classrooms and empowered to share their observations of student learning and assessment of their own practice with other practitioners and researchers. They are positioned to leverage the classroom as a site for and of disciplinary learning useful not only to other practitioners but also to administrators and researchers now engaged in their own deep learning as we seek a more inclusive and equitable system of higher education. The community of practice WPAs now foster aligns with the goals of inclusive, equitable, and sustainable practice.

Those programs now need contract and budgeting reforms that value the labor of the instructor-researchers and the students with whom they are engaged in the transactional learning of first-year general education courses. The organization of higher education has yet to learn how to grow the co-labor for inclusivity and equity (Bensimon 2005), relying instead on budgetary distinctions between adjunct and tenure-line faculty that undermine the faculty learning at the core of self-governance. Universities continue to enculturate siloed expertise that mitigates against a fully trained and self-regulating faculty in composition; individuals are trained and promoted along lines of increasing exclusivity, and perceptions underlying "basic writing" continue to define narrowly the expertise required to deliver writing instruction. Institutional functions reinforce this system. The stories of transforming labor in this section delineate what Paulette Stevenson calls our shared "epistemological terrain" across varied learning communities in higher education: the tenured and nontenured lines of labor that are mapped contractually and administered at the state level through general education policy and budgeting (Stevenson, chapter 2). At SJSU, we also need a contract language that names, promotes, and compensates faculty learning through shared service and professional development.

If we are to change policy, we must include administrators in our learning. If Stretch has taught us the value of reciprocity as a principle of the heart of learning transfer, we seek now to leverage this same collaborative "organizational learning mechanism" to drive the continuous learning that supports the system-wide value to efficiency in our next phase of reform (Popper and Lipshitz 2000, 185). Targeting resources to actual need—the function and directive of the Chancellor's Office in our state system—creates efficiencies that lower the time-to-graduation and thus expand our capacity to meet the mission of California State University (CSU): a higher education responsive to all graduates of high schools in our state. The work we have yet to do locally requires a policy and contract language from the Chancellor's Office that unequivocally espouses a postremedial learning structure and opens the state system itself to learning generated from within local classrooms, challenging the "pretargeted linguistic and pragmatic standards, preferred codes . . . , and preferred modes and genres" (Jordan 2012, 123). We have joined, through our statewide CSU English Council, to guide the language of policies regulating California's dismantling of remediation.

Along with four other CSU WPAs, we crafted a language for admissions messaging that is an extension of pedagogy, not an expression of policy. Such a language recognizes students as novices to the local idiom of our university learning practice; it does not predict their learning but mentors their transfer of learning inherent in the admission to and enrollment in university. The lessons learned in our own classrooms inform our current conversations with the Chancellor's Office, whose predictive modeling of writing studies continues traditional preconceptions about language difference and normative myths (Matsuda 2006; Jordan 2012). While such predictive models—grounded as Adler-Kassner (2017) points out, in correlative, not causal, logic—may help systems administrators predict dollars needed; their logic falls short of the causality that can direct any one student's success (326–29). The result is that—in the CSU for sure and, if discussions on the WPA_list are indicative, elsewhere in the country as well—admissions policies and processes may help us to predict stable enrollment patterns but continue to impede the flexibility necessary to supply demand and deliver the instruction students need. At risk because of this systematic policy impasse is our ability to meet student need across all the dimensions of learning, and to define workloads that allow for a healthy and consistent growth of faculty capacity within this new learning system.

Our work to transform the culture of writing is only just underway, not fully realized. But the changes we have made within our own faculty and in the committees and university workgroups who have come into contact with this program's goals, processes, and practices have sown the seeds of change. Most important, these changes teach us the functional value of collaboration as a learning model. A collaborative curriculum sees all stakeholders in a learning system as learners. It recognizes—and seeks ways to realize—for each learner their own agency in that learning, redistributing the labor of curriculum to create space for the dissensus that grows new norms and values transacted within the functional spaces of our campus.

Learning is work. I have done this work for the last thirty-seven years—almost exactly coincident with the forty years of our current Age of Migration, as linguists now name it. In that time, the university learning system has struggled to manage the growing diversity. Set in this historical context, the "work of composition" is central to the co-laboring of all who engage an academic life; it asks us to rethink how we translate learning through languaging practices across disciplines (Lu 2004). Our field is alive with this work of composition. And, as I sit here, writing this paragraph on the evening of November 6, 2018, the work feels more alive, more vital than ever, to me. The ground we stand in this moment of US history feels very much like a crisis. At the brink of a wall—our collective talk about language and our dispositions to it, to each other through it, feels urgent. It is only as we engage deep, system-wide learning—available to us because of our difference—that we trans-form. And so I seek, not just my own learning but a deep revolution in our collective learning that will transform and deliver all. I think that is the work of a university writing curriculum.

The specific "facts on the ground" at SJSU are these: In the last four years, only 24 percent of our first-year-writing students (N_1) come from English-only households; the norm on our campus among our students is multilingualism. The languages included among our multilingual students (N_2) span the globe: Spanish is our largest group, comprising 25 percent (2014) to 37 percent (2017) of the students surveyed. Another 18 percent to 20 percent are from Chinese-speaking homes. Two other Asian-speaking populations are Vietnamese (10–13 percent) and Tagalog (9–11 percent). In smaller numbers—less than 1 percent of the total—students also bring to our writing tables Arabic; Farsi; Amharic; Russian, Ukrainian, and other Slavic languages; Portuguese; French; and German (see table 10.1 for full list).

Historically, these languages were distributed across our courses-based student test scores, into one of two levels of remedial instruction or into English 1A, our entry-level college writing course (see table 10.2). While these students come from multilingual households, most were born in the United States (74 percent), and have graduated from US high schools (92 percent). Almost half (48 percent) report English as a first or primary language used at home. While 43 percent began learning English from birth, an increasing number began learning English between eleven and seventeen years of age; that number grows from 0.4 percent in 2014 to almost 10 percent in 2016 as SJSU, along with many institutions, invited more international learners among us.

These are not just our "facts" or our "grounds": Paul Matsuda (2006) describes the migration patterns that have produced these facts of our history (643–48); the Migration Studies project at Penn State terms these last forty years of increased migration an "Age of Migration." So it is not surprising that Bruce Horner, Min-Zhan Lu, Jacqueline Jones Royster, and John Trimbur (Horner et al. 2011) point to "growing numbers of US teachers and scholars of writing [who] recognize that traditional ways of understanding and responding to language differences are inadequate to the facts on the ground" in many universities (303).

Table 10.1. Home languages as portion of total first-year writing fall cohorts, 2014–17

Home Languages	Fall 2014 $N_1 = 2,324$ $N_2 = 1,775$	Fall 2015 $N_1 = 1,784$ $N_2 = 1,356$	Fall 2016 $N_1 = 1,593$ $N_2 = 1,158$	Fall 2017 $N_1 = 2,123$ $N_2 = 1,681$
English only (N_1)	23.6%	24%	27.3%	21.8%
Multilingual (N_1)	76.4%	76%	72.7%	79.2%
Spanish (N_2)	25.4%	26%	39.67%	36.9%
Chinese (N_2)	18.2%	18.4%	20.05%	20.52%
Korean (N_2)	0.9%	1.4%	1.41%	1.9%
Vietnamese (N_2)	9.9%	9.5%	11.96%	12.8%
Japanese (N_2)	0.8%	1%	2.05%	1%
Hmong (N_2)	0.6%	0.3%	0.4%	0.3%
Tagalog (N_2)	8.6%	6.5%	11.5%	10.6%
Panjabi/Urdu/Hindi/ Tamil (N_2)	3.7%	5.3%	7.27%	6.8%
Arabic (N_2)	1.9%	1.5%	2.62%	2%
Russian/Ukrainian/ other Slavic	0.7%	0.6%	0.8%	1.5%
Farsi (N_2)	1.1%	0.9 %	1.6%	1.2%
Amharic (N_2)	0.2%	0.3%	0.5%	0.2%
Portuguese (N_2)	1.1%	0.5%	0.2%	0.4%
French (N_2)	0.7%	0.6%	0.8%	1.1%
German (N_2)	-0.3%	0.1%	0.7%	0.4%
Italian (N_2)	0.7%	0.3%	0.1%	0.4%

Table 10.2. Home languages by California State University English Placement Test Score

Home Languages	Eligible 1A, Exempt EPT	Eligible 1A EPT ≥147	Remedial 2 EPT ≤146–139	Remedial 1 EPT ≤138	Student Doesn't Recall Score
English only	38.7%	24.5%	24.5%	16.2%	36.5%
Spanish	19.7%	26.1%	30.2%	24.0%	30.3%
Chinese	15.8%	14.8%	20.6%	35.0%	16.0%
Korean	0.5%	2.0%	0.3%	2.0%	0.8%
Vietnamese	9.4%	15.8%	8.2%	12.8%	7.9%
Japanese	0.4%	2.5%	1.4%	0	0.8%
Hmong	0.4%	1.0%	0.7%	2.4%	0
Tagalog	9.2%	10.8%	10.0%	5.6%	7.7%
Panjabi/ Urdu/ Hindi/Tamil	5.9%	2.5%	4.1%	2.0%	2.6%

APPENDIX 10.B

THE SUCCESS OF SJSU'S TRANSITION TO A POSTREMDIAL WRITING CULTURE

Tables 10.3 and 10.4 map the redistribution of labor out of remediated writing. The difference between these tables pictures our successful transition to a culture that admits difference and allows full access to our college writing curriculum in the first semester of enrollment. Figure 10.1 shows percentages of nonpassing grades. The rate of nonpassing grades in our freshman composition program (English 1A) has for seven years averaged 8 percent, with a high of 10 percent and a low of 5 percent. Stretch success data have demonstrated this same trend during the four years of Stretch (HA 96 during the pilot, English 1AF/1AS postimplementation). With Stretch in place, we have been able to maintain and extend to a greater number of students the rate of success in entry-level college composition courses.

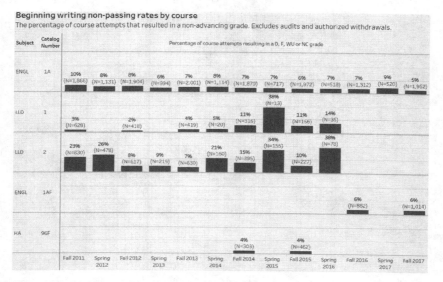

Figure 10.1. Beginning writing nonpassing rates by course. The percentage of course attempts that resulted in a nonadvancing grade. Excludes audits and authorized withdrawals.

Table 10.3. Units to satisfy the first GE writing requirement in SJSU's remedial curriculum

Written Communication Enrollment Category	Measures of Eligibility for College Writing	Course Enrolled Fall, Year 1	Course Enrolled Spring, Year 1	Course Enrolled Fall, Year 2	SJSU units to Satisfy 1 of 3 GE Writing Requirements.
Satisfied	AP, CLEP, IB scores	[Second writing requirement]	[Second Writing requirement]		0
Satisfied	Equivalent college units transferred	[Second writing requirement]	[Second Writing requirement]		3
Eligible	EPT 147 and above or Exempt (via SAT or ACT score)	Written Communication 1	[Second Writing requirement]		3
Remedial	146–139	Academic English 2	English 1A	[Second Writing requirement]	6
Remedial	138–120, or High Pass on Academic English 1 portfolio	Academic English 1 + Co-req lab	English 1A	[Second Writing requirement]	8 (5 are nonbaccalaureate units)
Remedial	138–120	Academic English 1 + Co-req lab	Academic English 2	English 1A	11 (8 are nonbaccalaureate units)

Table 10.4. Units to satisfy first GE writing's first course in the postremedial model

Written Communication Self-Placement	Course Enrolled Fall of Year 1	Course Enrolled Spring of Year 1	Course Enrolled Fall of Year 2	SJSU Units to Satisfy First GE Writing Requirement
Satisfied two requirements by test				0
Satisfied first requirement with units transferred	[Second writing requirement]			0
One-semester course	English 1A	[Second Writing requirement]		3 Baccalaureate
Two-semester course	English 1AF	English 1AS	[Second Writing requirement]	6 Baccalaureate

REFERENCES

Adler, Mortimer J. 1940. "How to Mark a Book." *The Saturday Review* (July 6): 11–12. The Saturday Review Archives. The Unz Review. https://www.unz.com/print/SaturdayRev -1940jul06-00011/.

Adler-Kassner, Linda. 2017. "Because Writing Is Never Just Writing." CCCC Chair's Address. *College Composition and Communication* 69.2: 317–40.

Adler-Kassner, Linda, and Chris M. Anson. 2011. Review of the Writing Programs: San José State University. Final Report. National Council of Writing Program Administrators.

Bawarshi, Anis. 2016. "Beyond the Genre Fixation: A Translingual Perspective on Genre." *College English* 78.3: 243–49.

Bensimon, Estela Mara. 2005. "Closing the Achievement Gap in Higher Education: An Organizational Learning Perspective." *Organizational Learning in Higher Education*, edited by Adrianna Kezar. *New Directions for Higher Education* 131 (Fall): 99–111.

Broad, Bob. 2003. *What We Really Value: Beyond Rubrics in Teaching and Assessing Writing*. Logan: Utah State University Press.

Canagarajah, A. Suresh. 2013. "Negotiating Translingual Literacy: An Enactment." *Research in the Teaching of English* 48.1: 40–67.

Canagarajah, A. Suresh. 2014. "ESL Composition as a Literate Art of the Contact Zone." In *First Year Composition, from Theory to Practice*, edited by Deborah Coxwell-Teague and Ronald F. Lunsford. Anderson, SC: Parlor Press, 27–48.

Canagarajah, A. Suresh. 2016. "Translingual Writing and Teacher Development in Composition" *College English* 78.3: 265–73.

Committee on Developments in the Science of Learning. 2000. "How Experts Differ from Novices." In *How People Learn: Brain, Mind, Experience, and School*, edited by John D. Bransford, Ann L. Brown, and Rodney R. Cocking, 31–50. Expanded ed. National Academy of Sciences. Washington, DC: National Academies Press.

Ferris, Dana. 2011. *The Treatment of Error in Second Language Student Writing*. 2nd ed. Michigan Series on Teaching Multilingual Writers, edited by Diane Belcher and Jun Liu. Ann Arbor: University of Michigan Press.

Glau, Gregory. 2007. "'Stretch' at 10: A Progress Report on Arizona State University's 'Stretch Program.'" *Journal of Basic Writing* 26.2: 30–48.

Horner, Bruce. 2016. "Reflecting the Translingual Norm: Action-Reflection, ELF, Translation, and Transfer." In *A Rhetoric of Reflection*, edited by Kathleen Blake Yancey, 105–24. Logan: Utah State University Press.

Horner, Bruce, Min-Zhan Lu, Jacqueline Jones Royster, and John Trimbur. 2011. "Opinion: Language Difference in Writing: Toward a Translingual Approach." *College English* 73.3: 303–21.

Hyland, Kenneth. 2004. *Genre and Second Language Writing*. Michigan Series on Teaching Multilingual Writers, edited by Diane Belcher and Jun Liu. Ann Arbor: University of Michigan Press.

Inoue, Asao B., and Tyler Richmond. 2016. "Theorizing Reflection Practices of Female Hmong College Students: Is Reflection a Racialized Discourse?" In *A Rhetoric of Reflection*, edited by Kathleen Blake Yancey, 125–45. Logan: Utah State University Press.

Jordan, Jay. 2012. *Redesigning Composition for Multilingual Realities*. CCCC Studies in Writing and Rhetoric, edited by Joseph Harris. Champaign, IL: NCTE.

Leaker, Cathy, and Heather Ostman. 2016. "Reflecting Practices: Competing Models of Reflection in Prior Learning Assessment." In *A Rhetoric of Reflection*, edited by Kathleen Blake Yancey, 84–102. Logan: Utah State University Press.

Lu, Min-Zhan. 2004. "An Essay on the Work of Composition: Composing English against the Order of Fast Capitalism." *College Composition and Communication* 56.1: 16–50.

Lu, Min-Zhan, and Bruce Horner. 2011. "Translingual Literacy and Matters of Agency." Plenary Address. Penn State Conference on Rhetoric and Composition: Rhetoric and

Writing across Language Boundaries. State College, PA. July 11. The Working Paper Series on Negotiating Differences in Language and Literacy. University of Louisville. ir .library.louisville.edu/cgi/viewcontent.cgi?article=1064&context=faculty.

Matsuda Paul K. 2006. "The Myth of Linguistic Homogeneity in US College Composition." *Cross-Language Relations in Composition,* a special issue of *College English* 68.6: 637–51. National Council of Teachers of English. http://www.jstor.org/stable/25472180.

Nilson, Linda B. 2016. "Self-Regulated Learning: Active Learning on the Inside" Key Note Presentation. What Works: Designing Teaching for Diverse Learners. CSU Summer Institute on Teaching and Learning, Long Beach, July 2016.

Nowacek, Rebecca S. 2011. *Agents of Integration: Understanding Transfer as a Rhetorical Act.* CCCC Studies in Writing and Rhetoric. Carbondale: Southern Illinois University Press.

Popper, Micha, and Raanan Lipshitz. 2000. "Organizational Learning: Mechanisms, Culture, and Feasibility." *Management Learning.* Sage Social Science Collections 31.2: 181–96. https://doi.org/10.1177/1350507600312003.

Reiff, Mary Jo, and Anis Bawarshi. 2011. "Tracing Discursive Resources: How Students Use Prior Genre Knowledge to Negotiate New Writing Contexts in First-Year Composition." *Written Communication* 28.3: 312–37. https://doi.org/10.1177/0741088311410183.

Schoenbach, Ruth, Cynthia Greenleaf, and Lynn Murphy. 2012. *Reading for Understanding: How Reading Apprenticeship Improves Disciplinary Learning in Secondary and College Classrooms.* San Francisco: Jossey-Bass.

SJSU. 2017. Demographics. Office of Institutional Effectiveness and Analytics. Accessed September 2, 2018. http://www.iea.sjsu.edu/Students/default.cfm?version=graphic. (n.d.).

Trimbur, John. 1989. "Consensus and Difference in Collaborative Learning." *College English* 51.6: 602–16.

Williams, Joseph. 1981. "The Phenomenology of Error." Language Studies and Composing. *College Composition and Communication* 32.2: 152–68.

Yancey, Kathleen Blake. 2016. *A Rhetoric of Reflection.* Logan: Utah State University Press.

11

WORLD ENGLISHES IN THE FIRST-YEAR COMPOSITION CLASSROOM
Perceptions of Multilingual Writers

Sarah Henderson Lee and Shyam B. Pandey

Colleges and universities in the United States continue to enroll large numbers of students from other countries. In fact, according to the most recent Open Doors report, the 2015–16 academic year marked the first time the number of international students studying in the United States exceeded 1 million, and while that number dropped by 3.4 and 1.5 percent respectively in the following years, it still remained above the million mark (Institute for International Education 2018). Since 2011–12, undergraduate international students have outnumbered graduate international students in the United States. This shift in the international student population stems from a number of factors, including increased globalization and the strong reputation and prestige associated with US higher education and related degrees. With a growing number of linguistically and culturally diverse undergraduate students on US college and university campuses comes "evolving roles and responsibilities of writing program administrators [and faculty] who are leading efforts to provide all students on their campuses, regardless of nationality or first language, with competencies in writing that will service them in the academy and beyond" (Rose and Weiser 2018, 5). This includes Aya Matsuda and Paul Kei Matsuda's (2010) call for writing instructors to "embrace the complexities of English and facilitate the development of global literacy" (373), which this chapter answers by exploring the role of World Englishes (WE) in the United States, first-year writing classroom context through the related perceptions of multilingual writers.

As the second-largest public university in the state, Minnesota State University, Mankato, enrolled 1,341 international students from 92 countries in Spring 2018, of which 1,068 were undergraduate students (Minnesota State 2018a). The University's English Department offers

https://doi.org/10.7330/9781646421428.c011

roughly thirty sections of the first-year composition course (ENG 101) each semester. On average, five of these sections are reserved for multilingual writers. Due to the limited number of ENG 101 seats, the multilingual sections are mostly filled by new international students who often arrive on campus and register for courses just days prior to a semester's start. ENG 101 is a one-semester course required of all undergraduate students that according to the undergraduate catalog "helps students develop a flexible writing process, practice rhetorical awareness, read critically to support their writing, research effectively, represent others' ideas in multiple ways, reflect on their writing practices, and polish their work" (Minnesota State 2018b, n.p.). The course is primarily taught by graduate teaching assistants (TAs) and contingent faculty. In the role of director of Second Language (L2) Writing, Sarah occasionally teaches a multilingual section of ENG 101 and invites L2 Writing TAs into her classroom as participant-observers, co-teachers, and co-researchers. In Spring 2016, Shyam, an MA Teaching English to Speakers of Other Languages (TESOL) student and L2 writing TA at the time, joined Sarah's ENG 101 class to help carry out a research project stemming from previous conversations about the intersection between WE and L2 writing scholarship.

The findings reported in this chapter highlight multilingual writers' perceptions of the incorporation of WE texts in an academic writing course through the four stages of resistance, curiosity and solidarity, acceptance, and resource, which were identified in data analysis. The participants' movement toward language variation as resource supports a revised first-year writing curriculum that prioritizes the development of global literacy among all undergraduate writers.

WORLD ENGLISHES AND PEDAGOGY

With more speakers of English now being from Braj Kachru's (1992) Outer (e.g., India and Nigeria) and Expanding (e.g., China and Nepal) circle countries than Inner circle countries (e.g., United States and United Kingdom), the extraordinary growth in the varieties of English represented in language classrooms across the globe is not surprising. Since the early 2000s, this reality has contributed to a growing interest in the relationship between two areas of applied linguistics: WE and TESOL. This intersection has facilitated, as Aya Matsuda (2013b) notes, "an increased sensitivity toward linguistic diversity in English and a shared concern toward and increased awareness of such problems as the construct of native English speakers and the dominance of English" (4).

In many English Language Teaching (ELT) contexts, this concern has resulted in a reexamination of standardized language teaching practices and, in turn, new research on language pedagogy with an emphasis on globalization and English for international communication.

The areas of communicative competence and language ideology, both of which inform this study, are at the heart of the WE paradigm. As a construct, communicative competence deals with issues of acceptability, appropriateness, and intelligibility in language use. Margie Berns (2009) describes the relationship between communicative competence and WE as "firmly rooted in recognition of the social realities of the users and uses of a given variety (or varieties, in multilingual societies)" (727) or context of situation. In terms of language pedagogy, communicative competence counters the prioritization of standard varieties of English as instructional models and supports a polymodel approach (Kachru 1992). Here, "assessment of teaching materials for linguistic tolerance, for correspondence with the sociocultural context for the use of English as well as the expressed or implied norms against which learners will be judged" (Berns 2009, 726) is critical for implementation. In addition, as Aya Matsuda (2013a) emphasizes, students must be made aware of and prepared to use both a "linguistic and strategic repertoire" to communicate cross-culturally and, moreover, must understand communication as a "two-way process" where "making one's own message clear and trying to understand the other is not the sole responsibility of non-native speakers or speakers of 'less standard' English varieties" (2). To further empower students as owners of their languages and prepare them as global citizens, adoption of a critical perspective in language classrooms has been promoted. Matsuda and Patricia Friedrich (2011) note the use of English as an international language especially "call[s] for awareness of the politics of English, including such issues as language and power, the relationship between English and various indigenous languages, linguistic ecology, and linguistic divide" (341). Understanding the sociopolitical and historical context of a particular variety of English heightens students' understanding of language choice, preparing them "to use English effectively to meet their own needs and resist any oppression from the dominance of English, while respecting the needs of others" (Matsuda 2013a, 4).

Grounded in these sociocultural constructs is research specific to the influence of WE on the teaching of ([first language] L1 and L2) composition, which has largely pushed for the pluralization of the field and the adoption of translingual approaches in the teaching of writing (e.g., Canagarajah 2013a, 2013b; You 2018). Here, A. Suresh

Canagarajah (2006) presents "code-meshing" as "a strategy for merging local varieties with Standard Written English in a move toward gradually pluralizing academic writing and developing multilingual competence for transnational relationships" (586). Building on the idea of code-meshing as a communicative tool and critiquing the prescriptive history of the US composition classroom, Vershawn Ashanti Young and Aja Y. Martinez (2011) advocate for code-meshing "as a way to promote the linguistics democracy of English and to increase the acquisition and egalitarian, effective use of English in school" and beyond (xx). While WE-informed pedagogical research in composition has increased in recent years, it remains relatively sparse with the majority of studies conducted in mainstream writing classrooms. Ana Maria Wetzl's (2013) investigation of American undergraduates' perceptions of WE, for example, notes increased acceptance of English varieties by students who experienced both explicit instruction related to WE and consistent exposure to WE texts. By introducing her students, many who communicate using varieties of English that are often stigmatized, to WE and creating multimedia space for them to engage in code-meshing, Melissa Lee (2014) also observes positive change in student perceptions, especially in terms of their self-perceptions as language users both in and out of school. Shifting the focus to L2 writing instruction, Shih-Yu Chang (2015) explores the use of a WE writing curriculum in L2 composition classrooms and reports increased confidence among multilingual writers, particularly at the idea generation stage of the writing process. As instructors of L2 writing, we are interested in knowing more about how multilingual writers, as WE users, perceive the incorporation of WE in the writing classroom and apply such content to their own academic writing journey. A better understanding of this, we believe, will contribute to local conversations on the pedagogical possibilities of using WE to benefit all student writers, which, in turn, will support to the larger programmatic, institutional, and professional work toward equitability and internationalization. Below, we share details of the WE-based pedagogical study we conducted in a composition course for multilingual writers.

THE STUDY

Eight class meetings were reserved for the WE project. During the first meeting, students completed an in-class writing task (appendix 11.A) exploring their beliefs of and experiences with language variation, and watched and discussed Jamila Lyiscott's (2014) spoken-word essay, "3 Ways to Speak English." Meetings 2–7 focused on a different assigned

WE text from the *Rotten English* anthology (Ahmad 2007). Students reread the text and completed a post-reading questionnaire which asked the following questions:

1. Is the text representative of good English? Why or why not?,
2. Is the text representative of strong writing? Why or why not?, and
3. How does the language variety used add to / detract from the author's essay?

Then, they engaged in a related class discussion and analysis activity. Meeting 8 concluded the project with an in-class writing task (appendix 11.A) revisiting students' language variation beliefs and applying their engagement with the six WE texts to their current academic writing development.

Twenty students were enrolled in the course and fully participated in the above class meetings. Seventeen of the students consented to share their in-class writings from these meetings as data sources for the Institutional Review Board (IRB)–approved study. Content analysis, referring to "any qualitative data reduction and sense-making effort that takes a volume of qualitative material and attempts to identify core consistencies and meanings" (Patton 2002, 453), was employed after the completion of the semester and revealed four stages through which multilingual writers' perceptions of WE in the writing classroom move.

FINDINGS AND DISCUSSION

Below we discuss the stages of resistance, curiosity and solidarity, acceptance, and resource based on our findings.

Resistance

At the start of the WE project, participants largely associated academic writing with the prescriptive approaches familiar to them from previous L2 instruction where standardized grammar and linear rhetorical patterns were prioritized for written communication. Many of the participants held a similar view to Participant 12, who emphasized, "In writing, you have to show your ideas without any mistakes in word choice and grammar" (Week 1). When presented with WE texts that did not conform to such standards, including the incorporation of background information and "advanced" lexicon, participants were quick to dismiss the text and/or author, often out of frustration from limited reading comprehension. Participant 17, for example, expressed, "It is weird to read [those] sentences. It makes me feel like 'Are you sure? You are an author? Seriously?' It detracts me from concentrating to the article" (Week 2). Such resistance was especially common in participants' Week 1 and Week 2 written reflections and related discussions.

According to Larry Smith and Cecil Nelson (2006), "the increasing numbers of varieties of English need not increase the problems of understanding across cultures, if users of English develop some familiarity with them" (441). In fact, their findings from an investigation of intelligibility, comprehensibility, and interpretability show that while students' self-perceptions of WE understanding are positively impacted by both increased familiarity of topic and language variety, their actual understanding is changed more by the latter. For student writers to move beyond the resistance stage, exposure to and engagement with a variety of Englishes is needed, including pre-reading, during-reading, and post-reading reflections and discussions that focus on factors influencing intelligibility, comprehensibility, and interpretability in cross-cultural communication.

Curiosity and Solidarity

When participants were asked the question, "How does the language variety used add to / detract from the author's essay?," several of them identified the use of an unfamiliar variety of English as motivation to read further and deeper in order to better understand the cultural context. Participant 9, for instance, commented, "The language variety helps the reader understand the cultural setting. The people's appropriation/ use of language depend[s] on the situation at hand" (Week 2). By "transcend[ing] their own [linguistic and] cultural experiences" (Nieto 2010, 258), participants started to view the incorporation of WE texts as a welcomed challenge. Here, Participant 11 noted, "But when one reads further. the language variety becomes more attractive and somewhat challenging to the readers. This makes the readers continue reading the whole readings" (Week 2). As instructors, we capitalized on the intrigue-based motivation of participants in this stage by providing collaborative spaces (i.e., discussions and activities) for students to analyze the texts from both a reader and writer perspective.

The majority of participants also viewed the incorporation of WE texts as a direct invitation to readers with similar lived experiences. As Participant 20 stated, "World English text makes the reader who has the similar background more easy to involve in or feel the situation" (Week 2). Because of their varied linguistic and cultural backgrounds, participants appreciated the diverse accounts of the WE authors. Similar to the participants, Shyam, as a multilingual writer, gravitates toward texts that represent linguistic and cultural experiences similar to his own, as opposed to those that offer no point of connection to his identity. To build on the themes of solidarity and curiosity as they relate to WE, writing instructors could design assignments and/or activities that encourage students' exploration of both their own variety of English and others through a variety of text types.

Acceptance

Participant data supported the following three areas in terms of students' acceptance of WE: (1) macro language features, (2) emotive language use, and (3) mixing/merging phenomenon.

Macro Language Features

In the acceptance stage, participants prioritized the macro features (e.g., genre conventions) of the WE texts over the micro features (e.g., grammar and mechanics). Participant 18, for example, reflected, "Every English is good English no matter what kind of method the author uses to interpret as long as the author can let the readers to understand his text. The English may not be standard but it does not mean it is not good" (Week 5). In the role of reader, participants like Participant 18 were more concerned about their comprehension of the overall ideas presented in the texts and less concerned with whether or not the authors deviated from standard grammatical and rhetorical conventions.

Emotive Language Use

Many participants also associated emotive language use with strong writing. Here, participants assessed their relationship with the text by considering the impression it left on them. Participants accepted the deviations of the English variety when they emotionally connected to the text. As an example, Participant 19 opined, "It is [strong writing]. I like the increase of vernacular use to show the emotional change the narrator experiences" (Week 5). Like Participant 19, other students identified a link between language use and readers' emotions in strong writing. Valuing the emotional proximity to the author and text, Participant 20 stated, "When I consider strong writing I think about if the writing could attract and influence readers' emotion, if the reader could 'feel' the author and story, then it is strong writing" (Week 4). Building on students' association of emotive language as strong writing in reading texts, writing instructors should provide space for student writers to explore the emotive language in their own writing and its effectiveness. With the added complexity of expressing emotions in an L2, Aneta Pavlenko (2001) advocates for the use of narratives, particularly as a starting point, which allows L2 writers "to assume legitimate ownership of their L2 and to provide the readers with new meanings, perspectives, and images of 'being American—and bilingual' in the postmodern world" (317).

Mixing/Merging Phenomenon

When asked "Is the text representative of good English? Why and why not?," several participants emphasized their willingness to embrace multiple varieties in writing. They described WE texts as representative of strong writing when different language varieties were used within the same text. Responding to the WE reading in Week 4, Participant 19 noted, "It is [strong writing]. There's a great combination of different English dialects that aid in understanding of the story." Negotiation of dialects within a single story, according to the majority of participants in the acceptance stage, indicated advanced writing skills of the author and ultimately representation of acceptable writing. With increased exposure "to a range of dialects in classrooms where English is studied," Young and Martinez (2011, xxii) argue that students are more likely to claim their own right to move between their accents, dialects, and varieties of Englishes both in written and verbal communication and in and out of the classroom.

Resources

Regarding the final stage, WE as resource, data analysis identified the following four areas: (1) cross-cultural understanding, (2) critical reading skills, (3) genre/audience awareness, and (4) self-representation through voice.

Cross-Cultural Understanding

Noting the bidirectional relationship between language and culture, participants identified WE as a resource for understanding cross-cultural issues in this final stage. They did not consider language varieties as barriers but rather as means through which they could better understand the particularities of context. Participant 12, for example, commented, "Using language variation can make reader understand well and know about different cultures" (Week 6). The incorporation of WE texts not only provides students with opportunities to explore the cultures of potential future interlocutors, but it also, as Matsuda and Friedrich (2011) point out, provides students with opportunities to gain knowledge of their own culture, as well as the ability to effectively communicate their culture to outsiders. Here, they remind educators of the following: "The purpose of using English is not solely to *learn from* others, as we may have believed in the past. Our goal now is to establish and maintain an equal, mutually respectful relationship with others, which requires the ability to perceive and analyze the familiar with an outsider's perspective" (340). Recognizing WE as a resource to achieve this is an important first step for language and more specifically writing instructors.

Critical Reading Skills

The majority of participants associated WE as a resource for developing critical reading skills. For many participants, the focus here was specifically on vocabulary. Participant 5, for example, noted, "[The author's word choice] is what attracted my attention. I was trying to figure out the meaning" (Week 4). The unfamiliar vocabulary encountered by students in the WE texts required them to adopt the identity of language detective, where they turned to strategies connected primarily to the use of context clues, L1s, and dictionaries. Regarding the latter, students questioned the limited representation of WE varieties in dictionaries, which prompted a discussion on the topic of legitimacy and languages. Here, Fredric Dolezal (2009) remarks, "Finding a word in 'the dictionary' gives the user not only information but also *confidence*; when we find the word we are looking for in a dictionary, we are assured that our language usage has been confirmed, even anointed" (695). For WE speakers and writers, including the participants of this study, to experience such confidence, comprehensive dictionaries of individual Englishes are needed. In the context of the writing classroom, an assignment that allows students to collect, analyze, and document data from their own Englishes would be welcomed.

Genre/Audience Awareness

For participants, the particular variety of English used in a text was beneficial in terms of increasing genre and audience awareness. Participant 9 asserted, "Also, language changes in terms of genres. The language choice in poetry is not the same in prose even if both are treated as literature branches. Therefore, a writer should be flexible depending on the context and the targeted readership" (Week 6). In addition to identifying known genre features based on the language used in a given text, participants were able to identify new genre features as well. Such identification of distinct features stemmed from close readings, class discussions, and individual and collaborative analysis tasks that explored both genre and style in terms of language use. Vijay Bhatia (2009) notes "genre and style . . . share a large area of common ground, which can be effectively used to distinguish variations of different kinds in language use in the context of world Englishes" (398). The incorporation of WE texts allowed participants to use language features to inform their understanding of genre and to use genre features to inform their understanding of a particular language variety, both important skills as a reader and writer.

Self-Representation through Voice

By the end of the WE project, the majority of participants viewed WE as a resource to more accurately represent their voice in writing. In this vein, Participant 11 reflected, "The freedom of writing outside the standard English makes my writing more authentic and creative" (Week 6). Such authenticity and creativity, according to Yamuna Kachru (1999), are critical to the future of academic writing: "If academic writing in general is not to become a sterile, formula-oriented activity, we have to encourage individual creativity in writing. It is the tension between received conventions and the innovative spirit of the individual that produces good writing in academic disciplines as well as in creative literature" (85). By nurturing students' linguistic creativity in the academic writing classroom, instructors adopt a polymodel (Kachru 1992) and empower students by providing space for them to navigate the balance between creative and academic discourses.

TOWARD A GLOBAL LITERACY FOCUS

Our data suggest that despite initial resistance by participants, the incorporation of WE texts into the L2 composition classroom positively impacted multilingual students' beliefs and attitudes about language variation and the relationship between WE and written communication. This finding supports Sonia Nieto's (2010) linguistic acceptance model, which recognizes "the necessity of affirming linguistic diversity at all educational levels and creating a pedagogical environment conducive to developing critical consciousness on the global spread of English" (Kubota 2001, 62). As US universities and, more specifically, first-year writing programs continue to diversify, it is imperative that writing instructors facilitate such linguistic and cultural awareness raising for all students. To do so, we recommend the following resources in addition to the two used in our study (i.e., *Rotten English* and "3 Ways to Speak English"):

- *The 5-Minute Linguist: Bite-Sized Essays on Language and Languages* (Rickerson and Hilton, 2019). This third-edition text provides accessible and brief readings on a variety language topics, many of which are directly related to language variation and change and the relationship between language and society. The mini essays address such questions as "What's the difference between dialects and languages?," "Do all languages have to change?," "Aren't pidgins and creoles just bad English?," "What causes foreign accents?," "What are lingua francas?," "What is African American English?," "How is language used on social media?," and "Is text messaging changing how I write and speak?" In the first-year writing classroom context, this text could be used to initiate classroom discussion and facilitate students' writing of reading responses or position statements, as well as their planning of related research projects.

- The Purdue Online Writing Lab (OWL). The OWL website houses several resources that highlight many of the fundamental aspects of WE (Purdue Online Writing Lab 2019). Some of the resource topics include "What counts as a 'new' English?," "How do new English varieties develop?," and "How do new English varieties function?" In addition to describing the differences between a few regional examples of English, the website also provides access to such pedagogically oriented resources as "How to Incorporate World Englishes in the Classroom," "Activities, Discussion Questions, and Writing Prompts," and a list of suggested readings. The OWL website is an accessible WE resource for first-year writing teachers looking to introduce their students to the topic of WE and its role in academic writing through focused classroom discussions and various writing assignments. The OWL YouTube channel also offers a supporting video of a short interview with WE scholar, Dr. Margie Berns (OWLPurdue 2019).

- Digital Archive of Literacy Narratives (DALN). The DALN is an open public resource of over 7,000 stories of individuals' literacy experiences from a variety of linguistic and cultural backgrounds (Digital Archive of Literacy Narratives n.d.). Also, the recent publication of the digital book *The Archive as Classroom: Pedagogical Approaches to the Digital Archive of Literacy Narratives* (Comer et al. 2019) provides writing instructors with a number of ideas for using this archive with students. This resource supports the idea of using literacy narratives to explore language variation.

- Tracy Luley's (2014) book review of *English with an Accent: Language, Ideology, and Discrimination in the United States* by Rosina Lippi-Green. In addition to detailed information about the related content in the book's second edition, this review includes a sample lesson plan based on Lippi-Green's use of Disney movies to explore linguistic and cultural discrimination. While designed specifically for an English as a Second Language (ESL) classroom, the lesson could be easily adapted for use with first-year writing students.

Noting the participants' positive movement through four stages, from resistance of WE to recognition of WE as a resource, we then ask: How can the transformative process of linguistic acceptance facilitate application of WE in the L2 composition classroom? Here, more pedagogical research is needed. Canagarajah (2006) and Young and Martinez (2011) propose the allowance of code-meshing in the composition classroom, which requires a reconceptualization of academic literacy as global literacy (Matsuda and Matsuda 2010). Such a reconceptualization should, according to Allison Skerrett and Randy Bomer (2013), highlight "flexibility across a wide range of discourses, genres, strategies, and practices that support and shape various forms of thinking and social action" (334). This pedagogical shift from monomodel to polymodel (Kachru 1992), however, requires advancing teacher development in composition from a pluralistic perspective (Canagarajah 2016). Writing instructors, for example, need hands-on training to effectively move between Matsuda and Matsuda's (2010) related principles of (1) teach the dominant language forms and functions, (2) teach the nondominant language forms and functions, (3) teach the boundary between what works and what does not, (4) teach the principles and strategies of discourse negotiation, and (5) teach the risks involved in using deviational features. Similarly, instructors would benefit from regular teacher collaboration "focused on (1) designing opportunities for students to interact in socially diverse activities and reflect deeply in writing on their communication experiences and (2) identifying key concepts instructors and students can use to make sense of the complex communication experiences in those contexts" (Martins and Van Horn 2018, 165). By prioritizing WE-based pedagogies in the training and development of writing instructors, composition curricula move toward a global literacy focus with teachers as local agents of change better positioned to advocate for the languages and literacies of their particular student writers. Such collective pedagogical change is needed to achieve more equitable first-year writing programs, academic institutions, and professional communities and to promote internationalization.

APPENDIX 11.A

MEETING WRITING PROMPTS

Meeting 1 Writing Prompts: Do you use different varieties of the same language (i.e., English or any of your additional languages)? If so, why? If not, why not? How would you describe the relationship between language and identity?

Meeting 8 Writing Prompts: After reading six World Englishes texts, what is your understanding of language variation? What role does language variation play in writing? In what ways has your study of World Englishes impacted your writing in English?

REFERENCES

Ahmad, Dohra, ed. 2007. *Rotten English: A Literary Anthology.* New York: Norton.

Berns, Margie. 2009. "World Englishes and Communicative Competence." In *The Handbook of World Englishes*, edited by Braj B. Kachru, Yamuna Kachru, and Cecil L. Nelson, 718–30. Hoboken, NJ: Wiley-Blackwell.

Bhatia, Vijay K. 2009. "Genres and Styles in World Englishes." In *The Handbook of World Englishes*, edited by Braj B. Kachru, Yamuna Kachru, and Cecil L. Nelson, 386–401. Hoboken, NJ: Wiley-Blackwell.

Canagarajah, A. Suresh. 2006. "The Place of World Englishes in Composition: Pluralization Continued." *College Composition and Communication* 57.4: 586–619.

Canagarajah, Suresh, ed. 2013a. *Literacy as Translingual Practice: Between Communities and Classrooms.* London: Routledge.

Canagarajah, Suresh. 2013b. *Translingual Practice: Global Englishes and Cosmopolitan Relations.* London: Routledge.

Canagarajah, Suresh. 2016. "Translingual Writing and Teacher Development in Composition." *College English* 78.3: 265–73.

Chang, Shih-Yu. 2015. "Toward World Englishes Writing: Is It Idealism in the Introductory Composition Class?" PhD diss., Purdue University, West Lafayette, IN. ProQuest (3736760).

Comer, Kathryn, Michael Harker, and Ben McCorkle, eds. 2019. *The Archive as Classroom: Pedagogical Approaches to the Digital Archive of Literacy Narratives.* Logan: Computers and Composition Digital Press / Utah State University Press. https://ccdigitalpress.org/book /archive-as-classroom/.

Digital Archive of Literacy Narratives. n.d. Accessed June 11, 2019. http://www.thedaln .org/#/home.

Dolezal, Fredric. 2009. "World Englishes and Lexicography." In *The Handbook of World Englishes*, edited by Braj B. Kachru, Yamuna Kachru, and Cecil L. Nelson, 694–707. Hoboken, NJ: Wiley-Blackwell.

Institute for International Education. 2018. "Open Doors 2018." Accessed June 18, 2019. https://www.iie.org/en/Research-and-Insights/Open-Doors/Open-Doors-2018-Media -Information.

Kachru, Braj B. 1992. *The Other Tongue: English across Cultures.* 2nd ed. Urbana: University of Illinois Press.

Kachru, Yamuna. 1999. "Culture, Context and Writing." In *Culture in Second Language Teaching and Learning*, edited by Eli Hinkel, 75–89. Cambridge: Cambridge University Press.

Kubota, Ryuko. 2001. "Teaching World Englishes to Native Speakers of English in the USA." *World Englishes* 20.1: 47–64.

Lee, Melissa E. 2014. "Shifting to the World Englishes Paradigm by Way of the Translingual Approach: Code-Meshing as a Necessary Means of Transforming Composition Peda-gogy." *TESOL Journal* 5.2: 312–29.

Luley, Tracy. 2014. "Review of *English with an Accent: Language, Ideology, and Discrimination in the United States*, by Rosina Lippi-Green." *TESOL Journal* 5.3: 546–50.

Lyiscott, Jamila. 2014. "3 Ways to Speak English." YouTube. https://www.youtube.com /watch?v=k9fmJ5xQ_mc&t=14s.

Martins, David Swiencicki, and Stanley Van Horn. 2018. "'I Am No Longer Sure This Serves Our Students Well': Redesigning FYW to Prepare Students for Transnational Literacy Realities." In *The Internationalization of US Writing Programs*, edited by Shirley K Rose and Irwin Weiser, 151–67. Logan: Utah State University Press.

Matsuda, Aya. 2013a. "World Englishes and Language Pedagogy." In *The Encyclopedia of Applied Linguistics*, edited by Carol A. Chapelle, 6224–30. Hoboken, NJ: Wiley-Blackwell.

Matsuda, Aya. 2013b. "World Englishes and Teaching English to Speakers of Other Lan-guages." In *The Encyclopedia of Applied Linguistics*, edited by Carol A. Chapelle. Hobo-ken, NJ: Wiley-Blackwell.

Matsuda, Aya, and Patricia Friedrich. 2011. "English as an International Language: A Cur-riculum Blueprint." *World Englishes* 30.3: 332–44.

Matsuda, Aya, and Paul Kei Matsuda. 2010. "World Englishes and the Teaching of Writing." *TESOL Quarterly* 44.2: 369–74.

Minnesota State University, Mankato. 2018a. "Spring 2018 MNSU International Student Population." ttps://www.mnsu.edu/international/statistics/Pop_Stats_20185_New _Format.pdf.

Minnesota State University, Mankato. 2018b. "Undergraduate Catalog 2018–2019." http:// www.mnsu.edu/supersite/academics/catalogs/undergraduate/2018-2019/2018-19 -undergrad_catalog.pdf.

Nieto, Sonia. 2010. *Language, Culture, and Teaching: Critical Perspectives.* 2nd ed. New York: Routledge.

OWLPurdue. 2019. "OWL Conversations: Dr. Margie Berns." https://www.youtube.com /watch?v=QAeWqckuuXI.

Patton, Michael Quinn. 2002. *Qualitative Research and Evaluation Methods.* Thousand Oaks, CA: Sage.

Pavlenko, Aneta. 2001. "'In the World of the Tradition, I was Unimagined': Negotiation of Identities in Cross-Cultural Autobiographies." *International Journal of Bilingualism* 5.3: 317–44.

Purdue Online Writing Lab. 2019. "World Englishes: An Introduction." Accessed June 30, 2019. https://owl.purdue.edu/owl/english_as_a_second_language/world_englishes /index.html.

Rickerson, E. M., and Barry Hilton, eds. 2019. *The 5-Minute Linguist: Bite-Sized Essays on Language and Languages.* Sheffield, England: Equinox.

Rose, Shirley K, and Irwin Weiser, eds. 2018. *The Internationalization of US Writing Programs.* Logan: Utah State University Press.

Skerrett, Allison, and Randy Bomer. 2013. "Recruiting Languages and Lifeworlds for Border-Crossing Compositions." *Research in the Teaching of English* 47.3: 313–37.

Smith, Larry E., and Cecil L. Nelson. 2009. "World Englishes and Issues of Intelligibility." In *The Handbook of World Englishes,* edited by Braj B. Kachru, Yamuna Kachru, and Cecil L. Nelson, 428–45. Hoboken, NJ: Wiley-Blackwell.

Wetzl, Ana Maria. 2013. "World Englishes in the Mainstream Composition Course: Undergraduate Students Respond to WE Writing." *Research in the Teaching of English* 48.2: 204–27.

You, Xiaoye, ed. 2018. *Transnational Writing Education: Theory, History, and Practice.* New York: Routledge.

Young, Vershawn Ashanti, and Aja Y. Martinez, eds. 2011. *Code-Meshing as World English: Pedagogy, Policy, Performance.* National Council of Teacher of English.

12

TEACHING WITH ARCHIVES
Transformative Pedagogy

Lynée Lewis Gaillet

The 2018 "A Changing Major: The Report of the 2016–2017 ADE Ad Hoc Committee on the English Major" (ADE Report) offers a descriptive national snapshot of the undergraduate English degree, including valuable data reports to support not only a summary status of the major but also recommendations for enriching the degree and attracting new majors in a climate of declining enrollments in the humanities. The report's primary aims are to suggest ways that English departments can build on strengths of concentrations typically housed in English departments (creative writing, literature, rhetoric and composition, and education), address student needs and demands, and connect the English degree to employment opportunities. The report hinges in great measure on curriculum reform, both to bring the English degree into the twenty-first century and to alleviate historical turf wars occurring among the various concentrations typically found within English departments. The course design I describe in this chapter directly addresses the issues raised in the ADE Report while also offering examples of potentially transformative pedagogy, one that asks students to merge personal experiences and interests, primary and secondary research, activist rhetoric, and community engagement. By integrating primary methodological instruction into writing classes, we can better prepare students for college success and for both academic and alt-ac employment. Additionally, within archival-based classroom spaces, students introduce and challenge one another to understand new issues by engaging in various interpretations of existing materials. They gain hands-on experience unsettling archives and in the process (re)examine and articulate their positions and beliefs.

The abundance of recent pedagogical scholarship focused on the "archival turn" in writing instruction (Hayden 2015, 2017; Gaillet and Eble 2016; Enoch and VanHaitsma 2012; Greer and Grobman 2016;

https://doi.org/10.7330/9781646421428.c012

Graban and Hayden in progress; Comer et al. 2019) offers practical research advice designed for both graduate and undergraduate students, resulting in a seamless vertical curriculum that attracts students from creative writing, education, literary studies, and rhetoric/composition concentrations. This Scholarship of Teaching and Learning (SOTL) connects archival investigation to specific venues, locales, and digital spaces while asking students to write about what they know, beginning with researching communities to which they already belong. The result is classroom research tied to what matters most to students, topics that often resonate with social justice, student rights, and career preparation issues.

The appeal and pedagogical significance of primary research and writing work at every level of instruction. Historically, scholars have adopted primary research methods in their own work but taught that method only to graduate students, particularly as they write theses and dissertations (alienating and often artificial/prescriptive writing exercises). However, archival investigation provides an organic method of work for students researching and composing at any level, one where the topic itself generates novel options for researching, organizing, and presenting findings. A dissertation, a graduation portfolio, a first-year writing (FYW) research paper, and the like often mandate that a student write to the form. In archival work, students select topics of personal significance or local interest, and the primary materials are frequently connected to a community who holds shared values and expectations. The community, materials under investigation, and intended audiences/stakeholders shape how findings are delivered—sometimes in ways that the teacher has not anticipated and that correspond with workplace literacies. Final course research isn't often delivered in traditional research paper formats.

In this chapter, I want to highlight a split-level graduate/undergraduate course in archival research methods, providing a rationale for the course along with dovetailed assignments that introduce students to digital and material primary investigations. Most important, this chapter relies on student voices that discuss the salient features of the class, along with some of the challenges. Students in this course see themselves as primary researchers, evident in their personal testimonies and descriptions of their work. They conduct interviews, surveys, and ethnographies while also visiting a broad range of local special collections (a papermaking museum, Tennessee suffragist papers) and digital archives (Digital Archive of Literacy Narratives, YouTube ContraPoints, QAnon). Some students investigate familial ephemera (immigration records, family photos, and letters), community records (blueprints and government documents), and collated business materials (Southern Labor Archives, SunTrust Bank archives) connected to their research questions that often investigate activist and workplace issues. In bringing together qualitative and quantitative research strategies, class participants create ways to code their findings and learn firsthand (and in self-driven projects) not only how to "do" primary research, but also how to enact much larger concepts integral to writing studies: participate in multidimensional collaborations with community organizations and stakeholders (Myatt and Gaillet 2017). Students become archivists in ways that open access to foundational and historical information that is available but often hidden in little-known collections' finding aids (Graban and Hayden in progress); engage in rhetorical activism by participating in marches, writing letters, and organizing dissenting voices (*College Composition and Communication* 2019, issue focused on pedagogical action in the world); and disseminate their research in academic and professional forums such as conferences, community talks, blogs, and newsletters (Gaillet and Guglielmo 2014). Along the way, many students engage in research and writing that is therapeutic, as they explain below. They seek archival evidence and solutions for building more inclusive communities, for finding historical antecedents and case studies relevant to contemporary social problems, and for understanding job opportunities that they thought were heretofore unavailable to them.

Archival research courses often dovetail with university initiatives in unique ways as well. For example, my university has recently adopted two student initiatives that I now fold into archival class structure. The Humanities Inclusivity Program (HIP), working under the umbrella of the Center for the Advancement of Students and Alumni into Graduate School and Professional Programs (CASA), mentors diverse undergraduates as they work towards admission into PhD programs, medical school, law school, and other professional programs. This initiative addresses the fundamental need to change who is in the pipeline in order to diversify hiring practices. Students accepted into the HIP program make a two-year commitment, and the positions include a paid research assistantship, required research presentations, participation in faculty-led reading groups, program-specific events, and professional development workshops. These program components correspond with archival and primary research assignments, ones easily added to existing course curriculum. My school's new quality enhancement plan (QEP) focuses on college-to-career preparation, presenting another rich opportunity for integrating primary investigation of professional work opportunities into writing and research classes. By incorporating local strategic plans into course designs, faculty may find a treasure trove of administrative support in terms of internal funding and Center for Excellence in Teaching and Learning (CETL) resources for implementing archival research. These two initiatives serendipitously resonate with my own historical research and antecedents for expanding course parameters.

COURSE ORIGINS

I became interested in the transformative power of student-centered pedagogy while investigating the work of innovative pedagogue George Jardine for my dissertation. Jardine, professor of moral philosophy at the University of Glasgow from 1774 to 1824, was committed to revising traditional curriculum in order to better meet the changing needs of his young students and to prepare them for careers in venues other than the bar and pulpit—jobs available to Scots in the wake of the 1707 Act of Union and subsequent political changes. In *Outlines of Philosophical Education* ([1818] 1825), Jardine meticulously describes his rationale for curriculum reform, new class designs, and the effects of asking students to engage in epistemic writing and learning. His influence is credited for introducing sequenced writing assignments in a wide range of courses across the Scottish University curriculum ("Evidence" 1837), and he relied upon a structured system of collaborative learning and peer editing, documented in *Outlines*. His nineteenth-century pedagogical plan for preparing Scots to advance by pursuing new employment opportunities holds merit for our students as well. As a new assistant professor, I too realized that introductory writing classes at my institution no longer met the needs of my urban students, many of whom, like Jardine's pupils, were first-generation college students from diverse backgrounds. A cadre of graduate teaching assistants and I began to design course materials to counter the policing Turnitin movement launched in 1997, burnout among teachers, and FYW programs that still viewed composition courses as weed-out opportunities. In seeking alternatives and solutions, we were guided by the certainty that students surpass abilities and are interested in research and writing when they see themselves as knowledgeable about a topic. Using that understanding as a starting point, we began informally restructuring FYW courses to include opportunities for archival and primary research based on students' curiosities and nonacademic interests.

Students began to see new possibilities in their academic work and to find ways to blend personal and local areas of interests and expertise with community and workplace issues. They no longer wrote traditional patchworked essays and papers but instead combined secondary and primary investigation to create finding aids for undocumented collections, compile commonplace books of research materials gleaned from diverse existing collections and undocumented sources, build wikis, write bibliographical essays for other researchers, and conduct and edit interviews. As archival pedagogy has caught on, recently, scholar-teachers have begun overtly sharing pedagogical plans for teaching with archives (Graban and Hayden in progress; Comer et al. 2019; Greer and Groban 2016), but we need additional SOTL addressing the how-tos of primary research.

Early iterations of the course asked students to interview a multitude of professionals, asking how they incorporated primary research in the workplace. Michelle Eble and I included a variation of this recurring feature, "Profile of a Primary Researcher," in our archival writing text based on our early pedagogical experiments (*Primary Research and Writing: People, Places, and Spaces* [Gaillet and Eble 2016]); profiles include interviews with professionals from across the disciplines: a historical fiction writer, a folklorist, a chamber of commerce executive, a newspaper journalist, ethnographers, an architectural historian, a professional interviewer/editor, a surveyor for national research center, a public relations professional, and an FDA quality investigator. In particular, asking students to conduct interviews reinforces salient components of a humanities degree that well serve current discussions (like the ones in the ADE Report) about ways to reshape majors in light of investigating a wider range of career opportunities. Another recurring course feature, "Communities in Context," highlights traditional and digital communities; teachers can point to ways in which specific archives are connected to characteristics of varied groups. This assignment asks students to analyze familiar sites and digital communities to better understand the numerous stylistic variations and genres that they may emulate in order to meet the expectations of a defined audience. Primary research is always tied to communities, and this initial assignment serves as a gateway, often suggesting other digital sites for investigation—and in the process expanding students' understandings of writing in a range of genres and professional settings.

COURSE DETAILS

I've paired *Primary Research and Writing* with *Working in the Archives* (Ramsey 2016) and the collected essays found in *Landmark Essays on Archival Research* (Gaillet et al. 2016), part of Routledge's resurrected

Landmark Essays Series. Following are the learning objectives for the split-level introduction to archival research course:

1. To demonstrate familiarity with archival methods and methodology (assessed by reading responses and by crafting a methodology section for each research assignment).

2. To understand and engage in digital archival research (assessed through digital archive project and in presentation of annotated scholarship to the class).

4. To demonstrate an understanding of positionality issues (assessed through research statements included with each major project).

5. To demonstrate an understanding of steps required to prepare for archival visits and to physically visit manuscript collections (assessed in site visit memoir and assignment, as well as final project reflection essay).

6. To design a primary research plan (assessed in memos for major paper assignments and in final project).

7. To understand and devise primary research tools (assessed in ethnography/interview/survey assignments.)

The assignments are designed to introduce archival skills, but the subjects of those investigations are not dictated by the teacher. Some students engage in stand-alone research projects for each exercise, while others integrate the course assignments around a central, self-selected topic (each exercise is accompanied by a detailed assignment sheet and requires a formal memo submitted to the instructor for discussion/ approval prior to beginning the project). Course assignments include (1) summarizing and presenting to the class a recent article addressing archival research methods, (2) a site visit to a local archival collection and accompanying report describing and detailing experiences accessing researching site materials, (3) an ethnographic paper describing two site observations, including both observational notes and a narrative/ analytical reflections on the observations, (4) a survey or interview, including a transcription of questions/answers and a short analysis of findings, (5) a digital archives paper investigating electronic materials (university/college libraries, public libraries, city/town/state government, or nonprofit and corporate organizations), and (6) a final project that unites the other distinct projects, explaining the significance of findings for interested communities members. The final assignment also asks students to engage in reflective practices about their research/ writing experiences.

At the end of the class, we hold a miniconference open to faculty and other students; class researchers present their final projects either as a poster board session, enactment, discussion session, paper, or other product appropriate to the project. Often, special collection librarians, family and community members, and interested stakeholders attend to hear how researchers address ways archival investigation can be used to (1) inform our understanding and explain situations or circumstances, (2) generate knowledge about a specific person's influence or a community movement, (3) recover people, events, or actions in the past that might have gone unnoticed, and/or (4) revise a common story given new primary materials, and so on. I also craft a roundtable of the best presentations for submission to local or regional conferences. Occasionally, the classwork leads to employment advancement or new job opportunities: one undergraduate student was promoted after he analyzed primary data to point out workplace inefficiencies and loss of revenue; another student volunteered to create a finding aid at her temple and was subsequently hired to continue the work; and one graduate student catapulted the class research into her thesis topic (researching archives of a nineteenth-century women's college) and a position as the full-time director of the town's Historical Society and Museum.

I asked class participants to illustrate course components and features by sharing their individual research, sampled in the following section, but what these seemingly disparate projects share, apart from reliance on primary investigation, is a firm grounding in author expertise. For each of these researchers, the subject matter is personal in some way or another, a part of their identity, reflective of social justice or familial interests, or connected to job aspirations. Because they are vested in their selected topics, students are willing to take on course exercises that initially seem alienating. They dig deep both to integrate and make meaningful the standard syllabus assignments, tailored for their specific research processes and findings. Students leave the class with a rich portfolio of ideas and materials to inform future private and academic projects; the work extends beyond the requirements of a single course. Many students gather evidence to support activist projects, as you will find within these testimonies, many connections and references to workplace rhetoric, and deliverables.

STUDENT VOICES

Students (both undergraduate and graduate) come to this course with a bit of trepidation—the archival research focus is alien to most of them, research topics are not assigned, and the format of the final project is fluid. The freedom that necessarily comes with archival research is daunting as well as liberating. As an instructor of archival research methods, I've come to embrace the unknown and am prepared to be the one who learns the most in any given course; however, this kind of abdication of authority in some areas of the course is alienating for many teachers. Teaching with archives means that you don't know exactly what subject student projects may tackle or what form projects may take—and both teacher and student must be prepared to change tactics when initial plans reach a dead end. In the passages below, students from the split-level archival research methods course select areas of the class upon which they wish to reflect (finding a topic, therapeutic nature of archival research, digital vs. physical primary investigation, creating a finding aid, familial projects, community projects and rhetorical activism, etc.). In many cases, students bring up insights that I had not anticipated. This chorale of voices captures the essence of archival research pedagogy. (Nota bene: while I have not taught this course online, Juliette Kitchens and Janine Morris at NOVA University developed and teach a successful online lower-division course grounded in *Primary Research: People, Places, and Spaces*).

On Finding a Topic

Selecting a research area is one of the first/biggest obstacles that students in archival-focused courses face. The assignments are intentionally vague. Margaret Kuhn discusses the confusion and frustration she felt initially, particularly as an undergraduate enrolled in a split-level course:

> I ventured into archival research methods with little understanding of how to conduct such research, plenty of interests in vague directions, and no idea where to start. Being surrounded by graduate student classmates who have all seemingly found their niches was somewhat intimidating—where was my niche? Why didn't I have a beautiful research question and intriguing commentary on a subject I wanted to pursue? However, while reading about serendipitous discoveries in the archive, I realized I was in the midst of my own string of serendipitous moments that led me to discover what may become my niche. The previous semester, I was in an experimental rhetoric class about decision making, when about halfway through, our professor switched the course focus to literacy studies. Immediately, I was enamored. Simultaneously, I was working on a grant application to teach English abroad and was having trouble with what to write about. When the idea of teaching a foreign language merged with a focused study of literacy, I knew not only what to write about, but remembered why I was interested in teaching English in the first place. The class finished, my Fulbright application was submitted, and I departed to Vietnam for the summer with my best friend, to visit her family that hadn't immigrated to

The States. There I learned bits of the language, lots of the culture, and ate a ridiculous amount of food. Upon return, I was more attuned to the interactions of my friend and her family in a country and culture they had adopted. One day, I was reviewing my application that focused on literacy and bilingualism (as I scarfed down homemade Pho) and realized I had the perfect course project at my fingertips—Vietnamese Americans and their bilingual literacy development. The topic dealt with concepts that interest me and that I had spent the last six months studying; I had a connection with the community and a basis of knowledge about it.

Margaret's final presentation was detailed, included a wide range of both primary and secondary research components gleaned from her friendships and experiences—and certainly stood toe to toe with the graduate student projects from the class. While the project was grounded in the personal, the final presentation was academic and inviting, particularly for researchers interested in cultural studies and current immigration issues.

On Therapeutic Writing

Student projects in this class often become transformative on many levels: students may explore issues that have intrigued them for years or personal concerns that they can now give scholarly attention; they learn something about themselves, families, or local communities by doing archival work; or perhaps they use class projects to engage in rhetorical activism that resonates in their lives. Marta Hess explains how her research of ephemera and club documents became therapeutic:

> Mary and Ross Catanzariti Bell, my grandparents, came from Italy to the United States when they were children, and they, as well as my mother and her sister, because they were Italian, faced prejudice and discrimination in their small Western Pennsylvania college town. For example, when they moved into their home, a neighbor told my grandparents not to expect visits from the other neighbors because the family was Italian, and therefore, dirty and dumb, and informed them that they really weren't wanted there. However, after one neighbor ventured into Mary's kitchen and she reported to the others that the "house was so clean, you could eat off her floor," things changed somewhat for my grandparents. Other relatives (including my Aunt and Mother) overcame similar personal barriers and career obstacles.
>
> Although I didn't experience the kind of prejudice that my relatives did, I've always felt sad when I imagined what happened to them. Several years ago, when I was researching the archives at the Heinz History Center in Pittsburgh, I happened on a treasure trove of material that documented the clubs and societies that were established in that area by the many ethnic immigrants who arrived in Western Pennsylvania at

the end of the nineteenth and early twentieth centuries. This material included minutes, membership books, scrapbooks, and photographs for the clubs established to help newly arrived individuals to both retain their identities and navigate the complicated and confusing "American" ways of doing things. These societies not only provided benefits for their own members, but raised funds for charities in the Pittsburgh area and in Italy. They were truly part of the fabric of the society of Pittsburgh. Of course, I knew that my relatives were not unique in their experiences, but immersing myself in this material provided me with concrete examples of the ways that other individuals in their same situations also exhibited strength, ingenuity, integrity, and intelligence that enabled them to thrive in their new country.

Marta explains the inherent therapeutic nature of archival research and the role serendipity can play in primary searches. Materials that she discovered during her research for the course led to Marta's dissertation topic: a feminist and cultural investigation of community cookbooks.

On Digital versus Physical Archival Research

In class, we discuss the limitations and advantages of both electronic and "in person" archival investigation (including issues of time, money, and access). Students are required to both make a site visit to a collection and conduct online research. Below, Meagan Malone recounts her research experiences, comparing and contrasting digital and physical investigation. Not only does she speak about sensory differences between the two kinds of research, but she insightfully comments upon the way meaning is made in different milieus and offers a novel perspective on finding aids:

My recent first experience visiting an archival collection and interacting with meticulously catalogued artifacts was an unexpectedly mysterious one. The William Dawson papers at the Rose Archives [Emory University] fit tidily into perhaps thousands of folders within 120 small, uniform boxes. To see, touch, smell, feel, and hear any of the items requires overcoming small but very real physical boundaries: lifting a lid, removing a folder, opening a cover. To preserve the original order of the materials, as a rule, researchers are allowed only one folder out of the box at any given time. While I examined the contents of one folder, the contents of others existed within reach but out of sight, tucked away behind their own set of boundaries. I worked through each box in a semi-constant state of anticipation. It was not until sifting through the last folder of a box that I felt a vague sense of what that particular container really held. The search itself was punctuated by individual, temporally disparate, multi-sensory moments, yet at the beginning and end of the process, I had before me a silent, drab-colored crate that was incapable of speaking for what was inside. I learned that the box-folder structure of the archival system resists affordance of, at least in a visual sense, a holistic, birds-eye view of the contents of the archive.

However, many, but not all, digital archives do afford a larger, over-arching perspective of their contents. When seen as digital archives, YouTube (YT) channels have a number of features that allow a creator or archivist to make clear, compelling arguments about the artifacts as a whole through the curation of the collection; furthermore, these features allow researchers or users of the archives to get a visceral, immediate sense of the contents of the archives. A YT channel's Home, Videos, or Playlist page each can be seen as a finding-aide that presents arguments or narratives about the collection as a whole in an audio and visual mode, stories that may go unnoticed if each video were cordoned off into individual physical containers, unable to be experienced simul-taneously on some level. This holistic viewing experience afforded by a digital archive contributes a richness and complexity to the way creators and archivists make meaning and to the work researchers must do to interpret the collection.

Meagan's final project included visual representations of the YT channel finding aids, an engaging and illustrative way to shape the next stages of her research on digital platforms. In the next iteration of this project (after the class has concluded), Meagan will address these research ques-tions: How can scholars in English studies harness the popular power of the YT platform to bring relevance to their own projects? In what ways might these scholars cultivate compelling alternative public defini-tions and narratives of marginalized populations and disseminate those narratives? How might English studies scholars answer Jean Burgess and Joshua Green's (2018) call for "professional archivists, librarians and cu-rators . . . to work within or alongside YouTube to achieve their organi-zational missions" (138).

On Creating a Finding Aid

While Meagan comments on discovering electronic arrangements of materials that can serve as a kind of organic finding aid, Sarah Bramblett took on an undocumented collection as her class project; she conducted the daunting background work required to create a finding aid for uncatalogued artifacts. Below she discusses ways in which she blended the assignments for the course toward her final goal of compiling a find-ing aid by working with donors:

> In 2016, experienced journalists Dr. Randall and Mrs. Kathleen Harber donated their collection of typewriters to Georgia State University. Two years later, the collection remained largely undocumented and

uncategorized, crammed into a storage closet. I set out to create a finding aid for the typewriters. I began with a site visit to the Robert C. Williams Museum of Papermaking, a university-sponsored archive that inspires a wide audience to ask new questions about historic yet commonplace technology. For the course's digital project, I investigated the Virtual Typewriter Museum, which provided exemplary information about the individual typewriters within the GSU collection. Through initial investigation of related, finalized archives, I was able to orient myself within the field and envision long-term possibilities.

The museum visits laid the foundation to begin a series of interviews. Speaking with faculty and administrators in various departments at GSU provided practical information on the difficulties inherent in displaying the typewriters locally. I learned about the costs of display cases, and I was provided access to the Gift-in-Kind record with serial numbers of the typewriters. These conversations also helped me find the Harbers and discuss the collection with the donors. From the interview with Dr. and Mrs. Harber, I matched the invaluable personal stories about the method of collection, the original owners, and the anecdotes about Communication's history to the typewriters. Though my research did not culminate in the creation of a complete finding aid or public display, the necessary foundation is now prepared. More importantly, these initial steps led to important questions that further justify a thorough finding aid so the research can continue.

Like many students in the class, Sarah's project is only just begun—not finished at the end of the term. The next step is to work with administrators, university foundation representatives, and craftsmen to create a rich display that honors the donor's legacy and the machines themselves. Teachers must be comfortable in archival research classes to design assignments that allow for assessing projects in progress. And students usually leave the class with research agendas and trajectories that they may continue in other courses or independently, as Jess Rose so beautifully recounts next.

On Familial Projects

Many students take on projects inspired by family history, as Marta Hess attests above; however, some students select topics that are woven into the fabric of their family histories. Jess's project, "American Song," explores the creation and provenance of "You Are My Sunshine," a part of the unofficial American songbook, alongside favorites like Mildred J. Hill's ditty "Happy Birthday," and Woody Guthrie's protest song "This Land Is Your Land." Jess's family contends that her great-grandfather, Oliver Hood, wrote "American Song"—a claim of documented, heated dispute. In the archival methods class, Jess began researching her family's claims in earnest. Below she explains the Sisyphus-like nature of her project, one that is likely to take years to fully investigate:

> The work for "American Song" is naturally transformative, requiring Yogic flexibility and demonstrating the shifting nature of archival research. In fact, the early research into informal and formal archives has actually forced the project to shift and reshape. It began as a small archival project about a quintessential American tune and a family's claim of authorship, but came to include a discussion of how technology and legal infrastructure innately privilege access. Along with this discussion came expanded concepts about the importance of multimodal and local literacies. The song, itself, has even transformed over the years, from a serious, lover's lament to a whimsical, timeless lullaby, where lyrics have been added, changed, and crowd-sourced. In fact, everything about this song identifies it as chase ephemeral, even though it has buried itself deeply into American culture.
>
> Hood's song was born of mill neighborhoods lined with houses built for families who worked at the town textile mill. These houses were modest, with small gardens, but whose surrounding lawns were devoid of grass, an expensive luxury. Only the most important things were spared—a family bible, photographs, instruments and a favorite suit. All else was considered disposable and burnable, or too showy and unnecessary. There is no Hood family archive, or collected papers; many of the official records went up in smoke with a courthouse fire in the 1960's; descendants all have some element of anecdote and theory, but anything published or legally concrete has yet to emerge. Thus, I am left with the task of building a mountain of circumstantial evidence that outweighs the legal copyright that was stolen so long. This work is, in a sense, part of Hood's legacy.

Jess's beautiful, if frustrating, class project will be the subject of her dissertation. While this work is deeply personal, its final iteration will take the form of a copyright case. Many of the projects in archival research classes begin as a kind of personal investigation or search for justice but eventually take on more universal, scholarly forms. Randall Morgan's course project is also integral to his identity, but with very different intentions and community outcomes.

On Community Projects and Rhetorical Activism

Understanding the connections between archives and communities is a fundamental goal of primary research. Randall, a lesbian, gay, bisexual, transgender, and queer/questioning (LGBTQ) Pentecostal pastor and undergraduate student, explains the transformative and personal significance of his community research in support of a local building project:

> Archival Research Methods helped me with a building project and an outreach strategy for our church, but more importantly, it's helped me build a personal, mental, planning space. Having now gone to an archival site,

something new is happening with the way I think about "where" churches meet. As an overseer of a network of churches, I've been a part of at least twelve churches moving into a new space or from one location into another. Often there has been very little strategic research done concerning the history of the new spaces; churches have simply seen a space (warehouses, storefronts, etc.) and have moved there without knowing the history of the building or the neighborhood.

Having gone through Archival Research Methods, I am now insisting that senior pastors go to the archives and find out the history of their buildings and spaces. The people who make up their cities and neighborhoods have corporate memories of these places, and if we don't know those memories, we can't honor or rewrite the history that affects the future of those buildings. New Covenant Church of Atlanta, a predominantly LGBTQ, Pentecostal church, bought 1600 Eastland Road from the United Methodist Church on January 19, 2018. On that day, we became a part of a building's sixty year old story. We didn't know this, but the archives taught us this. These wonderfully hopeful and awfully despairing archives speak, and they tell us what our challenges must be and where our greatest successes can be found. We have discovered the community without knocking on a door; we are finding allies and champions by simply looking somewhere so few ever do, the archives.

CONCLUSION

As these students' narratives richly illustrate, archival investigation has the potential to transform lives through a hopeful pedagogy. Offering students the freedom to research topics that resonate with their interests and experiences opens up a new world of pedagogical possibilities and venues ripe for investigation. These assignments and students examples provide unique and specific ways to discuss elements commonly characterizing composition courses, including selecting a topic and avoiding plagiarism (which rarely exists in archival research projects), digital research and composing, understanding audiences, developing an authentic voice, engaging in hybrid research methods and documentation, and learning to compose in a wide range of genres. Students find archival investigation to be both inviting and liberating once they learn to play by a new set of research guidelines, trust the teacher to be receptive to deliverables that often go against the norm, and embrace the idea that projects are rarely "finished" at the end of the term. In the process of engaging in what feels like real-world research, students come to learn something new about themselves and the communities to which they belong and communicate.

Both hybrid in nature and appropriate for students working across the disciplines, the archival research method is essential to academic and workplace investigation alike. It has the power to change students' fundamental understanding of ways to integrate life and school, experience and curiosity into component assignments that lead to novel and exciting larger research projects. In the preface to the ADE's "A Changing Major" report, MLA director Paula Krebs asks English departments to consider ways to reform curriculum in an effort to "meet our students where they are and help them become the readers and writers, the citizens and workers, and the parents, friends, and community members they want to be" (preface). Archival research presents a pedagogical solution for doing just that.

REFERENCES

Burgess, Jean, and Joshua Green. 2018. *YouTube: Online Video and Participatory Culture.* 2nd ed. Malden, ME: Polity.

"A Changing Major: The Report of the 2016–2017 ADE Ad Hoc Committee on the English Major." 2018. New York: Associations of Departments of English.

College Composition and Communication. 2019. Special Issue on Pedagogical Action in the World 70.3.

Comer, Katie, Michael Harker, and Ben McCorkle, eds. 2019. *The Archive as Classroom: Pedagogical Approaches to Digital Archive of Literacy Narratives.* Logan: Utah State University Press.

Enoch, Jessica, and Pamela VanHaitsma. 2012. "Archival Literacy: Reading the Rhetoric of Digital Archives in the Undergraduate Classroom." *College Composition and Communication* 62.2: 216–42.

"Evidence, oral and documentary, taken and received by the Commissioners appointed by His Majesty George IV., July 23d, 1826; and reappointed by His Majesty William IV., October 12, 1830; for visiting the universities of Scotland." 1837. London: W Clowes and Sons.

Gaillet, Lynée Lewis, and Michelle F. Eble. 2016. *Primary Research: People, Places, and Spaces.* New York: Routledge.

Gaillet, Lynée Lewis, Helen Diana Eidson, and Donald Gammill, eds. 2016. *Landmark Essays on Archival Research.* New York: Routledge.

Gaillet, Lynée Lewis, and Letizia Guglielmo. 2014. *Scholarly Publication in a Changing Academic Landscape: Models for Success.* New York: Palgrave Macmillan.

Graban, Tarez, and Wendy Hayden, eds. In progress. *Teaching Rhetoric and Composition through the Archives.* Logan: Utah State University Press.

Greer, Jane, and Laurie Grobman, eds. 2016. *Teaching Writing and Rhetoric at Museums, Memorials, and Archives.* New York: Routledge.

Hayden, Wendy. 2015. " 'Gifts' of the Archives: A Pedagogy for Undergraduate Research." *College Composition and Communication* 66.3: 402–26.

Jardine, George. [1818] 1825. *Outlines of Philosophical Education, Illustrated by the Method of Teaching the Logic Class at the University of Glasgow.* 2nd ed. Edinburgh: Oliver and Boyd.

Myatt, Alice Johnston, and Lynée Lewis Gaillet, eds. 2017. *Writing Program and Writing Center Collaborations.* London and New York: Palgrave MacMillan.

Ramsey, Alexis, Wendy Sharer, Barb L'Eplattenier, and Lisa Mastrangelo, eds. 2010. *Working in the Archives.* Carbondale, IL: SIUP.

13

DESIGNING AN OPEN-ACCESS ONLINE WRITING PROGRAM
Negotiating Tensions between Disciplinary Ideals and Institutional Realities

Joanne Baird Giordano and Cassandra Phillips

"A Position Statement of Principles and Example Effective Practices for Online Writing Instruction (OWI)" (2013) from the now-defunct Conference on College Composition and Communication (CCCC) OWI Committee outlines standards for online writing instruction.[1] The authors argue for disciplinary guidelines in an online teaching and learning environment that supports both instructors and students. The OWI principles lay a foundation for developing an online writing program based on writing studies theory and practice while also arguing for disciplinary values and ethical standards, including manageable class sizes, instructor control over course content and teaching, fair compensation, and faculty training. However, many of the OWI principles can be difficult to implement fully at two-year access institutions and some public four-year institutions because of institutional mandates, limited financial and professional resources, contingent staffing, and limited instructor agency. Disciplinary principles (including position statements from National Council of Teachers of English [NCTE], CCCC, and other professional organizations) that describe best or preferred practices are often unachievable ideals for writing programs that lack the financial resources, professional staffing, or autonomy within an institution to implement them. Program administrators and instructors working to improve curriculum, teaching, and student learning must figure out how to balance important principles for writing instruction within the lived realities of their teaching environments by making decisions that reflect locally situated constraints and giving up some ideals to move their work forward.

Beth L. Hewett describes the development of the OWI principles as "a story that admits of uncertainty and a need for 'A Position Statement

https://doi.org/10.7330/9781646421428.c013

of Principles and Example Effective Practices for OWI' to be organic; changing with research, scholarship, and experience; and one to which the practitioners in the field can contribute as well as from which they can benefit" (Hewett 2015, 37). Part of that story needs to include more professional knowledge about how to adapt principles for effective online teaching to diverse types of institutions, especially teaching environments with obstacles that affect how writing instructors implement disciplinary practices. In this chapter, we hope to contribute to conversations about online writing instruction and writing program transformations by focusing on challenges, limitations, and opportunities for bringing about change when institutional culture and/or a lack of resources impose constraints on instructors and program administrators. In particular, we explore the gap between disciplinary knowledge about how to create optimal conditions for teaching and learning online and the working conditions that many members of our profession face.

Using examples from award-winning program redesign work for a two-year, open-admissions OWI program, this chapter describes the process of negotiating tensions between disciplinary practices and the complex realities of designing and implementing change within an online writing program under conditions of austerity in a program that serves a wide range of diverse learners, including students who have limited experience with academic literacy and using technology as a tool for learning. As writing program and developmental education coordinators of a multicampus statewide institution,[2] we collaborated with department colleagues over several years to redesign a four-course writing program to support the literacy development of open-admissions students who are still developing the reading, writing, information literacy, and technology skills required for successfully engaging in college-level courses and working toward completing a degree. A major component of our program redesign efforts focused on creating a cohesive online writing program that reflected disciplinary best practices and the unique learning needs of online students at an open-access institution. Our online students faced barriers to course completion and college learning that complicated our work. As a result, redesigning our online writing program was by far the most time-consuming and labor-intensive part of our program development work, extending several years beyond the time frame for putting curricular changes and instructional resources in place for face-to-face courses.

Our work began with a review of published scholarship, disciplinary position statements, and research on student readers and writers conducted at our own institution, followed by intensive conversations about how to change our writing program to support transitions to college-level reading and writing for students at an open-access institution. Our goal was to redesign a program to support students who would be excluded from higher education at other institutions in our state and to identify learning goals, curricular revisions, and instructional methods that would provide accessible writing courses for all students regardless of their prior learning experiences or literacy skills. In contrast, our existing writing program at that time was structured around approaches to teaching that focused on well-prepared students and models for instruction that duplicated instructors' graduate teaching experiences at research universities. Our online program was disconnected both from disciplinary knowledge about students' development as college writers and from best practices for online teaching.

Drawing from our experience, we explore the challenges that constrain faculty and program administrators at open-admissions institutions as they attempt to implement disciplinary principles and best practices. We also describe the compromises that are a natural part of doing program change work within the structures of an institution, which may require writing studies professionals to selectively let go of some problems that can't be fixed with available time and resources. We hope that our experience illuminates the complexities that faculty face at any institution type as they seek to transform their programs while also dealing with institutional realities that conflict with disciplinary knowledge about how to teach writing and support student learning.

CONTEXTS AND CHALLENGES FOR OPEN-ACCESS OWI

The introduction to the *Principles and Example Effective Practices for OWI* describes the need to adapt principles for online teaching to institutional contexts: "In writing this document, the Committee agreed that so-called 'best' or effective practices are most usefully shaped in the context of particular institutional settings—such as 2-year colleges, 4-year colleges, state and private universities, and for-profit educational venues" (n.p.). However, implementing effective practices for teaching online poses complex challenges for open-access writing programs. Open-admissions institutions enroll students with limited proficiency in reading, writing, and using technology; have reduced funding and resources in comparison to more selective institutions (Kahlenberg et al. 2018); often lack a writing program administrator or cohesive writing program (Calhoun-Dillahunt 2011; Klausman 2008); often use scaled courses and publisher products; and face distinct administrative road-blocks to following OWI principles and other disciplinary standards.

Further, teaching diverse students who enroll in open-admissions writing programs requires professional development that goes beyond the initial graduate training of community college instructors (see Calhoon-Dillahunt et al. 2006). The Two-Year College English Association white paper "Characteristics of the Highly Effective Two-Year College Instructor in English" (Klausman et al. 2012) emphasizes the importance of adapting teaching to the diverse needs of students who enroll at community colleges:

> Highly effective two-year college English instructors understand and value student diversity. Their curriculum design and teaching approaches are genuinely inclusive and responsive to the broad differences in age; social and economic backgrounds; racial, ethnic, religious, and international affiliations; learning styles; and academic preparation that reflect the democratic nature of the typical two-year college classroom.

This particular disciplinary standard for teaching is an ideal that is typically not the reality for most two-year college writing programs, which often have a significant gap between students' college readiness and instructors' time and training to address the needs of underprepared readers and writers. For example, the Center for Community College Student Engagement (CCCSE) reports that 70 percent of community college instructors work off the tenure track and teach over half of two-year college courses but "have infrequent opportunities to interact with peers about teaching and learning" and "rarely are included in important campus discussions about the kinds of change needed to improve student learning, academic progress, and college completion" (3). They are more likely to teach developmental education compared to their tenure-line and tenured colleagues (CCCSE 7), working with the least-prepared and most academically at-risk students. The problem with contingent labor for online writing programs is not that instructors are not qualified but that institutions typically do not provide the financial and professional support required for learning how to teach diverse students in complex learning environments.

In addition to the disciplinary knowledge required for teaching diverse students in an open-access context, online writing instructors at two-year colleges would ideally have specialized expertise in online pedagogy. Principle 7 of OWI focuses on the training and experience for writing program administrators in online programs: "WPAs for OWI programs and their online writing teachers should receive appropriate OWI-focused training, professional development, and assessment for evaluation and promotion purpose" (n.p.). Another connected disciplinary ideal is that instructors engage in research that supports their development as online writing instructors. Principle 15 of OWI states that "OWI/OWL administrators and teachers/tutors should be committed to ongoing research into their programs and courses as well as the very principles in this document" (n.p.).

Without a doubt, professional development and scholarly activities focused on online writing instruction are a crucial part of developing high-quality OWI programs. Two-year, open-access online writing programs perhaps require the most extensive instructor training of any type of writing course, especially developmental writing and first-year writing in programs that accelerate students to credit-bearing courses with or without supplemental support. Ideally instructors would be proficient in both online pedagogy and writing studies theory and practices, while also having the experience and knowledge required for supporting structurally disadvantaged and academically at-risk students in an online learning environment. However, the lack of resources at two-year colleges to fund program administration, ongoing professional development for teaching online, and compensation for training contingent and adjunct faculty creates an enormous gap between unarguably important disciplinary standards and the material realities of open-access online writing programs. Further, the teaching-intensive nature of community colleges with accompanying workloads (annually 4/4 or more typically 5/5) makes it difficult for open-access OWI instructors to participate in research, which means that our discipline as a whole has limited scholarship and knowledge about how to implement the OWI principles and other effective teaching practices in open-access courses.

REDEFINING ACCESS FOR ONLINE WRITING PROGRAMS

For us, the most challenging aspect of designing an open-admissions online writing program was accounting for what *access* means in an online learning environment. At our statewide, two-year institution, a majority of the students in our lower-level courses had limited proficiency with critical reading, academic writing, and using an online learning management system. As we designed, assessed, and redesigned our online curriculum, we worked over a period of several years to identify strategies for supporting students who lacked the experience required for independent learning and who struggled in the absence of an in-person instructor. Taking traditional face-to-face classroom courses would have been a better fit for most of our students in developmental writing. However, many of them had no other low-cost alternatives for accessing higher education because they had full-time jobs or caregiver responsibilities, were place-bound in rural communities, or had mental health issues and medical conditions preventing them from attending on-campus classes. Unfortunately, the life circumstances that made attending a campus challenging also limited some students' access to the Internet and/or proficiency with using technology for learning.

Our process for redesigning a program to meet the needs of students was further complicated by the astonishingly diverse range of students who accessed writing credits for graduation through our online courses. Our two-year institution had the lowest tuition in our state system, universities in the state didn't offer developmental writing online, and few offered an intermediate composition course, which fulfilled graduation requirements for Research I (R1) institutions. Gaps in online course offerings at four-year universities meant that our online writing program also enrolled students from every public university in Wisconsin, state residents enrolled at R1 institutions in other states or living abroad, high school students (and even middle schoolers), and international students living in their home countries during the summer. Our intermediate composition course occasionally enrolled students with bachelor's and master's degrees who needed an additional writing course to meet the admissions requirements for medical school or other professional programs. Thus, our instructors taught students who were extraordinarily well-prepared for college reading and writing, some who might be considered to be expert writers (Sommers and Saltz 2002), and students who were inadmissible at any other type of institution—frequently enrolled together in the same online courses.

The student populations served by our program illustrate that (a) online education has redefined what access to higher education means and (b) online writing programs at open-admissions institutions likely serve the most diverse range of college writers. In the age of online learning, students pick up general education writing credits away from their home campuses because of cost, convenience, or scheduling. Our profession has yet to fully explore how these relatively recent changes in students' abilities to access writing credits away from a home campus impact writing programs, and few scholarly sources address strategies for teaching online in a truly open-admissions context. The widely varying prior literacy experiences and college readiness levels of our online students forced us to reconsider our thinking about the role of online education in providing students with access to writing instruction. At the same time, we had to design a program that would help underprepared students successfully complete online coursework.

Approaches to teaching students about technology are just one example of how the concept of access informs and shapes approaches to designing courses and teaching writing in an online learning environment. Perhaps more important, two-year college students' widely diverse experiences with technology as a tool for learning underscore the extent to which open-admissions writing instructors have to fundamentally redefine how to provide students with access to writing instruction in online courses. In our face-to-face classrooms, we tend to define writing program access in terms of college readiness, inclusive pedagogy, and accommodations for students with diverse needs. However, in an online teaching environment, *access* also includes students' literal ability to access and participate in the course through the use of technology. Our program work with principles of disciplinarity and adaptation put us in some conflict with OWI Principle 2: "An online writing course should focus on writing and not on technology orientation or teaching students how to use learning and other technologies." The CCCC "Statement on Principles for the Postsecondary Teaching of Writing" (revised 2015) complicates the issue by arguing that "sound writing instruction emphasizes relationships between writing and technologies . . . Instructors emphasize the relationships between technologies and writing by providing opportunities for students to gain access to and fluency with a wide range of writing tools and the possibilities for writing with them" (n.p.). Both statements seem to suggest that the focus on the use of technologies in writing classrooms should be on writing itself, which is a reasonable assertion but unrealistic for some students in open-admissions teaching contexts.

The OWI statement also assumes that students already know how to use basic technology before enrolling in college writing courses, and the rationale for Principle 2 asserts that "unlike a digital rhetoric course an OWC is not considered to be a place for stretching technological skills as much as for becoming stronger writers in various selected genres." The OWI statement suggests that the primary issue with teaching students to use technology in online courses is that instructors or programs might require students to use technology in advanced ways that aren't necessarily connected to college writing. However, the recommendation that OWI courses shouldn't provide students with an orientation to technology or instruction on using technology as a tool for learning doesn't take into consideration the students who enroll in online courses without a basic foundation in using technology for taking a course or for writing.

In some cases, the life circumstances that limit students' options for higher education to open-admissions online courses also create conditions that make it challenging for students to develop proficiency in using technology before they take an online course (e.g., living in a rural community or attending an underfunded high school and then subsequently lacking the financial resources to attend college full time). In an open-access online course, students often rely on their instructors to help them navigate the pathways to being more self-sufficient as college learners in comparison to students at more selective institutions who have more access to privileges and resources that help them develop proficiency in using technology as a tool for learning before attending college.

Our program redesign work had to consider the realities of students who do not even know how to use a computer when they enroll in online courses. Further, many of our students didn't have regular access to the Internet due to rural living conditions (including dial-up Internet and limited cell phone service), work schedules, or economic issues. We also had students who used their smartphones as the primary tool through which they did coursework. Griffin and Minter acknowledged these material realities in 2013, arguing that online education "poses challenges that may be less visible to instructors but just as much outside their ability to help or manage: irregular access to reliable computer equipment or Internet connections, limited knowledge and experience working with the technologies needed to navigate and work within and beyond the course shell" (146). This limited proficiency with and inconsistent access to technology significantly impacts the implementation of disciplinary best practices that rely on the presence of a writing community in an online course, including conferencing, early submissions for instructor feedback with subsequent revision, peer review, reading discussions, and workshops.

Our experience has shown us that open-access writing programs have to address issues related to technology if we are to expect many of our students to engage as writers in the discipline, participate in a course, and have a chance of completing a college degree. In our redesigned program, the entire first week of developmental writing focused on orienting students to the learning management system and using technology as a tool for learning, and we added a substantial review module to the beginning of credit-bearing writing courses for students with limited experience in using technology or taking an online course. Most instructors also spent much of the first month of developmental and first-year writing courses, providing one-on-one support to students for accessing course resources, buying online course materials, finding and reading online texts, using the discussion board, and submitting an assignment electronically. The support available through online videos and the institutional help desk was insufficient for helping students navigate their way through online course modules and figure out how to use technology for the unique requirements of a writing course, so part of our program development work included mentoring instructors in strategies for helping students use technology.

Without addressing technology through a substantial orientation and direct instruction connected to the writing course, nothing else in the entire course would matter because students would be unable to do *any* coursework and move on to the more important work of developing as college readers and writers and participating in an online writing community. The gap between disciplinary statements and the needs of students with limited resources or experiences with using technology in K–12 education illustrates the ways in which an open-admissions online writing programs have to design online courses differently from programs at more selective types of institutions. The technology gap for some students at open-access institutions also illuminates how disciplinary principles for writing instruction have to be adapted, reconsidered, or transformed in their implementation to reflect institutional contexts and instructors' daily experiences with students. Specifically, two-year college faculty need to adapt position statements to reflect their own teaching contexts, and professional organizations need to do more to reflect the needs of two-year college instructors and their students.

INSTITUTIONAL CONSTRAINTS AND INSTRUCTOR AUTONOMY

Two-year college writing and developmental English programs often have less faculty control over curriculum and program management compared to programs at more selective institutions. For example, open-access institutions frequently have mandates for developmental education, placement, writing course sequences, and curriculum placed on them by administrators, state systems, and even legislatures (Whinnery and Pompelia 2018), driven partially by legitimate concerns about low degree attainment rates for community college students. (See, e.g. Bailey et al. 2015; Hassel et al. 2015; Klausman et al. 2016; Toth et al. 2016.) However, a lack of autonomy for instructors (and sometimes departments) also stems from the culture and structure of underfunded open-admissions institutions, which require intensive teaching and service loads for faculty while also redistributing authority normally given to faculty to the administration.

In open-access contexts, writing program instructors face a complex set of challenges because they tend to work with the least-prepared and most-marginalized students in postsecondary education (those who are most at risk of not completing a degree) while simultaneously lacking the time, financial resources, and institutional support required for advocating for and maintaining disciplinary standards. Although recent scholarship on teaching English at two-year colleges has focused on teacher-scholar advocacy (Andelora 2008; Sullivan 2015; Griffiths 2017), constraints placed on faculty by administrators (and sometimes political forces external to the institution) are arguably the most significant obstacle that open-access writing programs face in aligning curriculum and instruction with professional standards and practices. As Brett Griffiths argues, "faculty members are often poorly positioned by administrators at institutions to engage such advocacy" (2017, 49). Our decision-making processes as online writing program developers highlight both the benefits of teacher-scholar advocacy in program development and the constraints of doing that work within the limitations of institutions that withhold autonomy from faculty.

Our institution had a team of instructional designers and administrators who had the responsibility for overseeing the development and revision of online courses. The online team worked with disciplinary experts appointed by an academic department to create a completely designed course with assignments, learning activities, and instructional materials. The instructional designers or the disciplinary experts put the entire course in a development shell within an online learning management system (Desire2Learn). Completed courses were then copied into each instructor's course site on a semester-to-semester basis after designated course leads from a department made course revisions. The course development process, structure, and time lines were mandated by the institution with minimal (or no) input from academic departments about when a course could be offered online or the process for creating it beyond determining which faculty members would participate.

Our experience in the course development and ongoing revision processes for four online writing courses (both as program administrators and as online course developers) illustrates the tensions that can occur when administrative control conflicts with professional standards and writing studies practices. The "Position Statement of Principles and Example Effective Practices for OWI" argues that "online writing teachers should retain reasonable control over their own content and/or techniques for conveying, teaching, and assessing their students' writing in their OWCs" (Principle 5). Our institutional administrators imposed several constraints on instructor autonomy, which made it impossible for instructors to have "reasonable control" over their own courses. First (and most important), the institution allotted funding in the form of course releases or summer stipends for faculty to develop courses for an entire department without providing access to resources that would give other instructors compensated time and technology support for creating an online course. This imbalance created significant workload issues for any instructors who chose to develop their own courses from scratch (which also required permission from their academic departments). Second, the practice of automatically copying a course into each instructor's course site left them with limited choices in how they would actually teach a course, including course content, the structure of the site, the course schedule, and when and how students completed assignments. Third, the culture of the institution gave more control to instructional designers than to disciplinary course developers in how a course was designed, organized, and presented to students in the learning management system. This created significant gaps between how instructors normally teach writing and the way that the online instructional team wanted the course to be organized within each instructor's class section site. And, finally, the culture of the institution's online program was so focused on the course development shell model of course design that instructors were prevented from editing and revising the content of their own courses beyond making their own weekly announcements.

Within the constraints imposed by these course development processes and available financial resources, one issue that we were unable to resolve in redesigning our online writing program was balancing instructor autonomy (or the idea from OWI Principle 5 that instructors should have "reasonable control" over the content and instructional methods for their courses) with the use of standardized online courses in our institution. In our case, standardization meant that instructors received a completely designed course created by disciplinary experts in consultation with instructional designers, which provided assignments, learning activities, and learning materials a few weeks before the start of each semester. Our own values and professional knowledge of how effective teaching normally works contrast sharply with this approach to developing a course. The statement on labor issues for contingent faculty that accompanied 2016 resolutions at the CCCC business meeting in Houston explains why required use of standardized course materials in writing courses is problematic:

The professional authority to make independent decisions based on disciplinary expertise may be limited for non-tenure track faculty. Many NTT faculty, including graduate students, are required to teach from a standard template or syllabus, leaving very little room for independent course design and/or implementation. These requirements can lead to intellectual and pedagogical stagnation. (CCCC 2016)

However, the ideal of instructor autonomy is often in conflict with what we see as even more important professional values connected to fair labor conditions for contingent faculty.

We firmly support the idea that writing programs should hire qualified professionals and then give instructors both on and off the tenure track the ability to create their own course materials, assignments, and methods for assessing student learning. However, instead of having instructors determine the content and focus of their online courses, we created an entire four-course sequence with assignments, discussion activities, workshops, and learning materials that instructors could use as is or adapt based on their own teaching preferences. Initially, the only pathway that our institution provided to us for redesigning our online writing program was a standardized course model with control over the content and instructional methods given only to course developers. Over time, we reshaped the culture of the online writing program in ways that ignored what had been mandated to us by the institution, and we started encouraging instructors to make their own decisions about how to teach their courses. We also provided structured opportunities for instructors to become involved in the semester-to-semester course revision process through feedback, one-on-one mentoring conversations, and opportunities for conversations with instructors who taught the same course.

However, given the choice between standardized courses and the freedom to design their own courses, our program instructors almost universally chose to use the standardized course and made very few changes. Issues related to contingent labor, faculty workload, and working conditions create challenges in implementing the theoretical ideal of instructor autonomy at an underfunded institution. The practical reality is that designing an online writing course, especially at an open-access institution, is a time-consuming endeavor that warrants compensation beyond the pay provided for teaching a course. In addition, the working conditions faced by instructors in our online program and at other two-year colleges (including last-minute hiring, frequently changing teaching assignments, 5/5 writing course teaching loads, and employment instability) meant that *not* providing them with a standardized course would result in an increased workload and less time for working directly with students. Our institution (like many others) did not provide the release time and stipends that would make it possible for contingent faculty to design their own courses without uncompensated labor. Because of the material realities of teaching writing online to diverse learners with intensive literacy needs, most instructors welcomed and wanted standardized online courses, and many even asked for permission to use the assignments and learning materials in their face-to-face courses. Our approach to using standardized courses illustrates the challenges of doing some types of program design work at an underfunded institution with limited resources, which can result in unresolved tensions between conflicting disciplinary values.

WHEN TO PUSH BACK AND WHEN TO LET GO

The most important part of implementing changes to our writing program was resisting administrative decisions and institutional processes that impeded instructors' abilities to follow best practices for teaching writing and create an online learning environment that responded to the needs of their students. We successfully negotiated with our administration to give instructors authority to revise and edit their own courses instead of going through an instructional designer for every change. Our requests to the online program for this change were futile, so we made an appeal to the provost detailing the specific ways that the practice of giving instructional designers control over courses created barriers to student success, conflicted with accreditation standards (HLC, 2014), and resulted in a situation in which instructors were not actually teaching their courses.

We were also able to push back against an institutional requirement that all online courses require the same format and structure in the learning management system regardless of disciplinary practices and student learning outcomes. The weekly course lesson formatting for most online courses in our institution didn't work for multistage writing projects that students developed over a series of weeks, and our writing courses needed a different discussion structure for writing workshops and critical reading activities compared to other disciplines that had different types of online discussions. We also resisted efforts by instructional designers to limit the number of hyperlinks and instructional resources included in our course pages, because students needed to access instructions and resources over the entire course as they revised their writing projects and worked toward creating a portfolio. Although we weren't able to change the culture of our institution that gave more authority to instructional designers and the administration than to faculty, we gradually managed to gain control over most decisions for the online writing program even while impediments to academic freedom continued to be imposed on other departments. We were eventually able to design the structure of our course development shells to reflect process approaches to writing that included revision, workshop-style discussions, and access to a variety of online resources that students could adapt to their individual needs.

The processes that we used to maintain disciplinary practices in course design were complicated and included a mix of negotiating with, fighting against, and eventually working outside the control of instructional designers and administrators. For example, we frequently edited and revised our course development shells to restore content, structure, and learning support resources that online program staff removed or changed in our courses. Initially, we asked for permission to make changes, but over time we completely bypassed the processes normally required by our institution for doing online course revisions after instructional designers repeatedly changed our writing course development shells in ways that created barriers to student learning (e.g., revising or rearranging assignment instructions in confusing ways, removing information about writing process steps, miscommunicating information about writing workshops to students, and eliminating hyperlinks in assignment instructions that helped students access the readings and resources required for completing writing projects). The conditions for designing courses imposed on us by our institution were in direct conflict with our professional knowledge about how to teach writing (NCTE 2016).

Through a lengthy process of actively resisting the work of nondisciplinary experts in making decisions about our courses and ignoring institutional procedures for course development, we eventually received almost complete autonomy over our four writing courses. However, we faced two consequences for insisting that our courses reflect disciplinary practices for online teaching and going outside the boundaries for online course development mandated by our institution. First, we had to do all the work of course design and development ourselves without receiving support with technology and our workload from an online team, including doing uncompensated work while also shifting some activities that would normally receive an online course development stipend to our program coordinator workloads. Second, we also used up some of our institutional capital, which affected how we were included in decision-making processes for online courses that took place outside of shared governance.

Throughout the process of improving our online writing program, we had to make difficult choices about when to push back against institutional practices that conflicted with our disciplinary values and when to let go. We effectively changed parts of the program that fell under our jurisdiction as program coordinators, but we were less successful in resisting administrative decisions that required additional funding or that were rooted in a need to use online program tuition revenue to fund other parts of the institution. Because the online program filled in large gaps in campus and department budgets, we were unable to change most administrative decisions that would reduce the revenue that our courses generated. For example, our institution outsourced tutoring to a for-profit company and explored but eventually rejected our suggestion that we develop a virtual writing center or learning center staffed by our own instructors with knowledge of our program and experience with online teaching. Our institution also distributed large amounts of revenue from the online program to departments to fund professional development activities for work that was rarely (if ever) connected to online teaching without providing *any* funds to support professional development for online instructors. Consequently, we ended up using a substantial portion of our time as statewide program coordinators to develop resources and a mentoring process for online writing instructors even though we believed that the institution had failed in its ethical obligation to fund professional development for online teaching.

Our institution also never implemented an online multiple measures placement process and corequisite support course that we developed with colleagues as part of transforming our writing program, which was used for moving students in face-to-face courses from developmental to credit-bearing composition with support. Even though our institution in theory gave our department control over placement, the administration permitted the online program to use a different process and sometimes different standards for online-only students who weren't affiliated with a physical campus. We faced challenges in maintaining control over how students from other institutions were placed into our courses, including those who had no placement data, had failed a course at another institution, or were concurrently enrolled in sixth-to-ninth-grade English courses. We created an appeals process that students could use for a department-level review of their placements and transfer credits, but online students were much less likely to know about and use the process unless they were affiliated with a bricks-and-mortar two-year college campus. Our experience illustrates the frustrating ways in which the most significant roadblocks to improving a writing program through disciplinary change can come from administrators who impede the process, especially in combination with financial constraints.

Beth Hewitt and Scott Warnock argue that "Good OWI should help the field of composition be better. We believe that OWI will—if allowed—change how people in our profession view their work as writing teachers overall and ultimately change how outsiders view us. Good OWI should move composition—the whole structure—forward" (560). We join them in asserting that online instruction and program development work have the potential to transform entire writing programs. Our experience was that the work of implementing change to online writing instruction in our institution fundamentally changed our perspectives on the meaning of access to higher education, ways to support contingent faculty, the material conditions of teaching and learning within our institution, and the importance of considering the diverse needs of writers within the contexts of varied learning environments. We also learned that the work of transforming a writing program is an imperfect and problematic struggle involving sometimes unresolved tensions between disciplinary standards and the lived realities of instructors and program administrators.

Writing studies as a profession has yet to address the challenges and complexities of designing, maintaining, administering, and teaching in open-access online writing programs in a comprehensive or systematic way. We recommend program development work accompanied by new research that focuses on creating and investigating supportive online learning environments for underresourced and underrepresented students and their instructors. For example, open-access writing programs need to operate from the assumption that students may not be familiar with using technology as a tool for learning or navigating the course and may lack access to the types of technology resources (including consistent Internet access) available to students at wealthier institutions. Program administrators and instructors need to account for gaps in students' access to technology, proficiency, and experience with using technology for learning, and their potentially limited understanding of information literacy both at the level of course design and as part of ongoing instruction throughout a course.

Another limitation for open-access writing programs is a lack of available scholarship on interconnections between reading and writing and how that influences students' literacy development, success, and retention in online writing courses. Instructors need professional resources that will help them account for community college readers and their challenges in accessing course materials, completing assignments in a text-heavy online learning environment, and growing as readers and writers in a learning environment where teachers have fewer opportunities for providing students with direct support and contact compared to face-to-face classrooms.

Finally, instructors teaching open-access courses have to rethink the traditional course structures and pedagogical models that drive online education at some institutions (like ours, initially), including the view that online students work independently or in a self-paced way to achieve learning outcomes with limited interaction with classmates or the instructor. Instructors have to consider ways to design their courses so that they are structured around opportunities for students to participate in and belong to an online community of writers. We see the potential for rich and rewarding (but challenging) work in reshaping how writing studies approaches future OWI position statements, scholarship, training, and disciplinary resources to account for the diverse needs of online students at two-year colleges and other open-access institutions.

NOTES

1. The Global Society of Online Literacy Educators (GSOLE) has taken up the task of revising the OWI principles and providing related resources to support online writing instructors.

2. A decade after we began our writing program redesign work, our institution was dismantled when the University of Wisconsin System merged its two-year open-access campuses with four-year institutions.

REFERENCES

Andelora, Jeffrey. 2008. "Forging a National Identity: TYCA and the Two-Year College Teacher-Scholar." *Teaching English in the Two-Year College* 35.4: 350–62.

Bailey, Thomas R., Shanna Smith Jaggers, and Davis Smith. 2015. *Redesigning America's Community Colleges: A Clearer Path to Student Success.* Cambridge, MA: Harvard University Press.

CCCC Committee on Computers and Composition. 2015. *CCCC Promotion and Tenure Guidelines for Work with Technology.* November 30. http://www2.ncte.org/statement/promotionandtenure/.

CCCC OWI Committee for Effective Practices in Online Writing Instruction. 2013. "A Position Statement of Principles and Example Effective Practices for Online Writing Instruction." March. https://prod-ncte-cdn.azureedge.net/nctefiles/groups/cccc/owiprinciples.pdf.

Calhoon-Dillahunt, Carolyn. 2011. "Writing Programs without Administrators: Frameworks for Successful Writing Programs in the Two-Year College." *WPA: Journal of Council of Writing Program Administrators* 35.1 (Fall/Winter): 118–34.

Calhoon-Dillahunt, Carolyn, Darin L. Jensen, Sarah Z. Johnson, Howard Tinberg, and Christie Toth. 2016. *TYCA Guidelines for Preparing Teachers of English in the Two-Year College*. National Council of Teachers of English. http://www.ncte.org/library/NCTEFiles /Groups/TYCA/GuidelinesPrep2YCEngFac_REVISED.pdf?_ga=2.16292670.94945 7624.1550012042-925470537.1535483756.

Center for Community College Student Engagement (CCCSE). 2014. *Contingent Commitments: Bringing Part-Time Faculty into Focus*. Austin: University of Texas at Austin, Program in Higher Education Leadership.

Conference on College Composition and Communication (CCCC). 2015. "Statement on Principles for the Postsecondary Teaching of Writing." NCTE. https://cccc.ncte.org/ cccc/resources/positions/postsecondarywriting#principle7.

Conference on College Composition and Communication (CCCC). 2016. "Overview of the Issues." Statement to Accompany Labor Resolutions at CCCC 2016 in Houston. NCTE. https://cccc.ncte.org/cccc/labor/overview.

Griffin, June, and Deborah Minter. 2013. "The Rise of the Online Writing Classroom: Reflecting on the Material Conditions of College Composition Teaching." *College Composition and Communication* 65.1: 140–61.

Griffiths, Brett. 2017. "Professional Autonomy and Teacher-Scholar Activists in Two-Year Colleges: Preparing New Faculty to Think Institutionally." *Teaching English in the Two-Year College* 45.1: 47–68.

Hassel, Holly, Jeffrey Klausman, Joanne Baird Giordano, Margaret O'Rourke, Leslie Roberts, Patrick Sullivan, and Christie Toth. 2015. "TYCA White Paper on Developmental Education Reforms." *Teaching English in the Two Year College* 42.3: 227–43.

Hewitt, Beth L. 2015. "Grounding Principles of OWI." *Foundational Practices of Online Writing Instruction*, edited by Beth L. Hewitt and Kevin Eric DePew, 33–92. Anderson, SC: WAC Clearinghouse, Parlor Press.

Hewett, Beth L., and Scott Warnock. 2015. "The Future of OWI." *Foundational Practices of Online Writing Instruction*, edited by Beth L. Hewitt and Kevin Eric DePew. Anderson, SC: WAC Clearinghouse, Parlor Press, 547–63.

Higher Learning Commission (HLC). 2014. "Criteria for Accreditation." HLC. https:// www.hlcommission.org/Policies/criteria-and-core-components.html.

Jaggars, Shanna. 2011. "Online Learning: Does It Help Low-Income and Underprepared Students?" *Community College Research Center* 52 (March): 1–4.

Kahlenberg, Richard D., Robert Shireman, Kimberly Quick, and Tariq Habash. 2018. "Policy Strategies for Pursuing Adequate Funding of Community Colleges." Report for the Century Foundation, October 25. https://tcf.org/content/report/policy-strategies -pursuing-adequate-funding-community-colleges/.

Klausman, Jeffrey. 2008. "Mapping the Terrain: The Two-Year College Writing Program Administrator." *Teaching English in the Two-Year College* 35.3: 238–51.

Klausman, Jeff, Judith Angona, Holly Pappas, and Shane Wilson. 2012. "Characteristics of the Highly Effective Two-Year College Instructor in English." National Council of Teachers of English. http://www.ncte.org/library/NCTEFiles/Groups/TYCA/Characteristics _Statement.pdf?_ga=2.11522236.949457624.1550012042-925470537.1535483756.

Klausman, Jeff, Christie Toth, Wendy Swyt, Brett Griffiths, Patrick Sullivan, Anthony Warnke, Amy L. Williams, Joanne Giordano, and Leslie Roberts. 2016. "TYCA White Paper on Placement Reform." *Teaching English in the Two-Year College* 44.2: 135–75.

National Council of Teachers of English (NCTE). 2016. "Professional Knowledge for the Teaching of Writing." NCTE. February 28. http://www2.ncte.org/statement/teaching -writing.

Sommers, Nancy, and Laura Saltz. 2002. "The Novice as Expert: Writing the Freshman Year." *College Composition and Communication* 56.1: 253–60.

Sullivan, Patrick. 2015. "The Two-Year College Teacher-Scholar-Activist." *Teaching English in the Two Year College* 42.4: 327–50.

Taylor, Tim. 2009. "Writing Program Administration at the Two-Year College: Ghosts in the Machine." *WPA: Writing Program Administration* 32.3: 120–39.

Toth, Christie, Patrick Sullivan, and Carolyn Calhoon-Dillahunt. 2016. "A Dubious Method of Improving Educational Outcomes: Accountability and the Two-Year College." *Teaching English in the Two-Year College* 43.4: 391–410.

Whinnery, Erin, and Sarah Pompelia. 2018. "50-State Comparison: Developmental Education Policies." Education Commission of the States, December 10. https://www.ecs.org/50-state-comparison-developmental-education-policies/?fbclid=IwAR0PtWtTt8i1gToFGnO0bAvZ1uY49Xc_ylj7VMDxrLqs8l1bo_sL9vNwyTo.

Epilogue

TEACHING AND WRITING DURING THE PANDEMIC, 2020

Holly Hassel and Kirsti Cole

We were in the late production stages of assembling and revising this manuscript when the March 2020 global COVID-19 pandemic hit and shifted many of the deeply held assumptions in higher education.

That sentence sat on its own in the manuscript for some time.

As we go to press, the United States is in crisis over federal malfeasance. Some of our states are banding together to save lives. Some are not. Some are callously playing with life in order to make a political point. The world is grappling with supply shortages and competing ideas about how best to help citizens manage the medical, emotional, and social consequences of illness and isolation.

But in all of this chaos, teachers keep teaching, using whatever tools are available to them: videoconferencing like Zoom and Skype, learning management systems (Blackboard, Canvas, Brightspace, Webex, Moodle), YouTube, PowerPoint, digital archives, e-books and libraries suddenly made available, Twitter, and many others. For the first time, teachers are teaching exclusively from home, some with babies, toddlers, school-age children, some with aged parents or caregiving responsibilities for ill friends, neighbors, and family members; some teachers are disabled, are in abusive homes, are food insecure, or have no or limited access to the resources of space, bandwidth (literal and figurative), and time required for teaching and learning. All of us are worried deeply about the quality of education we are providing, and for our students who may be in similar circumstances.

Since the pandemic closed K–12 and colleges and universities across the country, multiple online groups have sprung up in an attempt to support and give resources to teachers who are teaching online or in digital contexts for the first time. These online groups highlight triage pedagogy, which ostensibly is not something that most teachers engage in—but some of them do. Everyone tries to make sense of what

https://doi.org/10.7330/9781646421428.c014

is happening, and conversations online turn to arguments about what is the best way to manage what is for nearly all of us a completely different workload.

This context has deeply shaken (for better and for worse) some of the long-standing cultural scripts around teaching and teachers in the United States. While American anti-intellectualism prevails in some dark corners, more and more people recognize the value of teaching and the value of teachers—whether the expertise of scientists or the value of clear communication in confusing times and a chaotic information landscape. Prior assumptions about the value of online learning environments are being shaken (in many different ways), while the commonplaces about how we measure learning (seat time, credit hours, points, assignments, presentations, papers, tests taken from a classroom desk) have to be changed, by necessity.

In the same moment, administrators are scrambling to circumvent catastrophic budget shortfalls—and for composition instructors, when there is a budget shortfall at all, let alone a catastrophic one, the writing is on the wall. Contingent faculty who work part time, many without benefits, and at multiple campuses will be affected most immediately but not exclusively. We know that the pandemic will change labor practices in higher education. How? That has yet to be determined.

In the coming year(s), the long-term effects on pedagogy, on staffing and professional development, on higher education's sustainability, and on the assessment practices we've held on to for a long time are going to be in flux. We are, however, more convinced than ever that the authors in this collection who work to address equitable labor and cross-rank collaboration are on the right track: we must work, vocally, to support each other now and in the unknown future.

INDEX

emotive language use, 216–17
Emporium Model, 170–72
ENG 101, 211
ENGL 101A, 74–75
England, Paula, 91
English, Susan, 170
English as a Second Language (ESL), 6, 108–9, 132–35, 220
English department, 3, 5–7, 42, 45, 54, 68, 100, 109, 114, 132, 136, 142, 152, 155, 162, 168, 194, 200, 225
English Language Learners (ELLs), 134
English Language Teaching (ELT), 212
English studies, study of IT in, 152–59
English Techie, 153
Enos, Theresa, 81–82
epistemological terrain, 201
epistemology, centering, 22–27
ePortfolio, 150–51, 167, 175
essay prompts, 175
"Evaluating the Intellectual Work of Writing Program Administration," 77–78
"Everyone Writes," 112
existing literature, 169–72

F

faculty: contingent, 17–18, 39, 44, 51, 53–63, 67–70, 88, 211, 250–52; determining qualifications, 62–64; evaluating, 119; full-time, 55, 59–60, 78, 90, 95, 100, 137–38; non-tenure-track, 3, 5–6, 9, 17, 47, 77, 88; part-time, 5, 54–55, 58, 61, 66; qualified, 55, 62–63, 65, 70; seeing as writers, 115–16; transparency, 117–18; visibility of, 116–17. *See also* non-tenure track faculty (NTTF)
familial projects, 236–37
Family Educational Rights and Privacy Act (FERPA), 151
Feenberg, Andrew, 148
feminism, 22; collaboration, 28–31; Standpoint theory, 38
Ferguson, Margert, 44
Ferris, Dana, 187
finding aid, creating, 235–36
first-year writing (FYW), 123, 226
Fiscus-Cannaday, Jaclyn, 19; collaboration, 29–30; epistemology, 24–25
5-Minute Linguist: Bite-Sized Essays on Language and Languages, The, 220
fixated understanding, 193
Flaherty, Colleen, 41–42
Florida, remedial education in, 138
Foltz, Tanice, 30
Free Academy, 129

Friedman, Thomas, 148
Friedrich, Patricia, 212
funding, 139–40

G

Galin, Jeffrey R., 106
Gardner, Clint, 108
Gay, Geneva, 169
general education (GE), 197
generation 1.5, 168
genre/audience awareness, 218–19
Global Society of Online Literacy Educators (GSOLE), 256
Goodburn, Amy, 75
government, 179
graduate student instructor (GSI), 27
Graduate Student WPA (GSWPA), 76–77
graduate students: advocacy, 76–84; collaboration, 76–84. *See also* graduate workers
graduate teaching assistant (GTA), 5, 75–76
graduate workers, 19–22; epistemology, 22–27; feminist-based leadership, 28–36; stories, 31–36
GrammarPhobia, 117
Great Lakes Higher Education Corporation and Affiliates, 139–40
Great Recession, 137
Griffiths, Brett, 249
Grizz Writes, 59
Gunner, Jeanne, 72
Gutiérrez y Muhs, Gabriella, 90, 93

H

Harding, Sandra, 38
Harrington, Susanmarie, 131, 141
Harris, Joseph, 72
Hassel, Holly, 3
Heijstra, T. M., 87
Hern, Katie, 124
Hess, Marta, 233
Hewett, Beth L., 240–41
Hidi, Suzanne, 172
hierarchy, 79, 80, 82, 85; academic, 21, 24, 77; benevolent hierarchy, 30–31; care and, 93–96; teaching, 93–96
high bar, setting, 68
higher education: austerity crisis in, 136–40
Higher Learning Commission (HLC), 55. *See also* professionalization
Hitt, Allison Harper, 172
Hogan, Katie, 93, 97–98
Horner, Bruce, 184
Hostos Community College, 100

ABOUT THE AUTHORS

Leah Anderst is an associate professor of English at Queensborough Community College, City University of New York (CUNY), where she coordinates the Writing Program. She is also an affiliated faculty member of film studies in the MA Program in Liberal Studies at the CUNY Graduate Center. Her research has appeared in *a/b: Auto/biography Studies*, *Narrative*, and *Teaching English in the Two-Year College*. She is the editor of the essay collection *The Films of Eric Rohmer* (Palgrave, 2014), and she is a co–guest editor on a special issue (14:1) of the *Basic Writing e-Journal* focused on acceleration in basic writing pedagogy.

Cynthia M. Baer is an assistant professor and assistant writing program administrator at San José State University. Her research focuses on the systems of learning that have shaped her own thirty-three-year history as a college writing instructor—systems that are now being transformed as higher education seeks a more inclusive, equitable, and sustainable relationship with the students and public we serve. Of particular interest to her work, and to her institution, are the mechanisms to leverage multilingualism as a learning asset.

Ruth Benander is a professor of English at the University of Cincinnati Blue Ash College. She teaches both face-to-face and online courses in basic writing, first-year composition, and intermediate composition, as well as faculty professional development in online teaching. Her principal areas of professional interest are in researching how to teach cultural humility, how to foster equity and inclusion in composition, and how to cultivate mindfulness and mind/body awareness for students, faculty, and staff.

Rachel Hall Buck is an assistant professor of writing studies at the American University of Sharjah in the United Arab Emirates. She teaches academic writing, and writing for engineers, and she conducts writing workshops with the Iraq Public Leadership Program. Her work has appeared in *Currents in Teaching and Learning* and *Composition Forum*. Her current research and teaching interests involve disciplinary argumentation, second language (L2) reading strategies, and English for academic purposes.

Mwangi Alex Chege is an associate professor of English at the University of Cincinnati Blue Ash College. He teaches developmental writing, first-year composition, and intermediate composition. His research interests include scholarship of teaching and learning in developmental writing, as well as discourse on intellectuals and national development in Kenya's higher education.

Kirsti Cole is a professor of rhetoric, composition, and literature at Minnesota State University. She is the faculty chair of the Teaching Writing Graduate Certificate and Master's of Communication and Composition programs. She has published articles in *Women's Studies in Communication*, *Feminist Media Studies*, *College English*, *Harlot*, and *thirdspace*, and her collection *Feminist Challenges or Feminist Rhetorics* was published in 2014. Her collections, coedited with Holly Hassel, *Surviving Sexism in the Academy: Feminist Strategies for Leadership* (2017) and *Academic Labor beyond the Classroom: Working for Our Values* (2019), are available from Routledge Press.

Jaclyn Fiscus-Cannaday is an assistant professor of English at Florida State University. Her research and teaching are situated at the intersection of composition studies, linguistics, and feminism, broadly exploring how communication works, how people think it should work, and how we might address those ideologies through pedagogy and policy to better work across difference. Dr. Fiscus-Cannaday teaches courses in composition history, theory, and practice.

Lynée Lewis Gaillet is Distinguished University Professor and chair of the English Department at Georgia State University. Her book projects include *Scottish Rhetoric and Its Influence*; *Stories of Mentoring*; *The Present State of Scholarship in the History of Rhetoric: A Twenty-First Century Guide*; *Scholarly Publication in a Changing Academic Landscape*; *Publishing in Community: Case Studies for Contingent Faculty Collaborations*; *Primary Research and Writing: People, Places, and Spaces*; *On Archival Research*; *Writing Center and Writing Program Collaborations*; *Remembering Differently: Re-figuring Women's Rhetorical Work*; and *Composing in Four Acts*.

Joanne Baird Giordano teaches at Salt Lake Community College and previously coordinated the developmental reading, writing, and ESL program for the University of Wisconsin System's two-year campuses. Her professional work focuses on students' transitions to college reading and writing at open-admissions institutions.

Holly Hassel is a professor of English at North Dakota State University. Previously she taught for sixteen years at the University of Wisconsin–Marathon County, a two-year college. She served as editor of *Teaching English in the Two-Year College* for five years, and her research and scholarship have appeared in *College English*, *College Composition and Communication*, *Pedagogy*, *Peitho*, and *Writing Program Administration*. Her areas of professional interest are first-year writing, composition pedagogy, and institutional change work.

Allison Hutchison is a senior lecturer in the Engineering Communications Program at Cornell University, where she prepares students to challenge engineering stereotypes by developing their written, oral, aural, and multimodal communication skills. Her research and teaching interests include online writing instruction, writing centers, technical writing, and science communication. Her 2019 article addressing the limitations of using learning management systems to teach writing is available in *Computers and Composition*. Previously, she served as a graduate teaching assistant (GTA) in the Engineering Communications Program at Virginia Tech, as a tutor-training coordinator, and as a professional writing center tutor.

Sarah Henderson Lee is an associate professor of English at Minnesota State University, Mankato, where she directs the second language (L2) writing program and teaches in the graduate Teaching English to Speakers of Other Languages (TESOL) program. She also recently served as an English language specialist in Bahrain and Nepal, where she led multiple teacher training workshops on L2 writing. Sarah's research focuses on language teacher education, literacy practices of multilingual writers, and World Englishes and composition. She most recently published a coedited collection titled *Second Language Writing Instruction in Global Contexts: English Language Teacher Preparation and Development* with Multilingual Matters.

Jennifer Maloy is an associate professor and chairperson of the English Department at Queensborough Community College, City University of New York (CUNY). Her research focuses on working with multilingual writers in community college classrooms and the implementation of Accelerated Learning Program (ALP). She has published her work in *Teaching English in the Two-Year College*, the *Basic Writing e-Journal*, and *NYS TESOL Journal*.

Neil Meyer is an associate professor of English at LaGuardia Community College, City University of New York (CUNY), where he teaches developmental writing, Accelerated Learning Program (ALP), and first-year writing, and courses in early American and lesbian, gay, bisexual, transgender (LGBT) literature. His research interests include politics of developmental writing, religious writing, and early American culture.

Susan Miller-Cochran is a professor of English and director of the writing program at the University of Arizona. Her work has appeared in journals such as *Composition Forum*, *Computers and Composition*, and *WPA: Writing Program Administration*. She is a coeditor of *Composition, Rhetoric, and Disciplinarity* (Utah State, 2018); *Rhetorically Rethinking Usability* (Hampton, 2009); and *Strategies for Teaching First-Year Composition* (NCTE, 2002). She is also a coauthor of *An Insider's Guide to Academic Writing* (Macmillan, 2019), *The Cengage Guide to Research* (Cengage, 2017), and *Keys for Writers* (Cengage, 2016). She is a past president of the Council of Writing Program Administrators.

Ruth Osorio is an assistant professor of rhetoric and women's studies at Old Dominion University, where she teaches writing, rhetoric, feminist approaches to technology, and feminist disability studies. As a disability rhetoric scholar, she is interested in how activists rhetorically activate access in traditionally inaccessible spaces. Her work draws from her experiences in activism, community organizing, and motherhood.

Lori Ostergaard is a professor and chair of the Department of Writing and Rhetoric at Oakland University. She is also the coeditor of *WPA: Writing Program Administration*. In addition to her coedited collections—*Transforming English Studies*, *Undergraduate Writing Majors*, and *In the Archives of Composition*—her research appears in *College English*, *Composition Studies*, *Rhetoric Review*, *Journal of Basic Writing*, and *Composition Forum*.

Shyam B. Pandey is a PhD candidate in the Department of English at Purdue University, where he currently teaches professional and technical writing courses. Previously, he has taught a variety of composition courses. His recent research interests relate to multimodal composition, professional and technical writing, multilingual writers and their identities, World Englishes, and qualitative methodology.

Cassandra Phillips is a professor of English at the University of Wisconsin–Milwaukee at Waukesha, where she also coordinates the first-year and developmental writing program for the College of General Studies. Her research focuses on first-year writing and reading, program development, and writing pedagogy.

Brenda Refaei is an associate professor of English at the University of Cincinnati Blue Ash College. She was formerly the composition coordinator for the department. She is currently researching antiracist writing pedagogy and assessment. She is an Engaging Excellence in Equity Fellow. She teaches basic writing, Accelerated Learning Program (ALP), first-year composition, and intermediate composition courses and serves as the co-director of the college's Learning + Teaching Center.

Heather M. Robinson is an associate professor of English at York College of the City University of New York, where she has also served as English Department chairperson, writing program director, and writing center coordinator. Her research areas include applied linguistics, with a focus on translingual and transnational student composing, and queer-feminist writing program administration. Her writing has appeared in the *Journal of Basic Writing*, *Across the Disciplines*, and *Administrative Theory and Practice*, as well as in a collaborative volume, *Translingual Identities and Transnational Realities in the US College Classroom*, published by Routledge Press.

Rochelle (Shelley) Rodrigo is an associate director of the Writing Program, Online Writing, and associate professor in the Rhetoric, Composition, and the Teaching of English (RCTE) in the Department of English at the University of Arizona. She researches how "newer" technologies better facilitate communicative interactions, specifically teaching and learning. As well as coauthoring three editions of *The Wadsworth/Cengage Guide to Research*, Shelley also coedited *Rhetorically Rethinking Usability* (Hampton Press). Her scholarly work has appeared in *Computers and Composition*, *C&C Online*, *Technical Communication Quarterly*, *Teaching English in the Two-Year College*, *EDUCAUSE Quarterly*, *Journal of Interactive Technology & Pedagogy*, and *Enculturation*, as well as various edited collections.

Julia Romberger is the coordinator of the Professional Writing Program, the English Department Lab coordinator, and an associate professor of professional writing in the Department of English at Old Dominion University. She researches the environment's impact upon writing practices and the labor conditions of faculty who do technology-related service for writing programs. Her work has appeared in *Computers and Composition*, in *International Journal of the Image*, and in the edited collections *Pressures on Technical Communication Programs in a New Age of Austerity* and *The New Normal: Pressures on Technical Communication Programs in the Age of Austerity*.

Tiffany Rousculp is a professor in the English Department at Salt Lake Community College, where she is the founding director of the Writing Across the College program. She previously founded and directed the SLCC Community Writing Center. Her publications include *Rhetoric of Respect: Recognizing Change at a Community Writing Center* and the coedited collection, *Circulating Communities: The Tactics and Strategies of Community Publishing*.

Megan Schoen is an assistant professor in the Department of Writing and Rhetoric at Oakland University, where she serves as the director of first-year writing. Her articles have appeared in *Rhetoric Review*, *WPA: Writing Program Administration*, *WAC Journal*, and *constellations*. She is a cofounder and co–managing editor of *Present Tense: A Journal of Rhetoric in Society*.

Paulette Stevenson is a residential faculty member at Mesa Community College. She was formerly an instructor at Arizona State University, where she led the fight against an increased teaching load. Her research interests include labor activism within academia, transnational feminist rhetorics, and digital organizing.